The Isis (Yssis) Papers

The Isis (Yssis) Papers

Frances Cress Welsing, M.D.

Third World Press • Chicago

Third World Press, Chicago 60619

Printed in the United States of America

04 03 02 01 00   13 12

ISBN: 0-88378-103-4 (cloth)
       0-88378-104-2 (paper)

LCN: 90-071890

Manufactured in the United States of America

Dedication

This work is dedicated to the victims of the global system of white supremacy (racism), all non-white people worldwide, past and present, who have resolved to end this great travesty and bring justice, then peace to planet Earth.

"If you do not understand White Supremacy (Racism) – what it is, and how it works – everything *else* that you understand, will only confuse you."

— Neely Fuller, Jr. (1971).

The United Independent Compensatory Code/System/Concept

No persons who classify themselves as white living in the area of the world referred to as the United States of America (or for that matter, in any other area of the world) should presume to tell any Black person (or other non-white person) what racism *is* or *is not*, until they have read completely Kenneth O'Reilley's *Racial Matters: The FBI's Secret File on Black America, 1960-1972.*

No Black person living in the area of the world referred to as the United States of America should discourse on racism or deny the conspiratorial dimensions of the local and global system of racism until he/she has read *Racial Matters* completely.

All non-white people (black, brown, red and yellow) should read and discuss the implications of the book, *Racial Matters;* the implications for themselves as individuals and the implications for their collective should be discussed in depth. Then, all non-white people should view the docudrama videotape, *The Wannsee Conference* (which can be rented), to observe exactly how a white supremacy government calmly sits and plans the destruction of a people that it classifies as non-white. The Wannsee Conference took place in Germany, in 1941, to finalize the plans for the destruction of 11,000,000 Semites (non-whites) of the Jewish religion. The German white supremacists succeeded in killing six million.

After the above steps have been taken, all non-white people worldwide should read Neely Fuller's work, *The United Independent Compensatory Code/System/Concept: a text book/workbook for thought, speech and/or action for victims of racism (white supremacy)*.

Frances Cress Welsing
Washington, D.C.
August, 1989

CONTENTS

Preface

We now are nearing the final decade of the 20th century. The great African in America, the sociologist-historian W.E.B Du Bois, identified the problem of this century as the "problem of the color-line" (*Souls of Black Folk*, 1903). Thus, it is fortunate that in the final decade of the 20th century a basis for the solution to the problem of the color-line has been produced. This basis rests in an adequate analysis of the nature of the color-line – the exact nature of local and global racism. Ultimately, the conscious decision by people of color worldwide (the overwhelming majority of the world's population) to base their behavior in relationships on an exact analysis and definition of racism as white supremacy will change its appearance and activity on planet Earth. Just as the problem of the color-line (racism) has controlled events in the 20th century (and prior centuries), the *solution* to the problem will regulate events in the 21st century and beyond as we enter the era of justice.

Recently, there has been an unraveling and an analysis of the core issue of the first global power system of mass oppression – the power system of racism (white supremacy). Once the collective victim understands this fundamental issue, the ultimate organizing of all of the appropriate behaviors necessary to neutralize the great injustice of the white supremacy power system will be only a matter of time. The length of time required to neutralize global white supremacy will be *inversely proportional* to 1) the level of understanding of the phenomenon; plus 2) the evolution of self- and group-respect, the will, determination and discipline to practice the appropriate counter-racist behaviors – on the part of the non-white victims of white supremacy. Thus, the 21st century, and indeed the end of the 20th century, will be a time perhaps of great devastation. But, undoubtedly, it will be a time of great change. And the most critical factor in that change of circumstances will be non-white people's ever-increasing understanding of the behavioral phenomenon of white supremacy as a global, terroristic power system.

However, it must be understood that high levels of self-respect, will and determination, without an adequate understanding, analysis and definition of racism as the oppressing power system, will not be sufficient to bring the long-sought goal of neutralizing that injustice and establishing justice and peace for all people. Therefore, it is critical to have a comprehensive analysis and definition of the opposing force. As a Black behavioral scientist and practicing general and child psychiatrist, my current functional definition of racism (white supremacy) is as follows: *the local and global power system structured and maintained by persons who classify themselves as white, whether consciously or subconsciously determined; this system consists of patterns of perception, logic, symbol formation, thought, speech, action and emotional response, as conducted simultaneously in all areas of people activity (economics, education, entertainment, labor, law, politics, religion, sex and war). The ultimate purpose of the system is to prevent white genetic annihilation on Earth – a planet in which the overwhelming majority of people are classified as non-white (black, brown, red and yellow) by white-skinned people. All of the non-white people are genetically dominant (in terms of skin coloration) compared to the genetically recessive white-skinned people.*

When this definition of racism as a strategy for white genetic survival is mastered, one can understand precisely not only the present global power formations and realignments (i.e., U.S.A./U.S.S.R. linkage and European unification), but also all present urban (non-white) center epidemics. I am speaking of the concurrent urban crises of drug use, drug addiction, drug-related murder, teenage pregnancy, infant mortality, Black academic under-achievement, Black teenage unemployment, Black adult male unemployment, Black male incarceration, single parent (female-headed) households, chronic welfare dependency, poverty, AIDS and homelessness. (See Diagram I.) These very disturbing individual- and group-destructive pathological forms of behavior are the *direct* and *indirect* by-products of a behavioral power system fundamentally structured for white genetic survival, locally and globally.

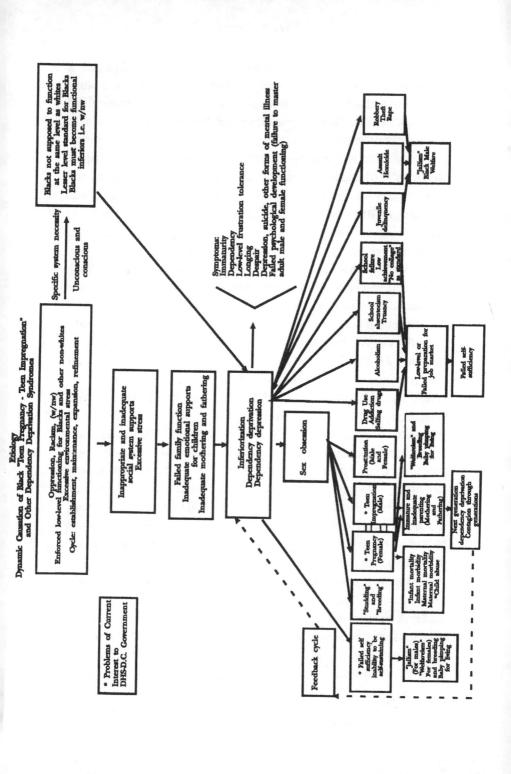

White supremacy domination and oppression of all non-white people is essential for global white genetic survival. The prevention of white genetic annihilation is pursued through all means, including chemical and biological warfare. Today, the white genetic survival imperative, instead of using chemicals in gas chambers, is using chemicals on the streets – crack, crank, cocaine, ecstasy, PCP, heroin and methadon (all "designer chemicals"). Ultimately, these chemicals are produced by whites and made available to urban Blacks, particularly Black males – upon whom the future of Black people is dependent. The core dynamic of white genetic survival eventually leads whites to a major act of genocide (destruction of the genes of non-white people), or toward *genocidal imperatives*. Such a genocide occurred in Nazi Germany (1933-1945), wherein the Semite and gypsy populations were classified as non-white and therefore were destroyed.

The reason that the Black male (as recently symbolized by Willie Horton) is and always has been central to the issue of white supremacy is clarified by the definition of racism as white genetic survival. In the collective white pysche, Black males represent the greatest threat to white genetic survival because only males (of any color) can impose sexual intercourse, and Black males have the greatest genetic potential (of all non-white males) to cause white genetic annihilation. Thus, Black males must be attacked and destroyed in a power system designed to assure white genetic survival. In the white supremacy mind-set, consciously or sub-consciously, Black males must be destroyed in significant numbers – just as they were in earlier days when there was widespread open lynching and castration of Black males, or during the Tuskegee Syphilis Study from 1932 to 1972 when a large number of Black males were used and destroyed by whites.

Today we are witnessing a more subtle systemic approach to white genetic survival. The destruction of Black males now is indirect, so that the Black male victims themselves can be led to participate in – and then be blamed for – their own mass deaths. However, through close examination and an understanding of the ultimate objective of white supremacy as collective white genetic survival, the steps to massive Black male death can be charted. The chain of events begins with the denial of full scale employment and advancement to Black males so that they cannot adequately support themselves, their wives and their children. In turn, large numbers of Black male children grow up without their fathers' guidance. This leads to frustration, depression and failure in school. Once this atmosphere is established, drugs are placed *deliberately* in the Black community. The drugs are then used to "street-treat" Black male frustration and depression. The high prices for which drugs are sold provide the Black male population with the *illusion* that finally they are beginning to make some money and to share in the "American dream." Guns are then placed at the disposal of the same Black male persons, supposedly to aid them in enforcing payment for drug sales. More important, the strategy is for Black males to kill and destroy one another and then carry the blame. (It must be realized that no Black males manufacture the chemicals for drug use, nor do any Black males manufacture guns.)

The same power system of racism has so ingrained a negative image and connotation of Blackness in general (i.e., Black Monday, blackmail, black sheep, black day), and of the Black male in particular, that for Black males to slaughter one another in the streets daily means next to nothing; indeed, it is treated as desirable and acceptable. "Good riddance of bad rubbish." This is in stark contrast to the urgency, alarm and concern that is generated in the same society when only 25 young white males commit suicide in the course of a 24-month period.

Failing to comprehend the environmental context of the white supremacy system and its ultimate goal of white genetic survival, Black people also fail to grasp the deeper sense of what actually is occurring in front of our eyes. We do not realize that the massive deaths of Black males constitute the genocide of Black people (as it takes Black males to make Black babies and ensure future Black generations).

The destruction of Black males for the purpose of white genetic survival is the reason behind the ever-increasing disparity between the number of Black females entering and graduating from high schools and institutions of higher education compared to the far lesser number of Black males. This becomes an additional facet of Black genocide. Furthermore, white genetic survival is the dynamic behind the high incarceration rate of Black males in the U.S., which is second only to that of South Africa. The high rate of Black male incarceration contributes in genocidal fashion to the prevention of Black births and the Black male-supported development of all Black children, particularly boys.

The genocide of non-whites must be understood as a necessary tactic of a people (white) that is a minority of the world's population and that, because it lacks the genetic capacity to produce significant levels of melanin, is genetically recessive in terms of skin coloration, compared to the black, brown, red and yellow world majority. Thus, the global white minority must act genocidally against people of color for the purpose of white genetic survival. This is the "kill or be killed" mentality. This is the reason that persons who classified themselves as "white" behaved genocidally towards Semites in the holocaust in Nazi Germany and Europe (1933-1945). (The word Semite is from the Latin prefix, semi meaning "half" – half Black and half white, and that means mulatto (non-white). This is also the reason that persons who classified themselves as "white" behaved (and still behave) genocidally towards the indigenous inhabitants of the Western Hemisphere who were classified as red (non-white).

Only the willingness of non-white peoples worldwide to recognize, analyze, understand and discuss openly the genocidal dynamic will bring this injustice to an end. Most important, Black males must help one another to understand that they are being led by the dynamic of white supremacy to inflict extreme damage upon themselves, one another and ultimately the Black race. Black males must understand that, contrary to what is said, the war being conducted in urban centers is not against *drugs* but against Black males – for the purpose of white genetic survival. Drugs are used simply as the means to achieve that end. That is why drugs are plentiful, while Black males are dying in ever-increasing numbers! (The recent proposal to treat drug addicts at military bases is only the first stage towards a more formal concentration camp placement, more formal than the ghetto.)

Mastering the above definition of racism as a strategy for neutralizing white supremacy will permit one to decode accurately the symbolism in the new Madonna video "Like a Prayer," designed consciously and/or subconsciously by whites to massage, stimulate and enhance further the collective instinct for white genetic survival. The same could be said about the recent films *Betrayal* and *Mississippi Burning*. Furthermore, such an understanding will help clarify the persistent and even violent behaviors on the part of persons associated with the so-called "right to life movement," which seeks to prevent abortions, especially amongst whites. Recognizing racism as the struggle for white genetic survival helps one to understand what is happening in South Africa; what is euphemistically referred to as "apartheid" is only the tactics and strategies of the minority white population, numbering only four million persons, attempting to survive genetically while surrounded by a majority Black population of 26 to 30 million. This is a microcosm of what is happening on the entire planet.

Finally, the time has come for unveiling the true nature of white supremacy (racism). For this reason, I have entitled this work, *The Isis (YSSIS) Papers: The Keys to the Colors*. Isis was the most important goddess of ancient Africa (specifically, Egypt). She was the sister/wife of the most important Egyptian god, Osiris ("Lord of the perfect Black"), and the mother of Horus. In the astral interpretation of the Egyptian gods, Isis was equated with the dog star Sirius (Sothis). According to the ancient African story, after the murder and dismemberment of Osiris by his evil brother Set (Seth), Isis discovered the crime, recovered the pieces of the body of Osiris, and put them together again, restoring his existence and his power. According to legend, Isis admired truth and justice and made justice stronger than gold and silver.

In the present era, truth and justice have been crushed by the global power system of white supremacy, making the existence of peace on the planet impossible under this reign of terror. The attempt in this work to reveal some aspects of the in-depth truth about the white supremacy power system for the ultimate purpose of establishing justice and peace in the world is in the tradition of the great African goddess, Isis.

I hope that with this knowledge the world's non-white people (black, brown, red and yellow) will work more effectively to neutralize this global and most monstrous form of injustice and chaos. Any person not interested in a definition, analysis and deeper understanding of worldwide white supremacy must have an interest (conscious or subconscious) in maintaining the same.

The subtitle of this work, *The Keys to the Colors*, came from a statement made to me by a patient in a Washington, D.C. public mental health clinic in the late 1960s. The patient was a tall, thin, middle-aged, Black-skinned man who, in a somewhat confused manner, talked earnestly to me about the problems he had experienced in his life. He said, "Doctor, if we could just find the keys to the colors!" And he repeated it slowly. It was a statement I never have been able to forget. This work is a portion of my response.

Frances Cress Welsing, M.D.
Washington, D.C.
1989

Introduction

The Isis (YSSIS) Papers: The Keys to the Colors is a collection of essays I have written over the past 18 years, following the presentation and publication of my first work, *The Cress Theory of Color-Confrontation and Racism (White Supremacy)*. That first paper was a theoretical statement, a psychogenetic theory and world outlook on the origin and meaning of the global white supremacy system. The theory summarizes and clarifies our experience as Black (non-white) people on a planet presently dominated by people who classify themselves as "white" and who are a minority of the world's people.

The Cress Theory was based upon the insightful work of Neely Fuller Jr., author of *The United Independent Compensatory Code/System/Concept – a textbook/workbook for thought, speech and/or action for victims of racism (white supremacy)*. Fuller, the founder of the racism/counter-racism concept, was the very first victim of racism to understand it as a global system of organized behavior (thought, speech and action) for white supremacy domination in all areas of people activity (economics, education, entertainment, labor, law, politics, religion, sex and war). In other words, he recognized that all activity and behavior encompassed by the white supremacy system had and has its origin in the dynamic of racism. Additionally, Fuller understood that racism contained the seeds and origin of counter-racism, the behavior dynamic of liberation for the non-white victims of white supremacy. His work led me to question the necessity of the global white collective to evolve such a system of unjust behavior. The result was *The Cress Theory of Color Confrontation and Racism (White Supremacy)*. (Cress is my maiden name.)

This thesis provided me with a "unified field theory" approach and understanding, in the Einsteinian sense, to all behavioral phenomena manifested with high frequency in the local and global system of racism.

The great physicist, Albert Einstein, in *The Meaning of Relativity* (1922) had the following to say about the "unified field."

> The object of all sciences, whether natural sciences or psychology, is to co-ordinate our experiences and to bring them into a logical system – the only justification for our concepts and system of concepts is that they serve to represent the complex of our experiences; beyond this they have no legitimacy.

The Cress Theory permitted me to see and understand many forms of activity (on the part of whites and their non-white victims) that have been either ignored or taken for granted. These behaviors, which can be viewed as symbolic of the fundamental objective of white genetic survival, are found in the social reflection of the white supremacy power system – the white supremacy culture. Together, the system and culture of white supremacy produce the phenomenon of racism. Thus, throughout this book, the terms *system* and *culture*, in reference to white supremacy, are used interchangeably.

This deep investigation and understanding is essential if Black and other non-white peoples are to succeed in playing the "black side of the chess board" (defense-offense) in contrast to the "white side of the chess board" (offense-defense) in the planetary game of chess (white supremacy) being played out between white and non-white. Currently, the players on the black side of the chess board are in a continuous state of checkmate (a losing streak that is centuries long). This has happened because of our failure to understand the game. Heretofore, non-white people have not decoded white genetic survival.

After presenting *The Cress Theory*, my brain-computer was flooded with new understandings specifically related to the global white supremacy system. Many things that I – as most people – viewed as commonplace, I began to see in a different light. It was as though an enormous window was opened in a room that had been without sunlight. I recognized many of the items I saw anew as *symbols* in the white supremacy system. Perhaps because I am a general and child psychiatrist with considerable experience in interpreting the symbolic play of children and the symbols in the dreams of children and adults, I was sensitive to the symbols in the behavior system of white supremacy once it had been defined and decoded.

Though symbols are usually visual entities, they also take the form of speech, or can be found in activities – such as games. Symbols are specific to people and their experiences, their evolved cultures and circumstances. As such, symbols are the entities that carry highly compacted messages pertaining to the origin, identity and survival of individuals and collective peoples.

In the form of visual entities, patterns of speech and/or activity, symbols contain complex messages distilled from the conscious levels of the brain-computer. These messages have been reduced to their essence in the subconscious functioning; there, these highly coded messages are stored and continuously referred to for existence and survival. Once a symbol evolves in a person's subconscious, that person uses the symbol with high frequency and has little or no necessary conscious understanding of its meaning.

A shared symbol speaks volumes, although contained in a relatively small visual or auditory package. A symbol speaks loudly, or even shouts its meaning without uttering a sound. Symbols communicate from one person's subconscious to the subconscious of another who shares the same identity and survival necessity. Such communication transpires at subconscious levels when the conscious levels of brain-computer functioning cannot bear to address certain issues. White supremacy is a topic that few can or dare discuss in depth at the conscious level of brain-computer functioning. Few dare to probe or research white supremacy as this could lead to the dismantling of the system. Therefore, it is not surprising that there are many symbols in the system of white supremacy that reveal its roots in the struggle for white genetic survival.

In the white supremacy system (often referred to as Western culture or civilization), there is little conscious focusing on symbols, their formation, use and interpretation. To the contrary, non-white peoples in their original cultures tend to focus on symbols and dream interpretation as essential aspects of their lives (i.e., African cultural objects referred to as African art, the Egyptian [African] systems of hieroglyphs and the symbols and interpretation of dreams in Biblical stories). Therefore, as an African, it is difficult for me to explain the ability to see and understand symbols; however, I am aware of making a certain shift to a lower frequency of brain-computer functioning (away from that frequency required for ordinary, day to day, conscious functioning) in order to see and interpret symbols. But I must repeat that *my* ability to explain a process for symbol interpretation is derived from my ongoing search for a firm understanding of the overall context in which these symbols evolved – the white supremacy system/culture.

Perhaps there will be persons, Black as well as white, who fail to appreciate the language of symbols. There will be those who demean the attempt to decode symbols and ridicule their value and my interpretations. Also, there will be those who seek to identify and to decode symbols but fail. Nevertheless, I am presenting certain symbolic aspects of the white supremacy system/culture in an effort to increase our understanding of racism and thereby assist in bringing justice to the world.

An examination of the Washington Monument in Washington, D.C. and recognition of it as a symbol of white power – specifically, white male power (thus, a gigantic white penis or phallic symbol) – may assist one who has difficulty understanding symbols. The law that no building in the District of Columbia can be taller than the white phallus-shaped Washington Monument (which, by the way, looks like a robed Ku Klux Klan) is not coincidental. The underlying meaning of the monument and law is that there can be no challenge to white power. It is not without significance that the Washington Monument, as a phallic symbol, towers over a predominantly Black population in the capital city of the most powerful government in the global white supremacy system.

If this is not sufficient, those who fail to understand the *symbol* should go to the East Wing of the National Gallery of Art in Washington, D.C. and view the painting (specifically commissioned for that building) by the artist Robert Motherwell entitled "Reconciliation Elegy." This work is a continuation of Motherwell's earlier series of paintings, "Elegy to the Spanish Republic." The entire "Elegy" series consists of massive black forms, some round or oval, some massive and vertical, positioned next to one another. All of the forms are black against a white background. In the book, *Reconciliation Elegy*, Motherwell states:

> White has always conveyed to me the radiance of life, so that if one – though this is too literal – if one takes the Elegies as a metaphor for 'life and death,' then obviously a sense of life as freedom and of death as the terminal vivifier, can be an endless obsession and preoccupation. In a curious way in the Reconciliation Elegy my black forms, the life-death forms, are becoming personages, instead of black stones...the black and white are beginning to merge.... Death has been a continual living presence to me.

The word *elegy* means a poem of lament or praise for the dead. The massive black oval and vertical forms, symbolic forms representing death, obsessively painted throughout the entire "Elegy" series were immediately seen by my eyes (the eyes of a Black person) as the imposing genitalia (testicles and phallus) of the Black male, dominating a white background (symbolic of the global white collective). While referring to the round objects he has painted as "stones," Motherwell seemed unaware that the word "stone" is an ancient term for testicles. However, in his own description Motherwell speaks of the black and white painting as a "metaphor for life and death" (white as life and black as death). Certainly he is not thinking consciously of his paintings of Black male genitalia as symbols of white death through white genetic annihilation (caused by Black male genitalia and Black genetic material). But symbols do not arise from conscious levels of thought. Still, however, it is astonishing that Motherwell is unable to see his forms as Black male genitalia and name them overtly as such. But does Motherwell consciously understand white supremacy?

According to Motherwell, the first part of his series, "Elegy to the Spanish Republic" (at the level of his conscious thought), refers to the aftermath of the defeat of the Spanish Republican Army by the Spanish fascists in the 1935 Spanish Civil War. However, at a much deeper level it occurred to me that Spain also was conquered for 700 years (from the eighth to the 15th century, C.E.) by Black men from northern Africa, the

Moors. During their occupation of Spain, the Moors damaged the efforts of white genetic survival, causing Spaniards to become darker in skin color (compared to the rest of the Europeans) because of the long-term admixture of African (black) genetic material. Only with this under-standing does the obsessive painting of the symbolic forms of the black phallus and testicles in a series entitled "Elegy" (poem for the dead) make fatal sense. Not understanding the underlying fear of white genetic annihilation (in the individual and collective white psyche) causes a mere surface interpretation of the paintings (even in the mind of the artist himself). Failure to reach the core issue of white genetic survival (resonat-ing in the subconscious), which is most threatened by the genetic power in the genitalia of the Black male, relegates interpretation to superficial levels with a failure to see and understand the symbols arising from that subconscious core.

Motherwell addressed the issue of white (Western) survival in his comments on the "Elegy" series, specifically on "Reconciliation Elegy."

> Against the background of possible nuclear holocaust, we must even reconcile ourselves to the fact that western man in choosing centuries ago to exploit nature rather than to marry her, has doomed himself – with an industrial technology for which there is neither the wisdom nor the political mechanism to control...

Yet, after having said all of the above, Motherwell still remains unconscious of the symbolic forms in his paintings. Indeed, the industrial technology and the nuclear weapons of which Motherwell speaks are designed by the Western (white) collective as protection against white genetic annihilation. Other Motherwell paintings of black figures against white backgrounds bear such titles as "Africa," "Study for Kilimanjaro" and "Ancestral Presence."

This same concern and subconsciously perceived threat (in the white psyche) of the Black male (via black male genitalia) to white genetic survival is played out in the symbolism of the bullfight. In the bull ring, the bull is usually black. The bullfighter is usually a white male or any male in a "suit of lights," meaning white. The bull is chased and tormented until it is killed. This killing goes on obsessively, as a symbol of white survival in the presence of the Black male threat; symbolic of white males conquering Black males or of white survival in a world populated mostly by non-white people. Further, we must understand symbols of com-munion" in the Christian religion; the wine and bread that are eaten by the communicants are symbolic of the blood and body of Jesus, respectively. It is important to keep in mind that Jesus was an African, a Black male whose color has been changed to conform with the white supremacy perception and ideology. Finally, *King Kong*, the film in which a gigantic black ape plays opposite a white female, addresses in symbolic form the threat of the Black male to white genetic survival. Of course, King Kong is killed by the end of the film.

The papers in this collection were written over the past 19 years. They are dated to give the reader some appreciation of the order in which they evolved in my thought processes. They are of a whole cloth; all are derivatives of the white supremacy power system/culture, which before now has not been understood in sufficient depth. Several essays address specific symbols in the white supremacy system/culture. I did not con-trive these symbols. On the contrary, I looked and there they were.

Some have asked, "Why is it that others have not penetrated these deep symbols of Western culture? Why only you?" My answer is that I neither saw these symbols nor understood their meaning until I had written *The Cress Theory of Color-Confrontation and Racism*. That analysis gave me access to the total spectrum of collective brain-computer products (sym-bols, logic, thought, speech, action, emotional response and perception) that emanate from those who have established and maintained Western civilization. Having probed to the central core of Western civilization, I was able to see into (intuition = in-to-it) the myriad energy phenomena that spin off from that dynamic core. Recognizing the specific injustice committed against non-white people in the framework of Western civilization and culture, it became clear that the entire Western civilization dynamic is fundamentally linked to the fear of white genetic annihilation and the subsequent need (as experienced by the global white collective) for the continuous battle against the genetically dominant global majority of black, brown, red and yellow peoples. The organization for that survival is none other than the white *race*, which carries out the global system of white supremacy.

Although initially it came as a great surprise, it is only logical that the myriad *symbolic manifestations* of the struggle for white genetic survival *abound* throughout the historic and global structure of white supremacy. These symbols manifest wherever one looks, wherever one steps and wherever one turns. That these subtle and once hidden symbols are everywhere serves as the strongest evidence of the validity of *The Cress Theory.*

It is as though I had written, "If *The Cress Theory* is correct, symbols so informing us will be found throughout the whole of Western civilization and culture." Indeed, without the specific theory, one can look at the symbols for decades and truly not know what one is looking at, even when one is handling the symbol in one's bare hands.

One then might ask, "Why is it necessary to *read* a civilization or power system at deep levels?" Western culture has produced much violence and destruction on the planet. It is like a cancer destroying the body. A physician attempting to treat or cure a disease (i.e., cancer) must examine the patient at deep levels. It is inadequate to stop at what is seen with the unaided eye. The physician attempting to solve the problem of a persistent and troubling cough in a particular patient may order x-ray studies to view the *inside* of the lungs and the chest cavity. He/she might perform a microscopic examination and bacterial culture studies on the sputum that comes from the lungs in order to understand the cause of the cough. When the cause is understood, chances that the disease can be treated effectively and cured are improved greatly, while that which is not understood in depth rarely can be treated or cured. Similarly, there are serious problems posed for the vast majority of humankind by the specific dynamic of Western (white supremacy) culture.

I hope that this collection of essays will assist Blacks and all other people – who have as their cosmic responsibility the resolution of the problem of injustice in the world – in identifying the problem of that specific injustice more clearly than ever before. Instead of engaging in our past practices of complaining, moaning, crying, groaning, begging, clapping hands and singing "We shall Overcome" when confronted with these death-causing, life-stultifying problems posed by white supremacy, Black people in the U.S. must dissect and analyze those problems to their core. With this knowledge, Black people can take the necessary steps to eliminate the problem.

Those who *will* to work for justice and who understand that work as their conscious responsibility will be found in all places and in all walks of life, at all levels of formal education and at all income levels. There are no class divisions nor language barriers for those who do this cosmic work. It is time to solve this problem once and for all. It is time for justice on the planet Earth.

1

The Cress Theory of Color-Confrontation and Racism (White Supremacy):

A Psychogenetic Theory and World Outlook

(1970)

Unlike religion, the body of knowledge known as science takes the position that all observable phenomena can be explained, or, at least, is grist for the mill of investigation, analysis and understanding by the human mind.

In today's very small world at least three-quarters of the people are "non-white," and the members of this "non-white" majority population are subjected to domination throughout their lives, either directly or indirectly, by a tiny minority of the world's people who classify themselves as "white." Racism (white supremacy) then, is revealed as one of, if not *the* most important observable phenomenon in the world today for which social, behavioral and all other scientists should be seeking an explanation.

Heretofore, racism has been defined and described variously, (see Gullattee, Comer, Butts and Pinderhughes). Yet in my view, the comment made by Oliver C. Cox in his 1959 award winning text, "Caste, Class and Race" (*Monthly Review Press*), still prevails:

> It is not ordinarily realized that, of all the great mass of writing on race relations, there is available no consistent theory of race relations. The need for such a sociological explanation is so great that recently, when one author succeeded, with some degree of superficial logic, in explaining the phenomena in terms of caste relations, the college textbooks and social-science journals, almost unanimously and unquestioningly, hurriedly adopted his theory.

Perhaps social and behavioral scientists have failed to develop a sound and consistent theory of racism because of their tendency to be less demanding and less stringently disciplined in sticking to observable and measurable data than the so-called "physical" scientists are required to be in formulating hypotheses. Frequently, contrary to all the basic premises of modern science, statements are made by some of these scientists "a priori" — that is to say, claimed as valid independent of observation. Similarly, society, in general, fails to impose a significant amount of pressure on behavioral and social scientists to yield viable theories and definitions. Such theories and definitions subsequently can stand and function as efficient and effective tools to be utilized by social engineers as guides for changing social reality. However, the contrary seems to be the case; if there is any pressure at all, it is to maintain the social status quo. And all too often, institutions of the society reward the superficial, inconsistent and dysfunctional theories of societal dynamics.

Neely Fuller, in his 1969 copyrighted *The United Independent Compensatory Code/System/Concept: a textbook/workbook for thought, speech and/or action for victims of racism (white supremacy)*, recognized the need for a functional statement on racism, one that could be utilized daily by those earnestly seeking to bring about social change. Fuller observed that, contrary to most present thinking, there is only one functioning racism in the known world — white supremacy. He challenges his readers to identify and then to demonstrate the superiority or functional supremacy of any of the world's "non-white" peoples over anyone. Concluding that since there is no operational supremacy of any "colored" people, Fuller reveals that the only valid operational definition of racism is white supremacy. He observes that in spite of any and all statements the world's "non-white" peoples may make about themselves having economic and/or political independence and the like, in the final analysis, they are all victims of the white supremacy process. He places major emphasis on the present realities of the world that can be verified and tested, rather than on what one could imagine to be the case (such as a black or yellow supremacy). He further emphasizes that, instead of focusing on individual cases or on specific locations, a perspective that examines the patterns of relationships between whites and "non-whites" worldwide must be developed.

Fuller explains that racism is not merely a pattern of individual and/or institutional practice; it is a universally operating "system" of white supremacy and domination in which the majority of the world's white people participate. He discounts the validity of theories that recognize the evolution of economic systems as the origin of this state of affairs. Instead, he reveals the inadequate analysis of such theories by suggesting that various economic systems – such as capitalism, communism and socialism – have been devised, used and refined in the effort to achieve the primary goal of white domination. In other words, the goal of the white supremacy system is none other than the establishment, maintenance, expansion and refinement of world domination by members of a group that classifies itself as the white "race." Fuller then suggests that the word "race," in this sense, has little biological validity but is translated more correctly as "organization," the sole purpose of which is to maintain white domination and world control. Fuller's emphasis on the concept of color amplifies the assertion made in 1903 by W.E.B. Du Bois (perhaps the greatest American social scientist) in *The Souls of Black Folk*, that the great problem facing the 20th century is that of the color-line.

Whether or not one is emotionally comfortable with Fuller's thesis and assessment is not germane. The question of such comfort never has been the important concern of scientific investigation. Of great significance in Fuller's work is the description of relationships between "non-white" and white peoples. Fuller defines and elucidates these relationships as a means of accounting for and illuminating many past and present observable social practices. Also, this examination reveals that, despite all kinds of programs and pronouncements to the contrary, for the past several hundred years, white supremacist social conditions have remained intact as the dominant social reality.

Impressed that the concept of a "system" of white domination over the world's "non-white" peoples could explain the seeming predicament and dilemma of "non-white" social reality, I tended to focus, as a psychiatrist, on what possible motivational force, operative at both the individual and group levels, could account for the evolution of these patterns of social behavioral practice that apparently function in all areas of human activity (economics, education, entertainment, labor, law, politics, religion, sex and war). While Fuller clearly suggests that this "system" consists of patterns of thought, speech and action, practiced to various degrees by the majority of the world's white people, the only comment on etiology he makes is that:

> Most white people hate Black people. The reason that most white people hate Black people is because whites are not Black people. If you know this about white people, you need know little else. If you do not know this about white people, virtually all else that you know about them will only confuse you.

To take Fuller's account a step further, it should be noted that, in the majority of instances, any neurotic drive for superiority usually is founded upon a deep and pervading sense of inadequacy and inferiority. Is it not true that white people represent in numerical terms a very small minority of the world's people? And more profoundly, is not "white" itself the very absence of any ability to produce color? I reason, then, that the quality of whiteness is indeed a genetic inadequacy or a relative genetic deficiency state, based upon the genetic inability to produce the skin pigments of melanin (which is responsible for all skin color). The vast majority of the world's people are not so afflicted, which suggests that color is normal for human beings and color absence is abnormal. Additionally, this state of color absence acts always as a genetic recessive to the dominant genetic factor of color-production. Color always "annihilates" (phenotypically- and genetically-speaking) the non-color, white. Black people possess the greatest color potential, with brown, red and yellow peoples possessing lesser quantities, respectively. This is the genetic and psychological basis for *The Cress Theory of Color-Confrontation and Racism (White Supremacy)*.

The Color-Confrontation theory states that the white or color-deficient Europeans responded psychologically, with a profound sense of numeri- cal inadequacy and color inferiority, in their confrontations with the majority of the world's people – all of whom possessed varying degrees of color-producing capacity. This psychological response, whether conscious or unconscious, revealed an inadequacy based on the most obvious and fundamental part of their being, their external appearance. As might be anticipated in terms of modern psychological theories, whites defensively developed an uncontrollable sense of hostility and aggression. This attitude has continued to manifest itself throughout the history of mass confrontations between whites and people of color. That the initial hostility and aggression came only from whites is recorded in innumerable diaries, journals and books written by whites. Also, records indicate that only after long periods of great abuse have non-whites responded defensively with any form of counterattack. This perplexing psychological reaction of whites has been directed towards all peoples with the capacity to produce melanin. However, the most profound aggressions have been directed towards Black people, who have the greatest color potential and, therefore, are the most envied and feared in genetic color competition.

The experience of numerical inadequacy and genetic color inferiority led whites to implement a number of interesting, although devastating (to non-white peoples), psychological defense mechanisms. The initial psychological defense maneuver was the *repression* of the initial painful awareness of inadequacy. This primary ego defense was reinforced by a host of other defense mechanisms.

One of the most important of these defense mechanisms was *reaction formation*, a response that converts (at the psychological level) something desired and envied but wholly unattainable, into something discredited and despised. The whites, desiring to have skin color but unable to attain it, claimed (consciously or unconsciously) that skin color was disgusting to them, and began attributing negative qualities to color – especially to blackness. Interestingly, the term "non-white" is a double negative resulting in a positive statement. This is perhaps a Freudian slip, wherein the use of language ultimately reveals the primary psychological dynamic. Whites' desire to have colored skin can be observed at the very first signs of spring or summer when they begin to strip off their clothes (as many pieces as the law will allow), often permitting their skins to be burned severely in an attempt to add some color to their pale bodies and rendering themselves vulnerable to skin cancer in the process. Most cosmetics are also an attempt to add color to white skin. Such coloring makeup is provided for the white male as well as female. And finally, untold millions are spent annually on chemicals that are advertised as being able to increase the tanning potential of whites.

The fact that some Blacks have attempted to change the color of their skin to white does not mitigate the force of this argument, as it can be demonstrated readily that these non-whites are responding to the already established social conditions of white supremacy. Such a process, as seen in Blacks and other non-whites, may be described as identification with the oppressor.

Another example of the reaction formation defense is the elaboration of the myth of white genetic superiority, which continues to be reinforced assiduously (note Jensen's latest elaborations and their acceptance at all levels of the white social structure). Acutely aware of their inferior genetic ability to produce skin color, whites built the elaborate myth of white genetic superiority. Furthermore, whites set about the huge task of evolving a social, political and economic structure that would support the myth of the inferiority of Blacks and other non-whites.

An additional psychological defense maneuver utilized by whites has been that of *projection*. Feeling extreme hostility and hate towards non-whites, whites began the pattern of stating that non-whites hated them. In many instances, this mechanism has served to mitigate the guilt whites occasionally experience for their impulse to aggress against Blacks and other people of color.

Another, perhaps special, instance of the use of projection is the historic and continuing desire of whites for sexual alliances with non-whites – a desire indulged by white males throughout the world. This deep desire has been projected onto Black males and females, and is manifest in the notion that people of color have sexual desires for white males and females. The Color-Confrontation theory postulates that whites desired and still do desire sexual alliances with non-whites, both male and female, because it is only through this route that whites can achieve the illusion of being able to produce color. The extreme rage vented against even the idea of a sexual alliance between the Black male and the white female, which has long been a dominant theme in the white supremacy culture, is viewed by the Color-Confrontation theory as a result of the white male's intense fear of the Black male's capacity to fulfill the greatest longing of the white female – that of conceiving and birthing a product of color.

There are other sexual behaviors practiced by some whites that can be illuminated by the Color-Confrontation thesis. For example, in his autobiography, Malcolm X stated that the sexual perversion he was asked to perform most often by white men was for him, as a Black male, to have sexual intercourse with white females in their presence, while they (white men) looked on. This behavioral pattern on the part of white males, instead of being dismissed as a perversion, can be understood when viewed as white males' fantasized identification with Black males' capacity to give conceptual products of color to white females — something white females desperately desire but white males cannot fulfill. Further vivid testimony is given by Black males who have engaged in sexual intercourse with white females. These men report that a frequent utterance of white females is that they wish to have Black babies.

The Color-Confrontation theory also explains why Black males' testicles were the body parts that white males attacked in most lynchings: the testicles store powerful color-producing genetic material. Likewise, the repeated and consistent focus on the size of Black males' penises by both white males and females is viewed by this theory as a *displacement* of the fundamental concern with the genetic color-producing capacity residing in the testicles. Since the fact of color-envy must remain repressed, color-desire can never be mentioned or the entire white psychological structure collapses. Therefore, attention is displaced to a less threatening object or symbol – the penis.

Finally, the degradation of sex in the white supremacy culture allows for yet another area of insight into the fundamental psychological dynamics of whites and their self-alienation regarding their physical appearance. At the most primordial level, sex can be viewed as the reproduction of one's own image, of self and of kind. According to the Color-Confrontation theory, white supremacy culture degrades the act of sex and the process of self-reproduction because for whites both are reflective of whiteness and, in turn, their inabilitiy to produce color. This self-deficiency clearly is despised and is stated most explicitly in the religious and moral philosophies of the white supremacy culture. Yet, this manner of degrading the sexual act is not found in non-white cultures. In fact, the very opposite is the case: the act of reproduction is held in the highest esteem, as reflected in non-white arts and religious practices. The artistic and religious practices of India and Africa give strong and continuous testimony to this fact. In whites, this initial core feeling of alienation from themselves and from the act that produced their image found subsequent expression in their thought processes, religious philosophies, moral codes, social acts, and the entire social structure.

Psychiatrists and other behavioral scientists frequently use the patterns of overt behavior towards others as indications of what is felt fundamentally about the self. If hate and lack of respect are manifested towards others, hate and lack of respect are felt most often at deeper levels towards the self. Facets of other behavioral patterns within the white supremacy cultural framework support this thesis. For example, many white writers, in all areas of the world, experience and write about their profound sense of self-alienation. Additionally, some of the current political, social and behavioral activity enacted by whites against the ideology and values of the white social structure, although not spoken of in the terminology used here, can be appreciated at one level as an expression of the same kernel of alienation against whiteness. Thus, the hippies and yippies, by allowing dirt to accumulate on themselves, in one sense, are adding color to their skins. They also, by allowing their head and facial hair to proliferate, cover themselves with the only part of their bodies that has substantive color, their hair. The present frantic attempts made by whites to counter this sense of alienation take the form of free and open sexual practices and sexual orgies. Such attempts will be unsuccessful because, again, the core problem is a sense of alienation primarily from their own colorlessness, and secondarily from the social practices and structure whites have built around that psychological core over the centuries.

Racism (white supremacy), having begun as a form of self-alienation, has evolved into the most highly refined form of alienation from others as well. The Color-Confrontation theory views all of the present battlegrounds in the world as vivid reflections of this reality; the destructive and aggressive behavioral patterns being displayed by white peoples towards all non-white peoples is evidence of the inner hate, hostility and rejection they feel towards themselves and of the depth of self-alienation that has evolved from the genetic and psychological kernel of color inadequacy.

The mass inability of whites to live and attend school in the presence of non-whites is expressed in the patterns of Black and white housing and education throughout this country and the world. In terms of the Color-Confrontation thesis, this inability is seen as the apparent psychological discomfort experienced by whites in situations where, in confronting their neighbors of color, they must face their color inadequacy daily . Also, the myth of white superiority is exploded in the presence of equitable social and economic opportunity. The white personality, in the presence of color, can be stabilized only by keeping Blacks and other non-whites in obviously inferior positions. The situation of mass proximity to Blacks is intolerable to whites because Blacks are inherently more than equal. People of color always will have something highly visible that whites never can have or produce — the genetic factor of color. Always, in the presence of color, whites will feel genetically inferior.

The difficulty whites have in according non-whites socio-political and economic equality within the white supremacy structure stems neither from a moral issue nor from political or economic need, but from the fundamental sense of their own unequal condition – in regards to their numerical inadequacy and color deficiency. They can compensate for their color inadequacy only by placing themselves in socially superior positions. The color inadequacy of whiteness necessitates a social structure based on white superiority. Only tokenism can be tolerated by such a motivational psychological state, wherein the evolution of the myth of the exceptional non-white is used, again, as a defense mechanism.

The thrust towards superiority over peoples of color, the drive towards material accumulation, the drive towards a technological culture and the drive towards power are all cornerstones of the universal white supremacy culture, and they are viewed – in terms of the Color-Confrontation thesis – as responses to the core psychological sense of inadequacy. This inadequacy is not measured in terms of infant size as compared with that of the adult, as postulated by Alfred Adler. Rather, it is an inadequacy rooted in the inability to produce melanin. This genetic state is, in actuality, a variant of albinism.

The Color-Confrontation theory further postulates that whites are vulnerable to their sense of numerical inadequacy. This inadequacy is apparent in their drive to divide the vast majority of non-whites into fractional, as well as frictional, *minorities*. This is viewed as a funda-mental behavioral response of whites to their own minority status. The white "race" has structured and manipulated their own thought processes and conceptual patterns, as well as those of the entire non-white world majority, so that the real numerical minority (whites) illusionally feels and represents itself as the world's majority, while the true numerical majority (non-whites) illusionally feels and views itself as the minority. Interest-ingly, the white collective, whenever discussing the question of color, never discusses any of its own particular ethnic groups as minorities, but constantly focuses on the various ethnic, language and religious groups of non-white peoples as minorities. Then great efforts are made to initiate conflict between these arbitrary groups. This is one of the key methods by which a minority can remain in power. The "divide, frictionalize and conquer" pattern, observable throughout history wherever non-whites are confronted by whites, results primarily from whites' sense of color deficiency and secondarily from their sense of numerical inadequacy. This pattern, then, is a compensatory adjustment to permit psychological comfort through dominance and control. (See Diagram I.) Similarly, the present-day frantic focus on birth control for the entire non-white world is another example of white peoples' conscious or unconscious awareness of their numerical deficiency status. There is never great emphasis on

The psychogenetic and social dynamic
of racism (white supremacy)

↓

Genetic Factor: color inadequacy state (white)
an albinism or variant

↓

Individual and group psychological response:
development of psychological defense mechanisms

↓

Compensatory logic system: white supremacy

↓

Compensatory behavioral practices: (economics, education, entertainment, labor, law, politics, religion, sex, war)

↓

White supremacy behavioral "system" and culture
on worldwide scale

↓

Systematic oppresion, domination and inferiorization of all
people with the capacity to produce significant amounts of melanin
skin pigment: black, brown, red and yellow peoples of the Earth

Diagram I

controlling the births of whites; in fact, there are some white governmental groups that give dividends to citizens for increased procreation.

The above are but a few examples selected from millions of large and small behavioral patterns practiced by whites in varying quantities. Yet, these examples effectively demonstrate the individual and collective neurotic need to focus on color, sex, genetics, numbers, superiority/inferiority, white supremacy and power. The Color-Confrontation theory contends that all of the above can be explained on the basis of the core psychological sense of color-deficiency and numerical inadequacy. The individual patterns of behavior that, over time, evolved into collective, social, institutional and now systemic patterns are seen as the origin of the "system of white supremacy," which operates at a universal level and is the only effective and functional racism existent in the world today. Further, racism (white supremacy), in this historical epoch, is viewed as a full-blown social contradiction and the major social dynamic superceding all others in influencing universal social practices and decisions. The Color Confrontation theory recongizes racism as one of the dominating forces determining character development, personality and formation type. Therefore, a functional definition of racism (white supremacy), is the behavioral syndrome of individual and collective color inferiority and numerical inadequacy that includes patterns of thought, speech and action, as seen in members of the white organization (race).

What then are the practical implications of this theory? Of major importance is the fact that for the first time in centuries non-white peoples throughout the world will have a rational basis for understanding the motivational nuances of individual and collective white behavior. The Color-Confrontation thesis theorizes that the majority of the world's people, non-whites, were manipulated into subordinate positions because, never having experienced such a state in terms of their own thought and logic processes and premises, they were unprepared to understand patterns of behavior predicated upon a sense of color deficiency and numerical inadequacy. This is analogous to the man with two eyes finding it difficult, if not impossible, to understand the behavioral patterns and motivations of the congenitally one-eyed man, who always looked upon the two-eyed state with jealous antagonism and, perhaps, aggression.

Armed with such insight, knowledge and understanding, non-whites will cease to be vulnerable to the behavioral maneuverings of individual or collective whites. Non-whites will be less vulnerable to the messages of white superiority that radiate throughout the known universe and permeate world cultures, which are dominated by the white supremacy system. This understanding will have profound effects on the developing egos and self-images of all non-white children, who suffer severe damage under the white supremacy culture. Moreover, whenever they are confronted by the ideology of white superiority/supremacy, non-whites will understand that it is only a compensatory psychological adjustment for a genetic, numerical deficiency state; thus the white supremacy message can be evaluated and negated more readily. This allows non-whites to gain psychological liberation from the white ideological domination that negatively affects the total functioning of non-whites. Further, non-whites will be less vulnerable to being maneuvered into conflict with one another, thus weakening the continued domination of the white supremacy system.

Also, white peoples of the world presumably also could benefit from such an awareness of the motivation behind behaviors that often baffle them. If they are sincere in their attempts to stop the practices of white supremacy (racism), whites may be able to find methods to do so once the cause is understood. Perhaps some psychiatrist will develop a method of mass psychotherapy (i.e., therapeutic counter-racist theater) to help whites become comfortable with their color and their numbers. However, one can foresee a major problem arising from the possible difficulty of motivating whites to release the secondary gains historically derived from the racist system.

The possibility of white people accepting this analysis of the white problem in human relations is not for me to answer. I do know that the majority of the world's people are looking for an answer to the dilemma that was once called the "American Dilemma." They are looking for a change. Perhaps *The Cress Theory of Color-Confrontation* will help them

13

to make that change. In any event, I am reminded of a statement made by Freud's biographer, Ernst Jones: "In the last analysis, the justification of every scientific generalization is that it enables us to comprehend something that is otherwise obscure." [6]

And, as James B. Conant has stated:

> The test of a new idea is...not only its success in correlating the then-known facts but much more its success or failure in stimulating further experimentation or observation which in turn is fruitful. This dynamic aspect of science, viewed not as practical undertaking but as development of conceptual schemes, seems to me to be close to the heart of the best definition of science. [7]

This essay analyzes the unique universal behavioral phenomenon of white supremacy (racism), and places it in a conceptual framework and context of a theoretical formulation. The fundamentals of the dynamics inherent in the spectrum of relations cover all areas of life activity between people who classify themselves as white, and those people whom whites have classified as non-whites.

REFERENCES

1. Gullattee, A.C...*The Subtleties of White Racism*. A paper presented to the American Psychiatric Association Annual Meeting, Miami Beach, Florida, May 1969.

2. Comer, J..."White Racism: Its Roots, form and Function," *The American Journal of Psychiatry*, Vol. 26: No. 6, December 1969.

3. Harrison, P.A., Butts, H.F.. "White Psychiatrists' Racism in Referral Practices to Black Psychiatrists," *Journal of the National Medical Association*, Vol. 62, No. 4, July 1970

4. Pinderhughes, Charles A. "Understanding Black Power: Processes and Proposals," *American Journal of Psychiatry*, Vol. 125: 1552-1557, 1969.

5. Cox, O.C.."Caste, Class and Race," New York: *Monthly Review Press*, 1959, p. ix

6. Fuller, N. *The United Independent Compensatory Code/System/Concept*, Copyrighted, Library of Congress, 1969

7. Fuller, N. *The United Independent Compensatory Code/System/Concept.*, Copyrighted, Library of Congress, 1969

8. X, Malcolm, *The Autobiography of Malcolm X* (with the assistance of Alex Haley). New York: Grove Press, 1966, p.120.

9. Jones, E. *Papers of Psychoanalysis*, Boston: Beacon Press, 1961, p. 73.

10. Conant, J.B. *On Understanding Science*, New York Mentor, 1953.

2

The Origin of Alienation, Anxiety and Narcissism (August 1980)

Dedication

This essay is dedicated to Genevieve Ekaete, a Nigerian journalist who, because of the profound pain of *alienation*, took her life on June 25, 1978 while residing in the United States of America. The world lost a brilliant mind and a generous person. Shortly before her death she stated, "My superstructure is solid. I need a formidable foundation..." This essay is my contribution to our understanding of the destructive dynamic of alienation.

Psychiatry as a discipline is floundering on its previously established conceptual and theoretical foundation imported from 19th century Europe. My continuing question to myself as a late 20th century precautionary in general and child psychiatry, practicing in the power capital of the world (Washington, D.C.) is, "Can a greater understanding be achieved in the study of human behavior as it is organized and manifested in the world's dominant power system/culture?"

My answer is affirmative. We can derive an ever increasing level of order out of the existing chaos, a diagnostic and statistical manual that gets heavier and wordier with each effort. Thereby, we can enhance our diagnostic and treatment skills and increase the possibility of prevention, allowing us to serve a suffering humanity better.

In *Have Astronomers Found God?*, Robert Jastrow states, "There is a kind of religion in science; it is the religion of a person who believes there is order and harmony in the universe, and every event can be explained in a rational way as the product of some previous event; every effort must have its cause." Jastrow continues, taking a quotation from Albert Einstein, "The scientist is possessed by the sense of universal causation."

As a social and behavioral scientist, I am convinced it is possible to understand, in depth, the patterns and system of behavior encountered in the individual and in the broad collective. My further conviction is that we can serve humankind maximally as behavioral scientists and physicians only when we adequately analyze the fundamental causation and logic of these patterns of behavior.

Three major foci of attention in Western social and behavioral science, particularly in psychiatry — alienation, anxiety and narcissism — are not unrelated, isolated syndrome abstractions, as they have been discussed by Western social and behavioral scientists. These separately described phenomena are not only interrelated, but they have a common origin and cause; they are derivatives of the same causal dynamic. Although that causal dynamic has remained unidentified, the source of these three phenomena is the origin of Western civilization itself.

Alienation. In the Color-Confrontation theory, I stated that racism (white supremacy), having begun as a form of alienation towards the self, now has evolved into the most highly refined form of alienation towards others as well. The Color-Confrontation theory views all of the present battle-grounds in the world today as vivid reflections of this alienation towards others. The destructive and aggressive behavioral patterns displayed throughout the world by white peoples towards all non-white peoples is the evidence of the inner hate, hostility and rejection they feel towards themselves and of the deep self-alienation that has evolved from their genetic inadequacy.

My extended definition of alienation centers around the recognition that it is a fundamental behavioral dynamic in Western civilization and culture. Alienation is a powerful centrifugal, genetic-psychological and societal dynamic that, over time, drives human beings further and further away from all effective, meaningful, emotionally supportive and truthful communications amongst one another. The alienation dynamic increas-

18

ingly forces people away from one another as Western civilization and culture evolves, as seen through each successive generation since its origin – including Greek civilization and the Roman Empire. Alienation is the very same dynamic that pushes human beings away from respectful and harmonious relationships with the physical environment, leading to the pollution and destruction of the planet. Most important, the alienation dynamic forces the individual away from all manifestations of self-understanding and self-respect, including the most fundamental respect — respect for one's genetic makeup.

The *Encyclopedia Britannica* records that the roots of the idea of alienation are found in the works of Plotinus, a Roman philosopher born in Egypt, who lived between 205 and 270 A.D., as well as in the theology of both St. Augustine and Martin Luther. The latter addressed the struggle to alienate oneself from one's own imperfections by identification with a transcendental perfect Being.

Entries on alienation did not appear in major reference books of the social sciences until 1935, but the concept of alienation was present in classical sociological texts of the 19th and early 20th centuries in the works of Marx, Durkheim, Tonnies, Weber and Simmel. Eric and Mary Josephson, in their *Man Alone: Alienation in Modern Society,* had the following to say about alienation:

> Indeed, ever since the great technological and political revolutions of the late eighteenth century, with their shattering impact on a rigid social order and their promise of individual freedom, one of the most disturbing phenomena of Western culture has been man's sense of estrangement from the world he himself has made or inherited – in a word, man's alienation from himself and from others. This theme of the alienation of modern man runs through the literature and drama of two continents; it can be traced in the content as well as the form of modern art; it preoccupies theologians and philosophers, and to many psychologists and sociologists it is the central problem of our time. In various ways they tell us that ties have snapped that formerly bound Western man to himself and to the world about him. In diverse language they say that man in modern industrial societies is rapidly becoming detached from nature, from his old gods, from the technology that has transformed his environment and now threatens to destroy it; from his work and its products, and from his leisure; from

the complex social institutions that presumably serve but are more likely to manipulate him; from the community in which he lives; and above all from himself – from his body and his sex, from his feelings of love and tenderness, and from his art – his creative and productive potential.

Contemporary contributors to the definition of alienation include such thinkers as psychoanalyst Erick Fromm; philosophers Lewis Mumford and Herbert Marcuse; existentialists Jean Paul Sartre, Albert Camus, Paul Tillich and Martin Buber; and sociologists David Riesman, Robert K. Merton and Talcott Parsons.

In summary, there are at least five causal theories concerning alienation: the economic, the technological, the sociological, the philosophic/existential and the psychological. Karl Marx is identified with the economic theory. Marx viewed alienation as a result of the private ownership of the means of production and the expropriation of man's labor by the capitalists – resulting in worker exploitation and class-struggle, money and commodities becoming the most meaningful things in man's existence and thus man's alienation from man. Technological theories attribute alienation to man's adjusted life-style to machines and automation. Sociological theories view the decline of the limited local community, the emergence of mass society and the simultaneous increasing sense of individual powerlessness as the cause of alienation. Philosophic/existential theories emphasize that alienation is inherent in the finite and isolated character of man's existence as a stranger and an alien in the world. Psychologic theories are dominated by the views of Sigmund Freud, who viewed alienation or self-estrangement as a resultant of the split between the unconscious and the conscious forces in the personality – the individual thus being out of touch, in the sense that repressed and unacknowledged desires motivate his behavior. More specifically, Freud pinpointed the Oedipal conflict and the frustrations inherent in civilized society, as expressed in his *Civilization and Its Discontents,* as the source of alienation.

The following are but a few items from a long list of suggested manifestations of alienation: child abuse, psychosis, suicide, neurotic depression, delinquency, psychosomatic disorders, prejudice, civil riots, wildcat strikes and the rise of fascism. All are believed to have derived from one or more of the following states: social isolation, self-estrangement, a sense of powerlessness, meaninglessness, normlessness, and cultural estrangement.

Whereas I agree with the existence of the alienation dynamic in Western civilization and culture, I disagree with all of the aforementioned theories of its causation. These theories remain superficial in their analyses, as each fails to reach the core of the origin of Western civilization. The multiplicity of theories on such a basic and pervasive dynamic as alienation reflects the failure to comprehend the origin and nature of Western man, who has created – at conscious and unconscious levels – the totality of the Western cultural imperative.

With a sufficiently deep investigation, the myriad aspects of the alienation dynamic that on the surface appear unconnected are recognized as highly interrelated and tied to a central core – a unitary causation. Anxiety and narcissism are tied to that same fundamental core, as illustrated in the following diagram. The three-dimensional cone-shaped figure represents the multiple levels at which reality (phenomena) may be decoded. The dots on the surface at Level 5 represent the seemingly isolated, multiple phenomena that can be examined at ever increasing levels of depth, indicated by Levels 4 through 1. The basic interconnections between the isolated phenomena are less apparent at Level 5 than at Level 2 or Level 1. The interconnections, however, become increasingly clear as a greater depth of phenomena penetration is achieved. (See Diagram I.)

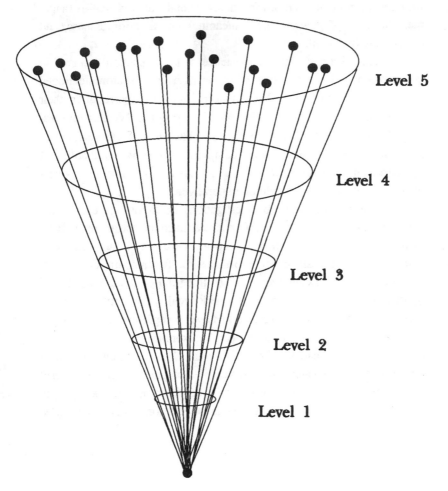

Level 5

Level 4

Level 3

Level 2

Level 1

Reality and Comprehension Levels
Diagram I

The term *Western* means "white." "Western" has become a comfortable (and for some, confusing), obfuscating euphemism or code for the word "white." The terms "Western civilization" and "Western culture" specifically refer to the civilization and culture evolved, determined, directed, developed and controlled by people who classify themselves as "white."

As mentioned in the Color-Confrontation theory, white-skinned people, who lack any substantial level of permanent melanin in their skin, historically have contrasted themselves with all people in the world who have substantial, recognizable and permanent levels of melanin. These skin-pigmented persons are referred to by the whites as "non-white" people, or when they are subdivided by the whites, they are referred to as "black," "brown," "red" and "yellow" peoples. Non-white peoples collectively constitute the global numerical majority. This skin-pigmented global majority is genetically dominant to the genetically recessive whites, and genetically they can annihilate the whites. These facts are essential to a thorough understanding of not only alienation but anxiety and narcissism as well. One cannot comprehend alienation, anxiety and narcissism as major phenomena in Western civilization and culture without an understanding of the origin of white-skinned people and their evolved thoughts and feelings (conscious and unconscious) about themselves.

White skin is a form of albinism. There is no difference, microscopically speaking, between the white skin of a white person and the skin of a person designated as an albino. My central thesis here is that white-skinned peoples came into existence thousands of years ago as the albino mutant offsprings of black-skinned mothers and fathers in Africa. A sizeable number of these Black parents had produced, rejected and then cast out of the community their genetic defective albino offspring, to live away from the normal black skin-pigmented population with the awareness of their rejection and *alienation* (as in leper colonies).

The white tribe's eventual migration northward, to escape the intensity of the equatorial sun of the Southern hemisphere, left the albinos eventually situated in the area of the world known as Europe – now recognized as the home of the white tribes. This early rejection of the albino offsprings might be viewed as a prehistoric (pre-Western civilization) instance of parental rejection, child neglect and abuse.

Sexual intercourse between the isolated albino mutants produced a white race — understanding race as an isolated population sharing a significant number of common identifying genes. This pattern of isolating individuals with defective genetic patterns is no different than the present-day practice of placing genetically abnormal individuals in institutions, away from the "normal" population group; another current practice is the isolation of those who are genetically different into "ghettos," which is an exact parallel to the albino isolation.

Support for my position is found in an article entitled "Albinism," by Carl Witkop, Jr., in the 1975 issue of *Natural History Magazine.*

> Historically, people with various depigmenting conditions, including albinism, have occupied a spectrum of social positions, ranging from outcasts to semigods. Montezuma, emperor of the Aztecs at the time of Cortez's conquest, maintained a museum of living human biological curiosities; prominent among these people were numerous albinos. Peoples with leprosy, which frequently causes a spotty depigmentation of the skin and hair, are described in biblical literature as the lowest outcasts...Among the San Blas, albinos are semi-outcasts; they participate less in daytime tribal activity and are not permitted to marry. Biological investigations show that as a group they are somewhat smaller and their muscles are not as well developed as those of pigmented San Blas.*

Similarly, in his article entitled "Cuna Moon-Child Albinism," in *The Journal of Heredity*, Clyde Keeler notes (among other findings on albinism):

> The voice quality of albino males is soft and higher pitched than in moreno (normal brown) males. In addition, they appear to be deficient in male sex hormone, and while they may be fertile, they have a lower phallic posture, due to flaccidity. Albinos usually have flabby muscles

---

*The San Blas are an Indian group in Panama, Central America.

and reduced muscular strength as shown by manometer readings....Psychiatric examination of six albinos showed their work to be generally in an intellectual sphere where overcompensation is the rule. Religion serves as a major support for many albinos who take a fatalistic view of life and blame their failures on their albinism which is God's will. As a usual thing sexual experience is much more limited in the albinos, who until recently, were not allowed to marry. While albino males have the reputation of being weakly sexed, albino females are said to be as active sexually as morenos, and they frequently have illegitimate children.

It should be noted that many of the San Blas albinos were indistinguishable from Scandinavians or other northern Europeans.

The 19th century German philosopher, Arthur Schopenhauer, made the following statement about white skin, in *The Philosophy of Schopenhaur, Metaphysics of Love of Sexes*, which illuminates both Witkop's and Keller's findings:

...the white colour of skin is not natural to man, but that by nature he has a black or brown skin, like our forefathers the Hindus; that consequently a white man has never originally sprung from the womb of nature, and that thus there is no such thing as a white race, as much as this is talked of, but every white man is a faded or bleached one.

Additional support is found in the work of Dr. Cheikh Anta Diop, the highly respected Senegalese anthropologist and Egyptologist, founder of the Radiocarbon Institute of the Fundamental Institute of Black Africa (Dakar, Senegal). Dr. Diop, in an interview in the winter 1976 issue of *Black Books Bulletin*, stated, "There is absolutely no doubt the white race which appeared for the first time during the upper Paleolithic – around 20,000 B.C. – was the product of a process depigmentation." Further, Dr. Diop informs us that much later the whites commenced their migratory movements towards the southern areas around 1500 B.C. Therefore, it should not be surprising that deep within the historic and current mythology and symbolism of Western civilization and culture (white supremacy system/culture) is evidence to strongly support the above outlined mode of origin as that actually traversed by the global albino (white) collective.

Major evidence for this theory of albinism (whiteness) is found in the symbolism of the Adam and Eve biblical mythology. Western civilization looks to this mythology in the Book of Genesis as the account of its beginning. The essential elements of the Adam and Eve story are that Adam and Eve were in the Garden of Eden, ate the forbidden fruit (the apple), had sexual intercourse, became ashamed of their nakedness and were chased from the Garden of Eden.

My decoding of that fundamental mythology and symbolism for Western civilization is as follows: Adam and Eve are the symbolic figures of the early albino mutants produced by Black parents; the Garden of Eden is Africa, the place where all knowledgeable anthropologists and paleontologists are informing us that human life began (and that the first human beings were black-skinned); the apple eaten by Adam and Eve is the presumed, orally ingested poison, looked upon as the cause of the mutation to albinism; this ingestion was followed by the act of sexual intercourse, which is also viewed as being responsible for the mutation to albinism and, therefore, the original sin; Adam and Eve's shame for their nakedness indicates their rejection and shame of their pale white bodies – colorless or naked – when compared to the black- and brown-skinned normals; their use of fig leaves to cover their genitals (as they are depicted) implies the shame and rejection of their genital apparatus, including their genes; their expulsion from the Garden of Eden represents the isolation of the albino mutants away from the skin-pigmented normals and their voluntary or involuntary migration out of Africa, northward into Europe.

Western culture goes further in the symbolism of its religious philosophy to pinpoint the eating of the apple by Adam and Eve, followed by their act of sexual intercourse, as "the act of original sin." Because of this act, Western culture conceives of all its people as being "born in sin" and in need of being "born again." Similarly, there are several other biblical references to skin-color change through God's punishment and leprosy, wherein the skin is described as becoming "white as snow" (2 Kings 5: 27). Of course, the further implication is that the skin originally must have been black, meaning melanin pigmented. Otherwise, how could it turn white? Numbers 12:10 states,

And the cloud departed from off the tabernacle; and, behold, Miriam
became leprous, white as snow: and Aaron looked upon Miriam, and
behold, she was leprous. And Aaron said unto Moses, Alas, my lord,
I beseech thee, lay not the sin upon us, wherein we have done foolishly,
and wherein we have sinned.

Contrary to this Western philosophy, there are no accounts of
skin-pigmented peoples, in their basic religious and/or philosophical
texts, conceiving of themselves as being born in sin or viewing their
genital apparatus (and therefore their genes) as the basis of sin and evil.

Further, Western civilization's religious and secular philosophy pin-
points the activity of Adam and Eve in the Garden of Eden as the point of
"the fall of man." "The fall" is the symbolic expression for the genetic
mutation to albinism and the negative projections regarding the white-
skinned self in a global population where the norm was black or brown
skin color. Likewise, today, the modern science of genetics views most
spontaneous mutations as negative and deleterious in terms of the welfare
of the organism in the environment, at least in the human population.

Additional symbolism in Western civilization and culture lends further
support to this thesis. For example, the *dog* rather than *God* proverbially
is considered Western man's best friend. This is contrary to the beliefs
of skin-pigmented peoples regarding their relationship to God. This
Western concept of the dog as man's best friend is linked to the mythology
of the founding of Rome. According to this mythology, Rome was
founded by two orphans, Romulus and Remus, who were suckled by a
wolf. (Both the wolf and the dog are canines.) These two presumably
white infants are said to have founded the state that began Western
civilization and culture. When this is decoded, Romulus and Remus are
the symbolic representatives of the early albinos who were abandoned by
their Black mothers in Africa as genetic mutant defectives and, in the
process of their northward migration for survival, were "left to the dogs"
– suckled by wolves. This decoding explains the worship and love of the
dog (canine) in Western civilization.

Western man's affection for the dog is reflected in the fact that in 1978
in New York City, dogs were permitted to put 250,000 pounds of fecal

27

matter on the streets each day, defiling the environment for human beings. And, is this love and worship of the dog reflected in the mirror-image of the words "God" and "dog" – even at this "advanced" stage in the expression and evolution of Western civilization and culture? Further, as relationships among people become more alienated, Western peoples and those non-white peoples who have been influenced most heavily by Western culture are gaining more satisfaction from feeding, clothing, loving and kissing canines than in feeding, clothing, loving and kissing human beings.

Western civilization's original symbolized relationship to the canine, following the African (Black) mothers' rejection of the albino mutant offsprings, undoubtedly has influenced the frequent use of the cursing expressions "bitch" and "son-of-a-bitch." These degrading expressions are used perjoratively because deep within the unconscious Western (white, albino) psyche, their rejected, mutant status is viewed perjoratively (in a world where the human norm is to have "hue").

Greater insight into the sense of alienation in Western culture is provided by the use of the word "mammy" when whites refer to a Black female caretaker, while referring to the white female caretaker as "nanny." Clearly, "nanny" is something less than "mammy." Also, the words "uncle" and "auntie," used by whites towards Blacks, bespeak an unconscious awareness of a deep and ancient familial relationship. The disrupted relationship is the origin of alienation, as supported by the symbolic rituals of Western fraternal organizations, such as the Masons and the Greek fraternities and sororities. The acting out of the "crossing of the burning sands" gives reference to the albino mutants' expulsion from Africa, across the burning sands of the Sahara Desert, out of Africa and into Europe. This was the original alienation experience of the albino whites first spawned in Africa.

From a more recent literary work than the Bible, the famous 19th century novelist Herman Melville, in his profoundly symbolic work about the white supremacy system/culture, *Moby Dick,* states:

> What is it that in the Albino man so peculiarly repels and often shocks the eye, as that sometimes he is loathed by his own kith and kin! It is

that whiteness which invests him, a thing expressed by the name he bears. The Albino is as well made as other men – has no substantive deformity – and yet this mere aspect of all-pervading whiteness makes him more strangely hideous than the ugliest abortion: Why should this be so?

Another famous American author, Mark Twain, in a collection of articles entitled *Mark Twain on the Damned Human Race*, compliments Melville's assessment in his essay, "Skin Deep." Twain's analysis suggests the depth of alienation experienced by whites (albinos).

...Nearly all black and brown skins are beautiful, but a beautiful white skin is rare. How rare, one may learn by walking down a street in Paris, New York or London on a weekday — particularly an unfashionable street — and keeping count of the satisfactory complexions encountered in the course of a mile. Where dark complexions are massed, they make the whites look bleached out, unwholesome, and sometimes frankly ghastly. I could notice this as a boy, down South in the slavery days before the war. The splendid black satin skin of the South African Zulus of Durban seemed to me to come very close to perfection. I can see those Zulus yet.... handsome and intensely black creatures, moderately clothed in loose summer stuffs whose snowy whiteness made the black all the blacker by contrast. Keeping that group in my mind, I can compare those complexions with the white ones which are streaming past this London window now...

Twain continues, detailing the negative attributes of white skin:

The advantage is with the Zulu, I think. He starts with a beautiful complexion and it will last him through. And as for the Indian, brown – firm, smooth, blemishless, pleasant and restful to the eye, afraid of no color, harmonizing with all colors, and adding grace to them all – I think there is no sort of chance for the average white complexion against that rich and perfect tint.

Finally, major documentation in Western literary symbolism that explains the origin of the global white collective's alienation – and unconscious awareness of this fact – is the stark symbolism of the profoundly important work of Edgar Rice Burroughs, the author of the

Tarzan series. The first of this series, *Tarzan of the Apes*, was copyrighted in 1912 and published in 1914. Before Burroughs died in 1950, he had produced 26 *Tarzan* books. So significant is the Tarzan symbolism for Western civilization and culture that Burroughs' company remains a multi-million dollar industry worldwide.

Edgar Rice Burroughs is one of the largest selling authors in the world. In 1975, his company estimated that more than 150 million copies of his books had been printed in 50 languages around the world. By 1980, the entire *Tarzan* series was being reissued. *Tarzan* is the story of a British baby, Lord Greystoke, who was abandoned in Africa at the age of nine months after his parents died. The great black "apes" then took care of him, as a passage from *Tarzan of the Apes* relates: "The hunger closed the gap between them and [Lord Greystoke] nursed at the breast of Kala, the great ape." It is a short leap through the symbolism to decode that nine months after conception, a white albino mutant was born to African (Black) parents and then abandoned. The child, in its anger and alienation, later returns to the scene of its rejection to dominate the Africans and all other non-white peoples.

Burroughs stated that the name Tarzan meant "white-skin" in the language of the apes. In the 1929 copyrighted *Tarzan at the Earth's Core* (13th in the series), Burrough's explains in more detail:

> The sun beating down upon his naked body, had no such effect upon his skin as would the sun of the outer world under like conditions. But it did impart to him a new confidence similar to that which he would have felt had he been able to retrieve his lost apparel. And in this fact he saw what he believed to be the real cause of his first embarrassment at his nakedness – it had been the whiteness of his skin that had made him seem so naked by contrast with other creatures, for this whiteness had suggested softness and weakness, arousing within him a disturbing sensation of inferiority; but now as he took on his heavy coat of tan and his feet became hardened and accustomed to the new conditions, he walked no longer in constant realization of his nakedness.

Just as Burroughs reveals this deep preoccupation of the white collective in *Tarzan*, we still find the white collective neurotically concerned with their white skin nakedness, developing suntanning parlors so as to produce a permanent state of brown skin coloration. For example, *Newsweek* printed an article in December, 1979 entitled "90-Second Suntans," in which one sunlamp devotee, when reminded of the hazards of suntanning stated, "If tanning is going to kill me at least I'll be a good-looking corpse."

The American Cancer Society estimates that the 1980 figure for new cases of skin cancer is 14,001, while an estimated 6,200 persons will die from the specific skin cancer melanoma. Despite these warnings, suntanning persists. A cursory glance at any beach or swimming pool today will provide a clear indication of the present number of white-skinned persons who are self-alienated even to the point of increasing their potential for cancer-caused death. They continue to pursue temporary skin pigmentation, even unto death, to become members of the "hue-man" family.

The symbolic profundity of all of the above should leave little doubt that whites' awareness of the origin of their alienation is in no sense superficial. This awareness goes deep to the genetic core of white peoples' status as mutated albinism variants and to the core of their concept and image of self as such. The Western brain-computer (individual and collective) then spawns patterns of its specific alienation in its myths, symbols, logic, thought speech, action, emotional response and perception in all areas of people activity: economics, education, entertainment, labor, law, politics, religion, sex and war.

Anxiety. More briefly, the core aspects of anxiety and narcissism in Western civilization and culture, which are integrally associated with the dynamic of alienation, must be discussed. Dr. Rollo May in his book, *The Meaning of Anxiety*, correctly informs us in the foreword to the 1950 edition:

> For the past hundred years,...psychologists, philosophers, social historians, and other students of humanity have been increasingly preoccupied with this nameless and formless uneasiness that has dogged the footsteps of modern man. Yet in all that time, to my knowledge, only two attempts have been made in book form – one essay by Kierhegaard and one by Freud – to present an objective

picture of anxiety and to indicate constructive methods of dealing with
it.

Twenty-seven years later, in the foreword to the revised edition, Dr.
May states,

> I believe a bold theory is necessary that will comprehend not only our
> normal and neurotic anxiety but anxiety in literature, art and
> philosophy as well. This theory must be formulated at our highest
> level of abstraction. I propose that this theory be founded on the
> definition that anxiety is the experience of Being affirming itself
> against Nonbeing. The latter is that which would reduce or destroy
> Being, such as aggression, fatigue, boredom, and ultimately death. I
> have rewritten this book in the hope that its publication will aid in the
> forming of this theory of anxiety.

Dr. May continues in his statement of the book's purpose:

> Despite the fact that anxiety has become a central problem to so many
> diverse areas in our culture, the attack on the problem has been
> handicapped by the fact that the various theories and studies of anxiety
> have, to date, been uncoordinated. In spite of the industrious work by
> skilled psychologists, this is as true in 1977 as it was in 1950. As is
> evident to anyone reading the papers from various symposia on
> anxiety, we do not even use the same language. Freud's description
> of the state of the problem in the opening paragraph of his chapter on
> anxiety published in 1935 is still largely accurate: 'You will not be
> surprised to hear that I have a great deal of new information to give
> you about our hypotheses on the subject of anxiety....and also that none
> of the information claims to provide a final solution to these doubtful
> problems.' What is necessary at the present stage of the understanding
> of anxiety is, the introduction of the right abstract ideas, and of their
> application to the raw material of observation so as to bring order and
> lucidity into it.

It is clear that the distinguished Dr. May, in regarding neurotic anxiety,
took into account Freud's discussion of neurotic anxiety as most fundamentally related to the birth trauma and to the fear of castration. Dr.
May later broadened the concept, writing: "It is very suggestive too that
the first anxiety state arose on the occasion of the separation from the

mother." Dr. May continues, referring to the danger of castration as "...a reaction to a loss, to a separation, of which the prototype is the birth experience." He also includes the analyses of other noted psychologists concerning anxiety: Otto Rank's view of anxiety as steming from the central problem of individuation – and then the fear of life and the fear of death; Alfred Adler's view of anxiety as related to feelings of inferiority; Jung's belief that anxiety is the individual's reaction to the invasion of his conscious mind by irrational forces and images from the collective unconscious; Karen Horney's view of anxiety as a reaction to a threat to something belonging to the core of the personality coupled with a hostility response; and, finally, Harry Stack Sullivan's view of anxiety as apprehension of interpersonal disapproval. However, Dr. May recognized that these theories, including his own ("Being affirming itself against Nonbeing"), remain insufficient.

I also view these approaches as insufficient and conclude, as argued in my earlier discussion of alienation, that *anxiety* in the Western civilization and culture, stems from the origin of that culture – which rests most fundamentally in the production of albino mutants from Black parents in Africa. Anxiety, like alienation in Western culture, is the result of the rejection of these albinos because of their genetic deficiency status and their subsequent abandonment and migration northward to form what is now recognized as the white race. This global white collective maintains a different appearance from the rest of humankind, and they dislike this difference. Therefore, they tan and use makeup. They remain a minority of the world's people, surrounded globally by a black, brown, red and yellow global majority. The white global collective remains genetically recessive to the black, brown, red and yellow global majority and lives each day and each minute of every hour in the continuous fear of white annihilation by the global majority of genetic dominants. This fundamental fear of albino isolation, abandonment and genetic annihilation, is at the core of Western civilization – a civilization structured to ensure white genetic survival. This survival plan necessitates the subjugation and control of all non-white peoples. I define this subjugation and control as the white supremacy system.

Because the conscious overt dialogue in the whole of Western civilization and culture is never about its global white minority status, its recessive (therefore vulnerable) genetic status, or its initial rejection by the Black parents and the Black majority, these feelings about self and fears of inadequacy and vulnerability reside underground in the brain-computer. These subconscious and unconscious thoughts become the basis for the pervasive neurotic anxiety that characterizes Western culture. Such is the specific nature and cause of this "nameless and formless uneasiness that has dogged the footsteps of modern man." Modern man means Western man, means white man, means the global white collective.

This is the reason that valium (diazepam) is the most prescribed drug in the U.S., the key unit of Western civilization and culture. It is this same anxiety that causes Western civilization's preoccupation with weapons, spending more money on armaments than on any other single budgetary item. These weapons surround all of the world's non-white peoples. The whites hope that the weapons will prevent white genetic annihilation and thereby ensure white genetic survival, but then whites hold the pervasive attendant fear that they will be destroyed in the conflagration also.

This fundamental anxiety relative to global white genetic annihilation pervades all patterns of symbols, logic, thought, speech, action, emotional response and perception in all areas of people activity within Western culture and civilization. Also, it pervades all aspects of family life, for whites and all non-white victims of white supremacy. All of the aforementioned theories of anxiety — by Freud, Jung, Rank, Adler, Horney, Sullivan and May — are encompassed in the above stated Cress-Welsing thesis on anxiety in Western civilization and culture.

Narcissism. Just as alienation and anxiety have become key foci of attention for Western behavioral and social scientists and other scholars, narcissism has become the most recent abstraction for intense intellectual involvement.

A January 30, 1978 *Newsweek* article entitled "The New Narcissism" outlines several qualities of narcissism:

> Long before social critic Tom Woefe labeled the '70s 'The Me Decade', scholars were exploring narcissism as a new – perhaps even

dominant – psychological pattern of both individual and social behavior. According to this theory, the New Narcissus suffers and emotionally dies because – like his mythological prototype – he cannot return anyone's affection. His fatal flaw, however, is not really self love but a grandiose expectation of himself that cannot be sustained and makes him vulnerable to chronic bouts of boredom and inner emptiness. In the eyes of the New Narcissus, the outside world is essentially a mirror that reflects his own alternating feelings of personal omnipotence and disintegration.

To Dr. Ernest Wolf of the Chicago Institute of Psychoanalysis, the identification of the new narcissism signals 'a major revolution in psychoanalysis', in which self-esteem is seen as just as important as sexuality. For social historian Christopher Lasch, narcissism is the key to understanding why 'self preservation and psychic survival' pervade the moral climate of contemporary society...At a recent conference on 'Narcissism in Modern Society' at the University of Michigan, several psychiatrists argued that there are still no solid clinical data proving that narcissism has increased in relation to traditional neuroses. Others, such as psychologist Kenneth Keniston, wonder whether a clinical term like narcissism can properly explain patterns of social behavior...Nonetheless, through a series of books, essays and symposiums, the new narcissism has emerged as a central intellectual concern. A post-Freudian school of psychoanalysis, based in Chicago, has proclaimed pathological narcissism the besetting psychological disorder of modern Western culture and has developed a 'psychology of the self' to explain its causes. And, some social scientists have adopted clinical descriptions of narcissism to help explain the declining interest in politics, social action and child-rearing, and the corresponding rise of an individual survival ethic.

'Pathological narcissists simply cannot depend upon others, which for me is a crucial characteristic,' says New York psychoanalyst Otto F. Kernberg, author of an influential study, 'Borderline Conditions and Pathological Narcissism.' Much as they crave admiration, says Dr. Kernberg, narcissists systematically exploit and devalue others. Frequently charming and charismatic, they tend to enjoy only fleeting emotional contacts, rather than genuine, long-term intimacy. Narcissists are often highly successful in business, bureaucracies, or other impersonal organizations; typically, such situations reward those who can manipulate others, while discouraging personal attachments and providing enough emotional feedback to satisfy self-esteem.

The third *Diagnostic and Statistical Manual of Mental Disorders* (1980), published by the American Psychiatric Association, contains a description of the narcissistic personality disorder, with the following stated criteria:

A. Grandiose sense of self importance or uniqueness

B. Preoccupation with fantasies of unlimited success, power, brilliance, beauty, or ideal love

C. Exhibitionistic: Requires constant attention and admiration

D. Responds to criticism, indifference of others, or defeat with either cool indifference or with marked feelings of rage, inferiority, shame, humiliation, or emptiness

E. Two of the following:

   1. Lack of empathy: Inability to recognize how others feel

   2. Entitlement: Expectation of special favors with reactions or surprise and anger when others don't comply

   3. Interpersonal exploitiveness: Takes advantage of others to indulge his own desires or for self-aggrandizement, with disregard for the personal integrity and rights of others

   4. Relationships characteristically vacillate between the extremes of over-idealization and devaluation.

Any non-white person who has had extensive experience with whites, collectively or as individuals, will find in the above a description of those relationships. At a superficial level, it seems ironic that those responsible for including this disorder in the *Diagnostic and Statistical Manual* have failed to recognize this as a statement that characterizes the global relationship of whites to non-whites, a description of the white supremacy dynamic (racism).

For further understanding of this perceptual failure, let us return to the Greek myth of Narcissus. According to Greek mythology, Narcissus was the son of the river god, Cephissus, and the nymph, Leiriope; he was distinguished for his beauty. His mother was told that he would have a long life, *provided he never looked upon his own features.* However, his rejection of the love of the nymph Echo or of his lover Anemias drew upon him the vengeance of the gods. He fell in love with his own reflection in the waters of a spring and pined away (or killed himself).

This ancient mythological symbolism displays the difficulty the white collective has in looking in the mirror to see itself for what it truly is in relationship to the vast majority of the world's people. Indeed, if it faces itself, with its puffed up attitude of white superiority, it will disintegrate.

Narcissism, as described but not deeply understood by Freud, is germain to this thesis. Freud viewed narcissism as a character disorder in which there was fixation of libidinal energy upon the self. Because of a lack of love or response on the part of the parents, the libidinal energy never can be discharged upon another person with satisfacton. Distrust of the other person in relationships persists into adult life, so that the narcissistic character prefers autoeroticism (i.e., masturbation) to normal sexual intercourse.

Freud and others have failed to understand that the failure of parental love is rooted in the original rejection by the Black mothers and Black fathers in Africa of their albino (white) mutant offspring, who were forced to try to love themselves if they were to survive; but they could not arrive at a point of true self-acceptance because there was never parental and group acceptance or validation at the time that the whites mutated from the Blacks. Because whites failed to be accepted by the original Black parents, they evolved the subsequent *compensatory* pattern of white supremacy. Yet, beneath the stance of white supremacy and white gran-diosity, the insecurity of inadequacy, inferiority and vulnerability remains to be displayed alternately. Long, long ago, the Greeks were cautioned by the Oracle of Delphi – whom the Greeks portrayed in the eponymous hero Delphas, as a Negro – to "Know Thy Self." Clearly, to date, the Western collective has failed in this task.

3

Unified Field Theory Psychiatry
(1980)

Yet do I marvel at this curious thing, to make a poet Black and bid him sing.
> — Countee Cullen

Is it conceivable that a Black who is also a woman can critique and dismantle the whole of Western psychiatry?

I will begin this essay somewhat differently than it was originally conceived several years ago. This alteration is occasioned by having read the article, "Retreat Behind New Walls Seen Posing Danger for Psychiatry," which appeared in the June 1980 issue of *Clinical Psychiatry News*. It is a report from San Francisco on the address given by Dr. Alan M. Stone, as outgoing president at the annual meeting of the American Psychiatric Association. Dr. Stone stated:

> The new walls are being built as psychiatrists attempt to deal with the issues of racism, homosexuality, and the situation of women....These are all issues which have confronted us in our practice, challenged the moral assumptions that lie concealed in our theories, and confounded us with disputes and acrimony in our association. It is no accident that each (issue) invites psychiatry to take a stand on human values. Human values, after all, are a crucial link in the chain that binds the self to society. To take a stand on them reveals something about our own selves, our own relations to society, and our own vision of what it means to love and to work. Many psychiatrists believe that the APA should limit itself to issues that are clearly psychiatric, but many others believe that these social issues are clearly psychiatric. I shall claim that what separates these two groups can only be understood as part of the deep theoretical dilemma in which American psychiatry finds

itself: its lack of conceptual clarity. This theoretical ambiguity is the core of the conflict that confronts psychiatry. As pragmatic eclectics, uncertain that we have put the pieces of the picture together correctly, we can never be confident that we can distinguish between the sick patient and the sick society. Psychiatry's contribution to what it means to be a person is its most powerful aspect. That contribution cannot be under psychiatry's control in a free society. However, the profession has a responsibility for the hidden values in its theories and therapies, which contribute to the shaping of 'contemporary consciousness.' It is in the issues surrounding the subject of women that perhaps the most convincing attack on the hidden values in psychiatry has been made.

Dr. Stone continued this discussion, asking if these issues cut deeper into American psychiatry than racism and homosexuality:

As far as I can see, the case against psychiatry as it regards women is far more damaging, requires far more than a minor adjustment of our composite sketch; indeed, it compels each of us to reexamine not only our theories, but also our lives and relationships. There can be no new psychology of women that does not require a new psychology of men. That makes necessary a new conception of all our human values and all the paradigms of psychiatry. Psychiatry does not stand outside of history or morality, but how do psychiatrists decide which history and which morality to accept? The rules about which history and which morality to accept are not clearly described in the biologic, psychodynamic, and behavioral paradigms. What is required of us is moral ambition. Until our composite sketch becomes a true portrait of humanity, we must live with our uncertainty. We will grope; we will struggle; and our compassion may be our only guide and comfort.

Originally, my essay began with the statement, "It is clear to many that grave problems are confronting the field of psychiatry at theoretical and conceptual levels. This crisis has important implications for treatment as well as problems encountered in formulating diagnostic categories as evidenced in the controversies surrounding the task of developing *Diagnostic and Statistical Manual III*." But who better should state the problems facing psychiatry in America than an outgoing president of the American Psychiatric Association? Indeed, who would be more readily believed than he?

While not accepting all that was said by Dr. Stone (most specifically his view of sexism as a more problematic issue than racism), I do share his awareness of a floundering chaos in psychiatry's current theoretical and conceptual state. It was this very awareness that led me to the consideration of a *unified field theory* in psychiatry.

The concept of a unified field theory is derived from the work of the great physicist Albert Einstein (March 14, 1879 – April 18, 1955). Einstein, a mathematical physicist, the most recognized and highly renowned scientist in the history of Western civilization, spent the greater portion of his productive years in search of a unified field theory, a theory that, in mathematical terms (by a single set of equations), would combine all of the different manifestations of energy phenomena in the universe.

Einstein studied the force of gravity and produced the General Theory of Relativity. He studied the forces of electromagnetism and produced the Special Theory of Relativity, which became a more accurate yardstick for measuring the characteristics of the physical world. Then, Einstein questioned the possibility of generalizing the mathematical foundations of the theory to derive not only the properties of the gravitational field, but also those of the electromagnetic field.

His work is reviewed in Ronald Clarke's 1971 *Einstein: The Life and Times.* In Einstein's own words:

> For years, it has been my greatest ambition to resolve the duality of natural laws into unity. This duality lies in the fact that physicists have hitherto been compelled to postulate two sets of laws — those which control gravitation and those which control the phenomena of electricity and magnetism...Many physicists have suspected that two sets of laws must be based upon one general law, but neither experiment nor theory has until now, succeeded in formulating this law....The relativity theory reduced to one formula all laws which govern space, time and gravitation, and thus it corresponded to the demand for simplification of our physical concepts. The purpose of my work is to further this simplification, and particularly to reduce to one formula the explanation of the field of gravity and the field of electromagnetism. For this reason I call it a contribution to 'a unified field theory'...Now, but only now, we know that the force which moves electrons in their ellipse about the nuclei of atoms is the same force which moves our earth in its annual course about the sun, and is

the same force which brings us the rays of light and heat which make life possible on this planet.

Not only did Einstein die before achieving this goal, but prior to his death his conceptualization of a unified field theory was being dismissed by younger physicists as the ideas of an old man whose scientific usefulness had passed long ago. Quantum physics and the physics of chance and statistical probabilities (the physics of Born and Heisenberg) were supplanting the Einsteinian physics of the whole. This was the new physics of *indeterminacy*. This new physics could be characterized by Sir George Thompson's following statements, which appear in *Einstein: The Life and Times*:

> Wherever a system is really complicated, as in the brain or in an organized community, indeterminacy comes in, not necessarily because of 'h' (Planck's constant) but because to make a prediction, so many things must be known that the stray consequences of studying them will disturb the status quo, which can never therefore be discovered. History is not and cannot be determinant. The supposed causes only may produce the consequences we expect.

I am almost certain that most workers in the field of psychiatry are not consciously aware that they too have assured a position in the respective scientific camps of either Albert Einstein or that of Born and Heisenberg. The camp of indeterminacy holds, as articulated by Sir George Thompson, that (in a system as complicated as the brain or in an organized community) one cannot uncover a unitary law or a unitary cause of the many complex forms of behavior, knowledge of which would enable prediction of expected consequences. On the contrary, the camp of determinacy concludes that in any finite energy system – no matter how seemingly complex at the surface level – a unitary law can be discerned simply because there is specific order in the universe and thus there is order in any given energy system. A unitary law would reveal the nature of *that* specific order. I reside in the Albert Einstein camp — the camp of determinacy.

Einstein's effort towards uncovering the unified field has great meaning to me as a psychiatrist/behavioral scientist because it is my developing conviction that the present confusion is largely a result of our failure to see the interconnections that exist between many seemingly isolated, disconnected behavior-energy phenomena in Western culture. Actually there are very few, if any, workers in behavioral science who perceive the necessity to search out, on the one hand, these interconnections and, on the other hand, to unveil the total unified form that is structured by these interconnections and their fundamental cause (etiology). This may be said in the reverse order: because there is the failure on the part of most investigators to perceive the total outline of the Western cultural dynamic, it is difficult, if not impossible, for them to make sense of the isolated behavioral patterns within the total behavioral system framework. Behavioral scientists, thus frustrated, have tried to find the answers in statistics, neurochemical molecules and genes. It was this same limitation and dependence on the statistical method of analyzing energy phenomena that depressed Einstein in the work of his colleagues in physics. He lamented that they just could not see the larger picture. They lacked his intuitive faculty to *see* at a deeper and more encompassing level.

This may best be understood if we look at the scattered pieces of a 1,000-piece jigsaw puzle for which the outlining border has not yet been set in place. Generally speaking, one cannot make heads or tails of the scattered, tiny pieces. Once the outline or context has been established, the order in which the small pieces are to be placed immediately becomes clear. I use this particular introduction for this brief essay because a total behavior-energy system also can be seen and understood as a *unified field* of energy phenomena. Once that unified field of behavior-energy is perceived and described, setting forth its etiology and dynamic, the once seemingly isolated, little understood, often unexamined, individual phenomena of behavior-energy within the field, are seen in brilliant coherence, whereas before, they were neither visualized nor understood adequately. A parallel process can be seen in the recent discoveries in physics of strange celestial objects such as quasars, pulsars and black holes, the discovery of which can be seen as dependent upon Einstein's concept of a unified field – the framework of his relativity concept.

43

The global white supremacy system (racism) is a highly specific system of behavior-energy. The force and energy of this system, through its ultimate goal objective and its patterns of logic, thought, speech, action, emotional response, perception and symbols, in all areas of people activity (economics, education, entertainment, labor, law, politics, religion, sex and war), determines the dominant patterns of behavior in the world today. The global system of white supremacy is euphemistically referred to as "Western civilization."

In Chapter 1, I explained that the global behavior patterns of racism are a survival necessity for the white collective. This racist activity is a compensatory attempt to prevent white genetic annihilation on a planet where the vast majority of peoples are genetically dominant to the melanin-deficient whites. The awareness of self (in the white global collective) as a white, genetic mutant population that was rejected by their Black parents in Africa (see Chapter 2), and the subsequent conscious and/or unconscious determination to survive as a global minority became the underlying law that determined the evolution of the now global white supremacy system/culture.

All major and minor behavior-energy crystallizations or behavior-units in the global white collective – no matter how simple or complex, old or new, short- or long-lived – must conform, in the final analysis, to the basic behavior-energy equation of *white over non-white* (or white power over non-white powerlessness). This is the necessary power or energy equation for *white* genetic survival. This behavior-energy equation is expressed in energy manifestations of patterns of logic, thought, speech, action, emotional response and perception in all areas of people activity.

From this basic law, it becomes possible to predict the ultimate output of individual and collective white brain-computers at the local and global levels. In energy terms, this means that it is possible to predict the fundamental patterns ("the bottom line") of all energy that flows from the white collective in its dynamic interactions with the non-white collective. That sum total of behavior-energy expression is always the energy crystallization of white supremacy (white genetic survival) – irrespective of the gross or subtle myriad behavior forms it assumes. Also, this energy formation can be understood as a finite unified energy field or force field, albeit that the force is behavior-energy.

This new theory of psychiatry is what I refer to as *Unified Field Theory Psychiatry*. It is a psychiatry that perceives a definable whole, global system of behavior-energy, wherein the behavior events lend themselves to prediction because the ultimate objective of the system remains constant. The basic considerations that Einstein proposed for physical energy in his concept of a unified field theory can be applied readily to behavior-energy in the concept of Unified Field Theory Psychiatry. Thus, the role of all major and minor patterns of behavior within the field can be understood and even predicted.

Now, the underlying interrelationships between seemingly unconnected patterns of behavior are visible. It is as though the end of a knotted ball or skein yarn has been discovered that, with patience, permits complete unraveling without breaks in the yarn. Heretofore, no Western behavioral scientist had recognized the single connecting thread of logic permeating seemingly unrelated phenomena such as lynchings, smoking objects, bullfights, chocolate candy with nuts, coffee, guns, umbrellas, automobiles, skiing, race, races and racing (horse, foot and car), the Adam and Eve mythology, *Moby Dick*, *Dracula*, *Frankenstein*, the play "Equus" by Peter Schafer, paper money, gold, Christian religious symbolism, the Nazi Swastika, anti-Semitism, sexual perversions, apartheid, child abuse, capitalism, nudism, the Holocaust, alienation, sexism, homosexuality, pornography, narcissism, gambling, rape, flags, men's ties, etc. All of the above are but a few of the major behavior-energy entities, myths and symbols included in the white supremacy system/culture that are related to the single underlying law governing the origin and continued existence of Western civilization.

Western social and behavioral science, particularly psychiatry, has been content with behavior fragment analyses and multiple theoretical explanations for different behaviors. This demonstrates a failure to comprehend the entire forest, while focusing on isolated trees or clumps of trees. Failure to comprehend the whole behavior-energy force field has resulted in isolated behavior modification techniques and programs, the inability to grasp the manner in which the total social structure determines the behavior of the individual personality, and the tendency to focus on isolated neurochemical sequences and mechanisms as causing certain behavior pattern constellations. This limited pattern of perception and the apparently necessary pattern of endless abstracting, with an inability to synthesize the whole, may be predicated upon a pattern of data reception in the nervous system of persons who possess insufficient levels of melanin in their nervous systems. The lack of melanin results from the genetic deficiency state of albinism or its variants, which in turn influences basic patterns of perception of energy messages from the physical/ social environment. (I will examine this possibility in a future work.) Understanding this, it is clear that current Western psychiatry's inability to identify the interrelationships existing between racism, homosexuality and sexism (articulated by Dr. Alan Stone) is due to an inadequate conceptual and theoretical base.

As stated previously, racism is the evolved behavior-energy system predicated upon the need for white genetic survival. Both homosexuality and sexism are derivatives of that fundamental dynamic. The forces in the white supremacy system that lead to a massive increase of passivity, effeminization, bisexuality and homosexuality in the Black male population as necessities for white genetic survival are discussed in Chapter 6. However, to specifically focus on white male homosexuality in the white supremacy system/culture, we must return to the male albino mutant's awareness of himself in contrast to the prototypic human male – the Black male, the father of the early albino mutants. Indeed, this fact is the true basis for the Oedipus mythology.

Historically, white males worldwide have suffered the deep sense of male inferiority and inadequacy because they represent a mutant, genetically recessive, minority population that can be genetically annihilated by all non-white people – males and females. Ultimately, this awareness in the white collective has produced high levels of masculine self-doubt, fear, anxiety and self-aliention. These difficulties have been intensified by the awareness that white reproductivity is far lower than the natural reproductivity of any non-white population.

Thus, the white male collective feels vulnerable to the global non-white male collective but most specifically to the Black male collective because of Blacks' ability to produce the highest levels of melanin and thereby the greatest potential for white genetic annihilation. This basic logic of disgust with the white genetic and genital self drives the brain-computer in the white male collective to self-negating patterns of behavior. Also, it is the basis for the continuing question in the white collective, "Who has the largest penis – the Black or the white male?"

At another level, white male homosexuality may be viewed as the symbolic attempt to incorporate into the white male body more *male substance* by either sucking the penis of another male and orally ingesting the semen, or by having male ejaculate deposited in the other end of the alimentary canal. Through anal intercourse, the self-debasing white male may fantasize that he can produce a product of color, albeit that the product of color is fecal matter. This fantasy is significant for white males because the males who are able to produce skin color are viewed as the real men.

This same sense of maleness-deficiency in the white supremacy culture causes the behavior patterns of smoking either *small* white phallic symbols called cigarettes, *large* dark brown or black phallic symbols known as cigars, pipes and the long brown cigarettes called *Mores*. (Or does it mean Moors?) These are sucked, swallowed, puffed and otherwise bodily ingested, ultimately leading to self-negation through potential cancer-caused deaths. Also, it should be noted that for the white male collective, the *greatest* sense of male power comes from smoking the large, dark brown, phallic smoking objects – cigars and pipes. Thus, cigars are given at the birth of a son! (See Chapter 11.) Similarly, this sense of maleness-deficiency elevates the gun to such important status in the white supremacy culture. (See Chapter 8.)

White male homosexuality is reinforced in the white family, wherein the white male's sense of genetic inadequacy causes him to project his sense of genetic inferiority onto the white female. She is forced to accept the concept of her own genetic inferiority compared to white males. In angry reaction to the white male attack, she causes her white sons to negate their masculinity and to become more like herself as a female. Also, the white male must oppress the white female because the latter proclaims that her ideal sex partner is, "tall, *dark* and handsome." Should the white female be permitted to have her freedom and to sexually aggress against the dark man (the non-white male), white genetic annihilation will occur.

The two above factors – 1) white males projecting their sense of genetic inferiority onto white females, and 2) white males' fear that white females (in their preference for Black and other non-white males) will become participants in white genetic annihilation – have resulted in what Western culture now refers to as "sexism" – the repression of white females by white males in the white supremacy system/culture.

Presently, white females are responding collectively to white males' imposed sense of genetic inferiority through their struggle for "equality" with white males. Large numbers of white females are proclaiming themselves lesbians, believing that this is a constructive response to their sense of inadequacy. They, of course, fail to realize that these behaviors arise from the fact that they have been taught to degrade their genetic makeup as white females in the subtle dynamics of white family life. Thus, they move into behaviors of non-self-reproduction and self-negation.

Also, in white females' drive to be "equal" to white males, they have increased greatly the practice of sucking on the white phallic symbols – cigarettes – causing a sharp increase in their incidence of self-negation through lung cancer. White females fail to understand that while they strive to become "the same as" white males, they become more alienated from their genetic selves. Thus, they fall victim to the dynamic of genetic alienation (the central core of racism) as they participate in the finite, unified energy field of white genetic survival.

Whether one examines the microcosm of the individual white personality or the macrocosm of the global white collective, the law of white genetic survival stands. That law can be stated in the following equation: white power over non-white powerlessness, or $\frac{W}{NW}$. Nonetheless, the implication of the law for whites is a *failure* of individual and collective white self-respect, based upon the negative image and concept of the self.

In the white collective, there is self-esteem, which is a compensatory inflated sense of the self, but there is *not* fundamental respect for the genetic white self. The implications for psychiatry are as follows: on the basis of a *negative* image and concept of the self, the brain-computer evolves patterns of neurochemistry, logic, thought, speech, action, emotional response and perception that are *self- and group-negating* and productive of *disharmony* in the universe. These are patterns of neurochemistry and behavior consistent with various degrees of *mental illness*. On the basis of a *positive* self-image and self-concept, the brain-computer evolves patterns of neurochemistry, logic, thought, speech, action, emotional response and perception that are *self- and group-supporting* and productive of *harmony* in the universe. These are patterns of neurochemistry and behavior consistent with mental health.

The following diagram shows the environmental factors that act upon the genetic and constitutional base to form the self-image and self-concept. Factors that support the self lead to positive self-images and self-concepts, whereas factors that deny the self lead to negative self-images and self-concepts.

Diagram of Dynamic Factors Contributing to End Product of Behavior

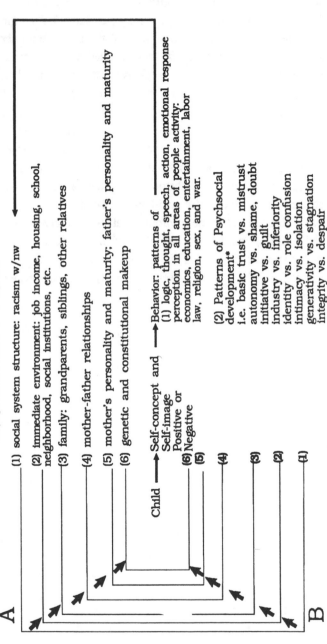

A

(1) social system structure: racism w/nw

(2) immediate environment: job income, housing, school, neighborhood, social institutions, etc.

(3) family: grandparents, siblings, other relatives

(4) mother-father relationships

(5) mother's personality and maturity; father's personality and maturity

(6) genetic and constitutional makeup

Child → Self-concept and → Behavior: patterns of
Self-image
Positive or
(6) Negative
(5)
(4)
(3)
(2)
(1)

B

Behavior: patterns of
(1) logic, thought, speech, action, emotional response perception in all areas of people activity: economics, education, entertainment, labor law, religion, sex, and war.

(2) Patterns of Psychsocial development*
i.e. basic trust vs. mistrust
autonomy vs. shame, doubt
initiative vs. guilt
industry vs. inferiority
identity vs. role confusion
intimacy vs. isolation
generativity vs. stagnation
integrity vs. despair

Negative self-concept

Positive self-concept and

*Patterns of Psychosocial Development from
Childhood and Society
by Erik H. Erikson
Norton 1930, 1963
Norton & Company Press, New York

Key: Levels 1-5 = Environmental Dynamic
A = Stress from Environmental Dynamic → Negative self-concept
and self-image → self-negating behaviors

B = Supports from Environmental Dynamic → Positive self-concept and
Self-supporting behaviors

The task of psychiatry is to help the individual and the collective achieve genuine genetic self-respect and thereby respect for others and for all aspects of the universe. Psychiatry's further task is to demonstrate that the white supremacy system (Western civilization) is unable to produce an environment in which mental health can evolve and flourish. Therefore, that power system needs to be abandoned for a more productive one.

This Unified Field Theory Psychiatry concept of mental health and mental illness challenges the dictum of Sigmund Freud — that mental health is the ability to work and to love. The global white supremacy system/culture constitutes a finite, unified behavior-energy field. The single, unitary law of white genetic survival governs its origin and its continuance. *Homosexuality and sexism* are necessary derivatives of this energy field and, just like all other significant behaviors in the global and local white collective, can be understood as derivatives of this finite, unified behavior-energy field. It is knowledge of the unitary, causative law that governs this field and enables the prediction of future behavior-energy patterns within it.

The above discussion then serves as background to the essays which follow. All dominant behaviors in the white supremacy system/culture are derivatives of this central concern and its secondary and tertiary elaborations and compensations, which also are concerned with white genetic survival. Together, these behavior patterns produce the white supremacy unified behavior field. Albert Einstein realized that we needed a law to guide us in and around the phenomena in the organized energy system of the physical universe, so that our movements and interactions in that universe could be facilitated. Similarly, we need a law to guide us in the evolved energy system of white supremacy behavior organization, in order to facilitate our movement in that system, with the ultimate goal being truth, justice, harmony and peace. Contrary to the fears of Dr. Alan Stone, new walls are being built in psychiatry. The old walls of artificial abstractions are being torn down, and in their place stands a new edifice, a unified field, which can be used to diagnose, treat and cure.

4

Learning to Look at Symbols
(February 1979)

A culture can be likened to a quilt of intricate geometrical design in which all of the many colored pieces, their shapes and stitching flow into one another, constitute the whole. This analogy is apt for yet a second reason. Often, the design on the upper side of the quilt is different from the undersurface pattern. Still, the undersurface design is essential for the outward surface appearance.

I have given myself the task of decoding the culture in which I find myself in time and space. That culture is the dominating global power system/culture of white supremacy (racism). This decoding amounts to turning over, examining and laying bare the intricate pattern pieces underlying the culture and power system – showing in sharp relief its lines of force and determination and thus its overall design. Only by so doing is it possible to see where we are going in the existing dense white fog.

Counter-racist psychiatry defines mental health as patterns of logic, thought, speech, action, emotional response and perception consciously practiced by the victims of white supremacy (racism) – with the objective of eradicating racism at the global level. Functionally speaking, for the victims of white supremacy, this means to act in a self/group-respecting and supporting manner in all areas of people activity, despite the specific conditions of racist domination and oppression. Submission to and cooperation with victimization and oppression are signs of individual or group mental illness or self-negation.

Once the victims of oppression accurately and completely decode the system and its objective of oppression and once they fully analyze the symbols and patterns of logic, thought, speech, action, emotional response and perception (consciously or unconsciously determined) that constitute the system, the oppressed will be able to reorganize their own behavior effectively. This reorganization will result in self/group-respect and support, and thereby end their oppression.

The process of decoding a power system and its culture is a necessary first step to achieve behavioral mastery over that system/culture. The attainment of such mastery is an essential step in the process of total liberation for the victims who wish to end that oppression and regain their self-respect and mental health. Without this process of decoding, the oppressed fail to fully understand what they are dealing with; they have minimal levels of consciousness and self/group-respect, and they are, functionally speaking, mentally ill.

This decoding activity entails the unraveling and analysis of all the various products of individual and collective brain-activity within the given culture. These brain products appear and are reflected in all areas of people activity: economics, education, entertainment (including games and sports), labor, law, politics, religion, sex and war. This means analyses of products of conscious as well as unconscious brain activity – patterns of logic, thought, speech, action, emotional response, perception, dreams, symbols and intuition – will be required. Of special importance are the brain products that issue forth from those who are white and who presently control the power balance in the global power system of white supremacy, and who thus produce the dominant themes and trends within the system and cultural framework.

Symbols are highly abstracted, condensed and coded messages that are developed by the activity of the brain-computer in the human organism. These messages are developed and evolved from energy (sensory) data received in the brain from the external environment. Various lines of energy data form the total environmental coverage on the brain-computer via the nervous system, which can then, under the proper circumstances, lead to the development of a symbol. Thus, symbols reflect certain aspects of the external environment and the total body's internal environmental response to the external environment.

Musical notes on paper, as well as written and spoken words, are symbols. There are other kinds of symbols that are not as immediately translated or fully understood because of their highly abstract forms and complexity. The impact of these complex symbols reach subconscious and unconscious levels of brain activity. These complex symbols are, in effect, full sentences, paragraphs or entire books of data stated in a highly abstracted single image or line configuration.

Once the symbol is formed, it is capable of acting upon the brain-computer, which receives it as an energy or data message. This message effects the end-product of behavior as carried forth in any area of human activity. The symbol, in turn, acts upon the external environment. These "single-picture-sentences" or "single-picture-paragraphs" commence in the brain-computer and act as powerful undetected persuaders, and thus, as powerful determinants of behavioral patterns.

These complex symbols are usually related to the deepest cultural themes of a people and have significant messages to convey about the people's and culture's reason for being. Furthermore, these reasons are passed on uncensored in the unconscious, via the total environmental experience, from the beginning of "people-time," generation to generation. In this manner, the symbols act as a stirring rod that agitates the unconscious, sending out energy responses in the form of thought, speech, action and emotions. In the opinion of the Hindu philosopher, Ananda K. Coomaraswamy,

> ...symbolism is 'the art of thinking in images,' an art now lost to civilized man – However, this loss, as anthropology and psychoanalysis has shown, is limited to consciousness and not to the 'unconscious,' which to compensate, is perhaps now overloaded with symbolic material.

He goes on to state, "To know the rational in the deeply irrational is the mark of truthful living, that is, of fully alive perception of the conditions of one's life."

The major forms of symbolism in a power system/culture constitute powerful and subtle messages about how and why the culture came into being, and what the people must do to survive and maintain itself.

Symbolism is thus the glue that holds the individual and collective psyche of the people and its culture together. The keys to the system/culture are found in the decoded symbolism of that system/culture.

Symbols and Brain Process

Carl Gustave Jung was the major European behavioral scientist to emphasize the importance of symbols, their production and their meaning in the brain's total process and behavioral output. Nevertheless, his massive volume of work has taken a lesser place to that accorded Sigmund Freud in the late 19th and 20th centuries of Western (white) thought.

However, it should be remembered that the understanding and use of symbols (including the interpretation of dreams), reached their highest development in African and Asian cultures and was of major significance in these cultures dating back to the earliest time (prehistory) – long before there was any European cultural development.

According to Jung, "the symbol is the primitive expression to the unconscious, but at the same time it is also an idea corresponding to the highest intuition produced by consciousness." Additionally, in his work *Psyche and Symbols*, he had the following to say about symbols:

> Since the symbol is the most complete expression of that which in any given epoch is as yet unknown – and cannot be replaced by any other statement at the time – it must proceed from the complex and subtle strata of the contemporary psychological atmosphere. Conversely, the effective living symbol must also contain something which is shared by considerable numbers of men: it embraces that which is common to a larger group. Consequently, it must include those primitive elements, emotional and otherwise, whose omnipresence stands beyond all doubt. Only when the symbol comprehends all those and conveys them with ultimate force can it evoke a universal response. Therein resides the powerful and redeeming effect of the living social symbol.

Also, it has been said that symbols are always paradoxical since they contain elements that do not exist in logic. Jung thought that the elements combined within symbols are contradictory only to the logic of consciousness, but that, nonetheless, they conform to a basic reality that eludes conscious thought processes. "A genuine symbol – is an image which possesses two essential features: it originates within the archetypal ground of the psyche, and secondly, there exists a consciousness to apprehend it."

In an article entitled "Contribution of Jungian Psychotherapy Towards Understanding the Creative Process" (*Creative Psychology*, No. 4), George Boas states, "The beauty of myth and symbol lies in their synthetic power; they can combine in one presentation disparate elements which would be self-contradictory if put in a declarative sentence." Norman O. Brown, in *Love's Body*, has stated, "The axis on which world history turns is symbolism. From figura to veritas." Translation: from symbol to truth. "The axis of world history is making conscious the unconscious." Brown further states, "Symbolism is between conscious and unconscious."

Jung explains in his book *Man and His Symbols (Approaching the Unconscious)*, "A symbol is a term, a name, or even a picture that may be familiar in daily life, yet that possesses specific connotations in addition to its conventional and obvious meaning. It implies something vague, unknown or hidden from us." He continues, "A word or an image is symbolic when it implies something more than its obvious and immediate meaning. It has a wider unconscious aspect that is never precisely defined or fully explained." He further informs us that, "As the mind explores the symbol, it is led to ideas that lie beyond the grasp of reason."

Jung's work indicates that a true symbol appears only when there is a need to express a thought one cannot openly think or what is only divined or felt.

Recent neurological studies suggest that the "silent" right cerebral hemisphere is the source of activity leading to phenomena such as symbol formation. Other studies demonstrate that the left cerebral hemisphere seems more concerned with the logical processes of directed, more consciously controlled thinking. By contrast, the activities of the right cerebral hemisphere may be subject to different laws that are, as yet, little understood. In addition, the right and left hemispheres appear capable of independent, simultaneous thought. Also, it has been suggested that collaboration of the two contradictory modes associated with right and left hemispheric activity may account for the symbolic process and for creativity.

Diagram I illustrates the process by which the brain-computer uses sensory data, received from the surrounding environment, to form symbols and other brain-computer products.

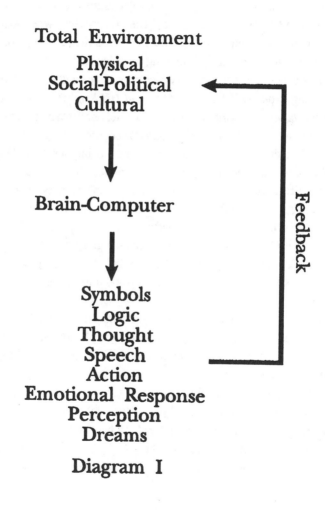

Total Environment
Physical
Social-Political
Cultural

Brain-Computer

Symbols
Logic
Thought
Speech
Action
Emotional Response
Perception
Dreams

Feedback

Diagram I

Clearly, many forms and levels of data messages from the physical and social environment are input in the brain-computer. Some of this sensory data is coded at the level of consciousness. But because of the large scope of unattended perceptions, much of the data is coded at the unconscious levels of brain activity. As some neurologist would state, this data is dispursed between the left and right cerebral hemispheres respectively.

For example, within the framework of a given system and culture, certain perceptions may exist that never are acknowledged overtly and certain ideas, thoughts, concepts and theories that are uttered rarely, if ever. These perceptions, words, ideas, concepts and theories that are repressed or channeled into the unconscious level of the brain-computer becomes an entire world of ideas treated as though they never existed in the form of concrete reality.

Nonetheless, the data from the environment that is encoded at the unconscious level of the brain-computer actually does not disappear – just as the objective data that produced the repressed ideas and concepts do not disappear. There simply ceases to be a clear focus on this body of data. This repressed data becomes the substratum from which symbols can be formed.

As stated previously, the dominant aspect of the total environmental reality on the planet is that the overwhelming majority of people are black, brown, red and yellow. This fact has created the most fundamental collective preoccupation and, perhaps, fear in the global white collective: *white genetic survival* – a survival that is threatened by the genetic material contained in the genitals of Black and other non-white men. Non-white people are genetically dominant to whites, and, thus, are potential genetic annihilators of the minority white collective. Due to this fear of white genetic annihilation, the global white collective has evolved, during the last 2,000 years, the global white supremacy system and culture that dominates all black, brown, red and yellow peoples in the world, determining their behavior in all areas of people activity.

REFERENCES

Jung, C.G. *Man and His Symbols (Approaching the Unconscious)*. New York: Dell Press, 1968.

Jung, C.G. *Psyche and Symbols*. Edited by Violet S. de Laszlo. New York: Doubleday, 1958.

McCully, R.S. "Contributions of Jungian Psychotherapy Towards Understanding the Creative Process," *Creative Psychiatry*, No. 4. Geigy Publications.

5

The Symbolism of Christ, the Cross, the Crucifix, the Communion
and Christian holidays
(August 1977, February 1979)

Dedication

This essay is dedicated to all of the Black men who are in "greater confinement" (prisons and jails) with the hope that they will be encouraged never to give up the struggle against white supremacy domination (injustice) once they understand what the struggle is truly all about. Then they never will return to jail, and their behavior no longer will be anti-racist (blind reaction to stress from ignorance, anger and fear), but effectively counter-racist. Many of these Black men, in their letters to me, also have given me great enouragement, support and help towards continuing our fight for justice. All Black people are still in confinement!

Foreword

This essay is not intended to be sacrilegious or offensive to anyone. I was baptized in the Baptist church and christened in the African Methodist Episcopal Church. This essay was written only to address the question Black people have been raising for a long time – "What's happening?" We ask that question of everyone that we meet because we truly have not understood and presently do not understand what really is going on. It is the responsibility of Black behavioral scientists in general, and Black psychiatrists in particular, to provide this answer.

The basic *discussion* of white genetic survival (through the possession and control of the Black male's genital apparatus) is carried forth unconsciously in the precepts and practices of the global white supremacy system's primary religion – Christianity. These fundamental concepts are manifested in Christianity's central pattern of symbols. In fact, it is in religious activity that the highest level of symbolic discussion emerges.

Whereas the testicles are those aspects of the male anatomy that contain the dominant genetic material, the penis is the aspect that transports the genetic material, which initiates the production of life and skin color. If one were to make a simple schematic diagram of the genital organs of the male anatomy, that diagram might look like Diagram I.

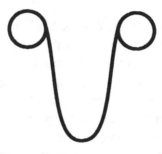

The Male Genitalia (diagrammatic sketch)
Penis and Testicles
Front View
Diagram I

A further abstraction of the same drawing could be represented as Diagram II.

Or, if further abstracted, it could be represented simply as two lines, one vertical, the other horizontal – one crossing near the top of the other. (See Diagram III.)

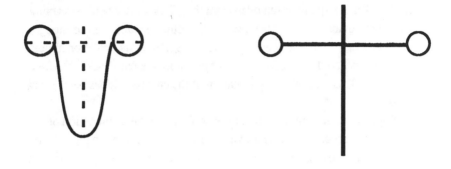

Drawing abstractions of male genitalia: penis and testicles
Diagram II

Highly abstracted line drawing of the male genitalia - the penis and the testicles
Diagram III

It is clear that Diagram III, a highly abstracted line drawing of the male genitalia, is a "*cross.*"

I submit that the cross, as an important and provocative symbol in the white supremacy system/culture, is none other than a brain-computer distillate of the white collective's fear-induced obsession with the genitals of all non-white men (of Black men in particular), who have the potential to genetically annihilate the white race. Furthermore, the cross represents the Black male's genitals removed from the Black male's body – meaning castrated genitals. Thus, the *cross* is a critical symbol in the thought processes of the white supremacy system, beginning its evolution almost 2,000 years ago during early white aggression against Blacks in Africa and Asia. This particular interpretation of the cross never has been given before.

Support for this interpretation may be found in the examination of the sword as a secondary critical symbol in the white supremacy culture. Here I am referring to the so-called "Western" sword with its straight blade, in contrast to the "Oriental" sword, which has a curved blade. J.E. Cirlot's *A Dictionary of Symbols*, relating to the symbolism of the sword, states, "Here one must recall the general meaning of weapons, which is the antithesis of the monster." In the same discussion, he notes, "There can be no doubt that there is a sociological factor in sword-symbolism, since the sword is an instrument proper to the knight, who is the defender of the forces of light against the forces of darkness." In the white supremacy system/culture, the "monster" is always the Black male (e.g., King Kong) and, more specifically, his white-genetic-annihilating genitals. As the white male (the knight) moves to control the monster (Black male genitalia), indeed he does become "the defender of the forces of light against the forces of darkness." The Western sword is shaped exactly as "the cross," the brain-computer distillate of the male genitalia.

In an article entitled "Values, Myths and Symbols," which appeared in the July 1973 issue of the *American Journal of Psychiatry*, Rollo May had the following to say about the cross: "For example, the Christian cross draws together the horizontal and vertical dimensions of life and unites them perpendicularly to each other, embracing their conflict." However, this is a superficial description of a cross, and it is totally inadequate as an in-depth interpretation of this major symbol in the white supremacy system/culture. The white collective seems unable to decode their own symbolism completely. Their own translations of their major symbols, and their analyses of their unconscious, remain superficial, incoherent and unconvincing. Therefore, the white collective remains unaware of itself and unpredictable to itself and to others who lack deep understanding.

If my interpretation of the cross symbol is correct (that in the white male psyche it represents the Black male genitalia in the context of the global white supremacy system), then it is possible to understand the portrayal of the white female in the popular book and film, *The Exorcist.* Here, the female used the cross to masturbate herself when she was possessed by the devil (i.e., the black monster). This symbolic portrayal emerged during a time period in which increasing numbers of white females were selecting Black males as "mates" or, more correctly stated, white females began sexually aggressing against socially powerless Black males to gain possession of the Black phallus.

The use of the cross as a symbolic object in white female masturbation also occurred when large numbers of white females actively were fantasizing about being raped by Black males and were establishing organizations and societies to prevent it. This was a reaction formation to their own unconscious desires. The white female's preoccupation with writing books on being raped also occured during this time period. In the white supremacy culture, the historic symbol of the rapist of white females is the Black male. The white female, until recently, has been held back in her sexual desires of the Black male by white male constraint. Since "white-female-liberation" has been granted to white women in small measure, the white female finds herself unable to hold her own desires and aggressions in check. Still she is unable to admit these desires and aggressions consciously. (It is common knowledge that the ideal male for the white female is "tall, *dark* and handsome.") Interestingly, following *The Exorcist*, the movie *King Kong* became a major focus of attention in 1976. The entire movie suggests an impending sexual attack on the white female by the giant black ape (the symbol of the Black male). Finally, the black ape is shot dead by white males. The gun is also a phallic symbol in the white supremacy culture. (See Chapter 8.)

At yet another level of the white supremacy cultural dynamic, white females (Jane Goodall, Diane Fossey and Birute Galdikas Brindamour) in the role of "scientists" are tracking (chasing) down large black apes in the African and Asian jungles (e.g., Tanzania). Some of these white females actually have attempted to get very, very close to these great black apes so that they can touch the apes and, perhaps unconsciously, so that the great black apes can touch them!

It is of further interest that the above mentioned films, *The Exorcist* and *King Kong*, simultaneously emerged in an atmosphere where increasing attention had been given to Christian symbolism and religion, and during the period when the man who was elected to occupy the "White House" referred to himself as a "born again Christian" – making frequent references to Christian symbols and scriptures. Thus, the culture simultaneously focused on the threat (Black male genitals) and the need to control the threat via castration of the Black genitals (the cross symbol).

This discussion of the cross as a symbol of the Black male genitalia, in the context of the white supremacy system/culture, would not be complete without noting that some of the most outspoken and aggressive white male and female members of the white supremacy system refer to themselves as the Ku Klux Klan. Since the termination of formal enslavement of Blacks, the Klan openly has espoused white genetic purity and survival via the castration, lynching and killing of Black men. The historic symbol for this group in the white supremacy culture is "the cross" and, more specifically, the burning cross. After Black men were lynched and castrated, they often were burned, thereby reinforcing the interpretation that the cross symbolically is tied to the Black male's genitalia and that the burning cross is the burning Black male and his genitals. When the Black male genitalia with the dominant Black genes are burned, cut off or otherwise destroyed, white genetic survival is assured.

Constantine I ("The Great"), the Roman emperor who ruled 306-337 A.D., built Constantinople and made Christian worship lawful in the beginnings of the white supremacy system, had the following words placed on the cross, "In Hoc Signo, Vinces" (meaning, "In this sign you will conquer"). Indeed, by controlling the Black (non-white) male genitals, which the cross symbolizes, whites have conquered Blacks and the entire non-white world majority. Currently, the majority membership of Christian churches is non-white, and all are held in control under the sign of the cross. The authority is maintained by whites, under white supremacy, white purity and white survival.

More recently, the fury of the white supremacy dynamic was expressed in the form of *Nazism*. The dominant symbol used by this group in the white supremacy system was and is the black swastika. The central element of the swastika is the cross. A spinning or whirling cross (the cross in motion) gives the visual illusion of the swastika. (See Diagram IV.) Hitler's and the Nazi movement's central theme was white racial genetic purity and the elimination of all persons classified as non-whites (i.e., Semites and gypsies), who were viewed as having Black genetic heritage from Africa and who were considered genetically dominant to the Aryans (whites).

The symbol of the swastika, the cross in motion, spurred the whites on to destroy those who were classified as genetically dominant non-whites.

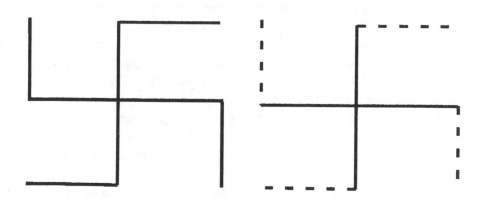

The Swastika
Diagram IV

To the extent that it can be accepted that a man named Jesus lived in Africa some 2,000 years ago and that he was a member of the indigenous peoples, that man was undoubtedly a Black man, a man with skin pigmentation – not a white man lacking in skin pigmentation. Albinism, like leprosy, causes the skin to turn white and was considered a serious disease in ancient Africa. The victims of albinism and leprosy were cast out from the skin-pigmented peoples. Jesus never was discussed as having such a disease state. (Recall that pigmented skin is the norm for the hue-man race, not albinism.)

In contrast to this Black man and the Black peoples of Africa, the peoples on the northern side of the Mediterranean Sea, some of whom referred to themselves as Romans, were then aggressing against and establishing conquests in Africa. They were men without skin pigmentation (white men).

The most likely essence of the story of Jesus, who only later was referred to as "Christ," was that he was a poor Black man, a carpenter, a member of the non-white oppressed population, whose ideas as expressed in the Beatitudes threatened the power, control and authority of the conquering Romans. If Jesus and the other Blacks got out of control, the Romans (the whites) could be annihilated genetically. Of course, then as now, under white supremacy domination, Jesus (the non-white) was turned over to the white oppressors who then used some of his fellow-victimized (self-hating non-whites who wished to ingratiate themselves to the white oppressors) to kill him. Jesus, this Black man, was then hung on a cross, a peculiar invention of the Roman (white) psyche. In other words, the white brain-computer that feared annihilation by the Black male genitals unconsciously invented an instrument or weapon of Black male destruction, exactly (in abstract form) analogous to the part of the Black male's anatomy that whites knew could destroy them. Jesus was not only hung on the cross and stabbed, but undoubtedly, was also castrated.

In Christian religious tradition, it is stated that Jesus died on the cross and suffered so that "we" (whites) can be "saved" (survive). White (Christian) theology goes even further to speak of Jesus "shedding his blood" so that we (whites) can "live" and have "everlasting life." Only in recent years has genetic material ceased being referred to as "blood." Always there has been (and in some circles it continues) discussion about individuals having "black blood" or "white blood" when what was really meant was Black or white genetic material or genes, respectively.

Thus, Christian (white supremacy) theology can be translated: Jesus (a Black man) shed his Black genetic material in a crucifixion, which in reality was a castration and a killing, so that the white genetic recessive population, in fear of its genetic annihilation, could be saved (genetically survive). Thus, Jesus is called "savior" by the whites. Is it little wonder that the holy day celebrated for the death of Jesus is referred to as "Good Friday?" And a television series that represented a socially and politically castrated Black male similarly was referred to as "Good Times." The historically "good nigger" has been the "dead nigger."

In keeping with this symbolic order, there is a song in the Christian religion called "Nothing But The Blood of Jesus." The chorus is as follows:

> Oh precious is the flow,
> That makes me white as snow
> No other font I know
> Nothing but the blood of Jesus.

This can be translated as, "As long as the genetic material from the Black male is spilling on the ground from castration, whites can remain white as snow."

The pattern of worshipping a suffering, dying Jesus on the cross, is fully comprehended only when it is understood that Jesus was a Black man and that the black wooden cross represents the Black male genitalia separated from the man. Only by the removal and destruction of the Black male genitals can whites have "everlasting life" in the most fundamental genetic sense. Jesus, of course, had to be rationalized as willing to make this "castration-sacrifice" – giving up his genes so that whites might live.

There is a profound and striking parallel between the above interpretation of the crucifixion and the destruction of black bulls with swords at bullfights. Bullfighting became a prominent sport in Spain after the Moors (Black men) finally had been chased out of Europe, back across the Mediterranean, into Africa. The Moors had conquered Spain for seven hundred years. By the time they left, the once white population had become dark (via the dominant Black genetic material): dark skin, dark hair and dark eyes. Cirlot's *A Dictionary of Symbols* states that the bull as an historic symbol represents the superiority of the *Aryan* over the *Negro*. This could not possibly be the logically correct meaning of the symbol. If this analysis were correct, there would be no need for "whites" to kill a *black* bull with a sword. Obviously, a more logical and accurate interpretation of the bull symbol is the opposite of Cirlot's interpretation – the bull represents the superiority or genetic dominance of the Blacks over the genetic recessive whites. Again, the sword used to kill the black bull, as Cirlot also noted, comes into play as the weapon of the "forces of light" over the "forces of darkness." The sword signifies the weapon of the possessor of the white genitals or recessive white genetic material, against the dominant Black genitals and their genetic material.

By the fourth century A.D., Jesus had been changed in color from Black "Jesus" to white "Christ" (then to be known as "Jesus Christ" or simply, "Christ"). This was the conscious or unconscious attempt to further repress from the collective white consciousness the true source of white anxiety and fear – the Black male and his genitals. Instead of a lynched *Black* Jesus, a frail, weak, effeminate, suffering and dying *white Christ* was hung against a black wooden cross as the dominant symbol in the religious practices of the white supremacy system/culture. Instead of the woolly, kinky head of the "Lamb of God," there was the straight, almost blond hair of the white Christ hung up against the black wooden cross. However, this symbolic image achieved a more important goal. In a single-picture-paragraph it states, "The weak, genetic recessive, white male, will be destroyed genetically-speaking, when up against the white-annihilating, genetically dominant, Black male genital apparatus (the cross)."

Arnold Toynbee, in *Mankind and Mother Earth,* states,

Fifteenth Century western Christians were obsessed with the horror of death (the antitheses of the Pharonic Egyptian's pleasurable anticipation of a post-mortem eternity), and they were fascinated by the physical suffering of Christ on the Cross. Contemporary western painters, engravers and sculptors – especially in the Transalpine countries – extended their art to portray these themes with gruesome realism.

The 15th century also heralded the Europeans' (the whites) world travel to conquer and control the entire non-white world, in order to prevent white genetic annihilation and death. This horrendous fear was then translated in European art.

Joel Kovel, in his book *White Racism (A Psychohistory)* writes:

Christianity spread over the West and created a community out of what had been barbarian splinters. It did this through the power of a concrete institution, the Catholic Church. It was the church's immediate influence that held aloft the subliminatory ideal of Christ and, through that ideal, gave Europeans a scaffold of identification with which to bind themselves into a unified civilization.

Men, however, remained men, torn and driven by their obscure passions into striving for greed and domination which culture could scarcely regulate. Intense aggression resisted the Church's unification, continued to plague European culture, and delayed its growth. Within the original world-view, there was no way to rationalize or include the striving for greed and domination that persisted within civilization. After all, the Christian revolution was superimposed upon a basically dominative way of life. It could only account for the guilt that arose from the dominative style of society by turning away from the given world.

What Kovel fails to understand is that the fundamental reason Catholic Christianity, from its early days of European organization and interpretation of the Jesus theology, was able to unite the global white collective (then the warring white tribes of Europe) was because of the cross symbolism and the deep meaning it projected. When Christianity projected "the cross," especially the cross with the limp, pale body of

Christ hung on it, everyone in the global white collective unconsciously understood that they must unite against the threat of Black (non-white) male genital material, which the black wooden cross represented. White genetic survival could be achieved only by a united, continuous offensive attack by the global white minority. This organized attack is now at least 2000 years old. The greed and the strivings for domination, which Kovel fails to fully understand, were compensation for a profound sense of genetic inadequacy.

Only in this context of symbol translation can the Christian hymn, "Onward Christian Soldier," be appreciated. This is not only an important religious song, but also a significant battle song in the white supremacy culture. One stanza of the song is as follows:

> Onward Christian Soldier,
> Marching as to war,
>
> With the cross of Jesus,
> going on before.
>
> Christ our loyal master,
> leads against the foe,
>
> Forward into battle,
> see his banners glow.
>
> **Chorus**
>
> Onward Christian Soldier,
> Marching as to war
>
> With the cross of Jesus
> going on before.

My translation in prose of the above words and symbol-images in this song is, "Onward white male (and white female) soldiers, marching to war to establish and maintain white genetic survival. You have the symbol of the Black male genitals before you keeping your true purpose in mind so that you can unite to subdue this common threat. *Christ* (the white male image) is your loyal master, who is leading you in the attack against the

Black male genital-monster enemy. The white male leads you into battle behind our glowing flags (phallic symbols)."

With the picture of a dying, weak white man held firmly in mind, white people fully understand what they must prevent from occurring, and why they must fight and, if necessary, die so that whites can survive. "Onward Christian Soldier" is a marching religious song for the white supremacy culture, but "Were You There When They Crucified My Lord?" in stark contrast, is a song of deep pain and sorrow about the castration and destruction of the Black male by the marching white supremacy army or its individual storm troopers.

In modern times, the gun has become the contemporary symbolic weapon used against the non-white male and his white annihilating genetic potential. Also, the gun is an abstraction of the male genitalia, functioning exactly like the male genital apparatus. (See Chapter 8.) Thus, it is no accident that Dr. Martin Luther King, Jr. – the modern day Jesus – was killed by a gun after being brought into focus on the cross of the cross hairs on the telescopic gun site. Dr. King brought only love to the white collective, but mating love (Black with white) causes white genetic annihilation, so he had to be destroyed.

The Communion

Since the 16th century, Protestants have believed that the act of communion is a symbolic reenactment of the crucifixion, with the bread and wine becoming the body and blood of Jesus. The Christian worshipper ingests the bread and wine as an act to remove sin (not to internalize divinity). The Orthodox Christian believed that the communion was a spiritual act that could not be explained. In August 1976, the Catholic Church, the Orthodox Christians and the Protestants came together and agreed that the communion, or the Eucharist, conveys Christ's real presence and represents his sacrifice (the giving up of his body and blood), although it is not to be viewed as an actual reenactment of the crucifixion.

The author's analysis of this symbolism of the communion, in the context of the white supremacy system/culture in which it evolved, reveals that the white population has had an historic awareness (albeit now largely unconscious) that they suffered bodily or genetic impairment, which made them different and separated them from the "hue-man" majority of black, brown, red and yellow peoples. They were not whole. This same genetic deficiency was the basis for the consideration of "original sin" and the shame of body "nakedness" (body whiteness), as discussed in the Biblical mythology of Adam and Eve, an important myth in the white supremacy culture. The view that the act of sex was the original sin is an extension of this same logic because the sex act produces the body and its appearance via genetic transfer and/or genetic mutation.

Having rejected the appearance of the white body as the equivalent of "sin" and "shame," the white psyche attempted to correct the white body's defect. Thus emerged the symbolic and ritualized acts of ingesting the body and blood (genes) of Jesus (the Black male), in the unconscious desire to correct the existing color deficiency. The symbolic attempt to correct the genetic deficiency state of skin albinism (skin whiteness), as performed in the Eucharist, is the central religious rite in the religion of the white supremacy system/culture. Therefore, it is not surprising that wearing black or dark-colored clothing, generally covering the entire body, is the primary and most acceptable pattern of dress for Christian religious leaders: priests, ministers, nuns, etc.

One finds curious the over-determined, highly intense abhorrence that many in the white collective continue to verbalize over the idea of cannibalism, always relating acts of cannibalism to so-called "primitive" Blacks in Africa. This continuing discussion is most interesting behavior on the part of those who symbolically practice cannibalism in the central rite of their own religious practice on a weekly or monthly basis. Even more significant is the fact that the Blacks are portrayed as eating missionaries (Christians) when it is the "Christians" who always are concerning themselves with their own ingestion of the body and blood of an African – Jesus. This is a classic example of projection.

Reinforcement for this interpretation of the communion symbolism comes not only from whites' obsessive pattern of suntanning to make their bodies colored, but also from major eating practices in the white supremacy culture, especially in the U.S. The most favored drinks are all dark brown in color: coffee, tea, coke, beer, and whiskey. These are all symbolic of the blood or genes of Jesus. A favorite meat is steak, which comes from the bull or cattle. (See Chapter 7.) We need not mention the hot dogs, half smokes and all the other varieties of sausages. Also, are not bulls castrated to make them taste better when eaten? Are not football players fed steak before they attempt to go out and capture the large brown balls? (See Chapter 10.) I further understand that "bull's balls" are eaten as delicacies in some bars and other eating establishments in the white supremacy culture. The favorite candy is chocolate candy (chocolate comes mainly from Africa), preferably with nuts. Recall chocolate kisses and all of the myriad chocolate candy bars. Nuts are also important in the white supremacy culture. Some have focused on peanuts and become millionaires and the most powerful persons in the world. Finally, given the symbolism behind such eating practices, it follows that oral sexual practices would be a favorite in the white supremacy system/culture.

Likewise, the symbolism in the major holidays of the Christian religion is supportive of my interpretations. At Christmas, the tree is one of the most important symbols. The Christmas tree is, in its abstracted form, a cross – the symbol of the Black male genitals. (See Diagram V.) First, the Christmas tree is *chopped down* in the *forest.* Then it is taken home. In the U.S., when the Christmas tree is decorated, *colored* "balls" are hung on the tree. When the tree is taken down and burned, the "balls" are first *taken off.* Then all can dream of a "white Christmas" and a surviving white Christ.

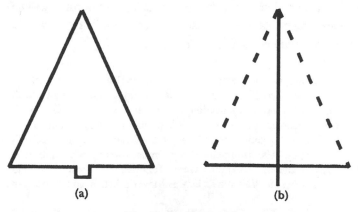

(a)   (b)

**The Xmas Tree and
Its Abstraction
Diagram V
(Cross is turned upside down)**

Similarily in Europe, small white wax candles were placed on the Christmas tree. In the Catholic religion, the Christmas tree is said to represent "the tree of the cross," while the wax candles are thought to represent the "body of Christ."

Thus, again, we have the symbol of the white, weak (melting) Christ hung on the symbol of Black male genitalia. At the Easter holiday in the U.S., it is traditional to have colored eggs, colored jelly beans and a chocolate rabbit and eggs in an "Easter basket." These colored items are eaten. The white albino bunny rabbit that sits amongst the colored eggs as though he laid them generally is not eaten. By ingesting the colored items, the sin of being without color is symbolically removed – being "born again whole" has been achieved through symbols.

Other important holidays in the white supremacy culture further reveal the intricate workings of this symbolism. On both St. Valentine's Day and Mother's Day, the white male gives gifts of chocolate candy with nuts. In the first instance, he gives it to his sweetheart, and in the second to his mother. If his sweetheart ingests "chocolate with nuts," the white male can fantasize that he is genetically equal to the Black male. And if his mother had ingested "chocolate with nuts," he would not have to worry about white genetic annihilation – as he would have been "colored" and then could be an annihilator of white genes like the feared and envied Black male. Both the valentine shape and the chocolate candy have a symbolic meaning not previously recognized, examined nor understood by Western culture investigators. However, once the unified field of the Western culture dynamic (behavior dynamic) is set forth, it will be seen that these fragments of symbolism take on a brilliant clarity. The *Encyclopedia Britannica* defines *valentine* as,

> a special form of greeting card exchanged in observance of St. Valentine's Day (February 14), a day set aside as a lover's festival. The custom has no connection with the two St. Valentines or with known incidents in their lives. It is probably that the valentine was the first of all greeting cards. The paper valentine dates from the 16th century; by 1800 hand-painted copperplates were produced to meet large demands. These were followed by woodcuts and lithographs....St. Valentine's Day as a lover's festival and the modern

tradition of sending valentine cards have no relation to the Saint but,
rather, seem to be connected with either the Roman fertility festival of
the Lupercalia (February 15) or with the mating season of birds.

The relationship of the valentine to an ancient *fertility rite* suggests that
the so-called "heart" shape of the valentine may be less associated with
the anatomical heart of the human body, as is commonly thought, than
with the symbolic drawing of the female genital organ, the vaginal
opening. As explained in Ajit Mookerjee's and Madhu Khanna's *The
Tantric Way*, in Tantric worship in India, this organ is frequently drawn
in the form of a heart or an upside down triangle, with the base upward.
It is clear that the organ of the heart in the human body has much less an
association with *fertility* than the vagina or the vaginal orifice.

Cirlot states, "The importance of love in the mystic doctrine of unity
explains how it is that love-symbolism came to be closely linked with
heart-symbolism, for to love is only to experience a force which urges the
lover towards a given centre." Indeed, in Tantric philosophy and art, the
symbol of *unity* was the union of the male and female genital organs, and
this unity was reverently portrayed in sculpture and graphic arts.

An explanation of the symbolism of chocolate in Western culture will
expose further the significance of heart-shaped valentines as well as the
importance of chocolate. In an article entitled "The Sweet Taste of Sin"
(*The Washington Post,* February 8, 1979), Marion Burros quotes food
critic Gael Greene: "I have always thought a good chocolate mousse is
an aphrodisiac, the more intense the taste of chocolate, the more erotic the
spell." Marion Burros continues, "Some chocolate mousse lovers go even
further. 'It's not a food, it's a concept,' says one indulgent male. 'It's like
illicit sex. It's so good but so fattening. It gives you pimples. It's a sin.'"
Burros concludes quoting Gael Greene, "...wonderful, wicked deeply
chocolate." One certainly must question why, in a culture produced by a
people that refers to itself as the "white race" and that historically has
denounced people with natural chocolate complexions, a *dark brown*
food, namely chocolate, causes such orgasm-like ecstacy and is associated
with eroticism when orally ingested.

This pattern of logic and thought surrounding *chocolate* (dark brown) candy and other deserts most certainly cannot be held in isolation from the previously mentioned preoccupations over suntanning and the white female preference for males who are tall and *dark* or the preoccupation in sports of placing large brown balls (testicle symbols) in *white* net (vaginal) orifices and between goal posts (white upright legs). A unified field theory in the behavorial sciences demands that gross and subtle interconnections, between behavioral phenomena, be *perceived* before they can be *understood.*

That there *should* be myriad behaviors in the white supremacy behavior system that reflect a deep desire to counteract and compensate for the perceived genetic deficiency of white skin should not be at all surprising. Thus, the customary and traditional little packets of chocolate candy (often with nuts), placed inside of the heart or vaginal orifice shaped box, are like little sperm packages of Black genetic material being placed in the vaginal orifice. When presented by the white male to the white female, in the context of the skin color deficient culture, the act is the exact parallel to the white male coaches who coach their Black basketball and football players to place dark brown balls in white net orifices or in white upright legs. (See Chapter 10.) One must conclude that the white male realizes consciously or unconsciously that the most desired mate for the white female is the Black male, just as he realizes that his most desired sexual mate is the Black female. This illuminates the white male's fascination with black stockings, black underwear and black negligees as sexual symbols.

Conclusions

The conscious and/or unconscious acceptance and internalization of a symbol system based upon the castrated Black male genitalia is essential to the global system of white genetic survival. This symbol system necessitates the oppression of Blacks and all other non-whites in the global context of white supremacy. Generally, the victims of a system of oppression have no alternative other than to accept blindly the patterns of symbols, logic, thought, speech, emotional responses and perceptions that are imposed forcefully upon them by their oppressors. After hundreds of years of oppression, the oppressed, having lost the sense of their own identity, begin to believe that the brain-products of their oppressors are one and the same with their own, failing completely to realize that they do not control their own brain-computers nor their brain-computers' output. The slave's fate is not to see nor reason why, but only to do or die. However, the process of liberation is one wherein the oppressed begin to clearly distinguish their perceptions, logic and thought processes from the oppressors'. The oppressed, then, begin to respect and validate their perceptions and their logic and thought processes, realizing fully that they can never free themselves with the thought processes and perceptions that were a part of the process of their enslavement.

As long as the Black (non-white) collective consciously and/or unconsciously accepts a powerful and dynamic symbolism of Black male castration, they never will be self/group-respecting and forever will remain mentally ill. Mentally ill people, persons who do not respect themselves and have self/group-negating patterns of logic, thought, speech, action, emotional response and perceptions, never can liberate themselves from their oppressors. Black psychiatrists have the responsibility of clarifying for Black people all aspects of the oppressive dynamic of white genetic survival. This includes exposing and decoding all of that power system's major symbolism.

6

The Politics Behind Black Male Passivity, Effeminization, Bisexuality, and Homosexuality
(August 1974)

Black male passivity, effeminization, bisexuality and homosexuality are being encountered increasingly by Black psychiatrists working with Black patient populations. These issues are being presented by family members, personnel working in schools and other social institutions or by Black men themselves. Many in the Black population are reaching the conclusion that such issues have become a problem of epidemic proportion amongst Black people in the U.S., although it was an almost nonexistent behavioral phenomenon amongst indigenous Blacks in Africa.

As Black psychiatrists and behavioral scientists, we need to understand fully the individual and social dynamics involved in these patterns of behavior. We must be able to help our patients understand their conduct and change it if they so desire. Also, we should be in a position to comment on the ultimate implications of these behaviors for the well-being of Black people – not simply as individuals, but as a whole organism of people seeking life and maximal development.

In the final analysis, behavior is not simply an individual affair, for when multiplied by thousands, it has profound effects on the life, future existence and well-being of the total people.

In 1973, I presented my definition of Black mental health:

The practice of those unit patterns of behavior (i.e., logic, thought, speech, action and emotional response) in all areas of people activity: economics, education, entertainment, labor, law, politics, religion, sex and war – which are simultaneously self- and group-supporting under the social and political conditions of worldwide white supremacy domination (racism). In brief, this means Black behavioral practice which resists self- and group-negation and destruction.

The above are the criteria used to judge Black mental health or Black mental illness. The reader should be forewarned that my conceptualizations do not rely on the currently utilized, late 19th and early 20th century "European" psychoanalytic theories of Sigmund Freud. If Freud's insights into behavior were truly adequate, they would have aided his six million fellow Semites in preventing their destruction by the anti-Semitic white supremacy power organization of Nazi Germany. Failing to understand this major behavioral dynamic, Freud had to flee to save his life. Furthermore, my conceptualizations do not rely on the recent position taken by the American Psychiatric Association – that homosexuality is no longer categorized as a form of behavioral illness. This pronouncement has nothing to do with the mental health of Black people.

The human brain – the organ responsible for all patterns of logic, thought, speech, action and emotional response – is an organ of the nervous system that evolved over many thousands of years. Its purpose has been to decode and solve problems in the external environment – both its physical and social aspects. Thus, specific patterns of behavior may be looked upon as functional or dysfunctional solutions to the problems posed by the external environment.

When the brain's purpose is understood, patterns of male passivity, effeminization, bisexuality and homosexuality may be looked upon as functional or dysfunctional solutions to specific problems posed in the environment, even though consciously they are not understood as such. But for what environmental problems are these behaviors considered answers – functional or dysfunctional – and for whom?

These questions cannot be answered without first understanding the nature of the environment (the specific dynamic and structure of the social system) in which these behaviors occur.

As explained in Chapter 1, racism (white supremacy) is the dominant social system in today's world. Its fundamental dynamic is predicated upon the genetic recessive deficiency state of albinism, which is responsible for skin whiteness and thus the so-called "white race." This genetic recessive trait is dominated by the genetic capacity to produce any of the various degrees of skin melanination – whether black, brown, red or yellow. In other words, it can be annihilated as a phenotypic condition. Control of this potential for genetic domination and annihilation throughout the world is absolutely essential if the condition of skin whiteness is to survive. "White" survival is predicated upon aggressiveness and muscle mass in the form of technology directed against the "non-white" melaninated men on the planet Earth who constitute the numerical majority. Therefore, white survival and white power are dependent upon the various methodologies, tactics and strategies developed to control all "non-white" men, as well as bring them into cooperative submission. This is especially important in the case of Black men because they have the greatest capacity to produce melanin and, in turn, the greatest genetic potential for the annihilation of skin albinism or skin whiteness.

During the past 400 years, Black men in the U.S. have been forced into passive and cooperative submission to white men. The major strategy has been the installation of an overwhelming *fear*. Specific tactics range from actual *physical castration* and lynching, to other overt and more subtle forms of abuse, violence and cruelty. We should not be ashamed to recognize these tactics used to oppress Black men. It is the truth. It is reality. Ultimately, this is the meaning of Black oppression.

All Black people are oppressed. I emphasize here that Black men are oppressed because ultimately, it is male muscle mass that oppresses a people, and only male muscle mass has the potential for achieving liberation. If the men of a people are oppressed, the women are brought under oppression – as they are dependent on their men for protection and defense. Women do not have the muscle mass to liberate a people and protect the young. Women develop the young, but their men must provide the protection and the security apparatus.

The global white male collective understands the priority of white domination. They fully understand, consciously or unconsciously, the threat that Black men represent to them. Also, white males realize that in the final analysis, the vast majority of females must submit to males because of their lesser muscle mass. Additionally, white males fully understand that males who are forced to identify as females will be programmed simultaneously into submission to the males they call "The Man," as opposed to aggressing against those same men.

White men in this world area have at least a vague, perhaps unconscious, understanding that after 20 generations (400 years), male passivity has evolved into male effeminization, bisexuality and homosexuality. These patterns of behavior are simply expressions of male self-submission to other males in the area of people activity called "sex." Males also can submit to males in any of the other eight areas of people activity – economics, education, entertainment, labor, law, politics, religion and war. Oppression is forced submission and cooperation in any of the areas of people activity.

However, the white male arrives at his deeply repressed sense of "femininity" because not only can he be dominated genetically by all Black and other men of color, but more profound from the white male perspective is the fact that he is dominated genetically by all Black and other non-white *females*. For the offspring of a white male and non-white female will be non-white like their mother rather than white like their white father; thus, the offspring are genetically dominant in respect to the white male. This sense of genetic weakness, when compared to the majority of the world's women, propels the white male to project weakness, passivity, effeminization, bisexuality and homosexuality onto the Black male, who is his arch potential challenger. Furthermore, the white male collective structures the social environment to transfer this mental protection into a functional reality.

The more the Black male strives to stand, the weaker the white male feels by comparison, and the greater the white male's thrust to effeminize the Black male – to weaken the Black male's psychological potential for aggressive and assertive challenge, forcing him to remain submissive to "The Man."

The American Psychiatric Association's decision to remove homosexuality from the list of mental (behavioral) disturbances resulted from the increasing number of white males seeking this mode of sexual expression, due to an increasing consciousness of true white male weakness. Male bisexuality and homosexuality can be viewed as the sexual expression of male weakness, passivity and effeminization. The motivation for these feelings and their sexual expression results primarily from the developing challenge by "non-white" men throughout the world to white male power and projected superiority. This challenge has assumed various subtle and overt forms during recent decades.

For example, in the U.S., heavyweight boxing, basketball, baseball and football have all been taken away from white males (by Black males) as symbolic expressions of white male virility and manhood. White males have been left with only two major sports wherein they dominate (tennis and golf), and both consist of hitting *small white* balls. I need not even mention that Black men have been blocked effectively from participating in these remaining white stronghold sports. (See Chapter 10.)

It is also crushing to the collective white male ego and sense of power to be told by "colored" men called Arabs that the whites cannot have any oil to run their machines to maintain and extend their technology – their major control apparatus. Increasingly, the white male is being forced to see himself as he really is.

The white females' liberation movement is another disturbing threat to the white male's sense of power and masculinity, helping to push him to a weakened and homosexual stance. However, white females are reacting to the oppression imposed on them by white males. Feeling inferior to "non-white" males and *females*, the white male said to the white female, "Well, at least I am going to be superior to you." The white female reaction in the form of women's liberation is contributing further to white male/female alienation, pushing white males further into the homosexual position and, incidentally, pushing white females in that direction also.

The long-standing white male/female alienation in the white family has pushed the white female, perhaps unconsciously, to mold her sons to be more like herself than like their father. Thus, she creates a female with a penis. Additionally, she proceeds to fight back at the male and finally achieves, symbolically, a penis for herself – resolving the white female's penis envy complex, a compensation for her sense of inferiority imposed by men. In a similar way, she fights back at the white male when she captures a Black male's penis and taunts the white male, who believes "her" black penis is stronger than his own.

From another perspective, white male and female homosexuality can be viewed as the final expression of their dislike of their genetic albinism in a world numerically dominated by colored people. This dislike of their appearance, though deeply repressed, causes a negation of the act of self-reproduction (sex), in various forms. This is the eventual origin of homosexuality. It is a parallel activity to the all familiar discussions of "population zero" and "birth control," now current articulations in the white supremacy culture.

All of the aforementioned dynamics are components of the total dynamic of racism. Some of the methodologies used to achieve Black male submission or effeminization warrant further examination. Unlike the white male, the Black male does not arrive at the effeminate bisexual or homosexual stance from any deeply repressed sense of genetic weakness, inadequacy or disgust, which I refer to as *primary effeminacy* (effeminacy that is self-derived and not imposed forcibly by others). Instead, the Black male arrives at this position *secondarily,* as the result of the imposed power and cruelty of the white male and the totality of the white supremacy social and political apparatus that has forced 20 generations of Black males into submission. This pattern of imposed submission is reinforced through every institution within the white supremacy system, but especially in the fundamental social institution of the family or, in this case, the Black survival-unit.

I make the distinction in terminology between family and survival-unit because "the family," by definition, is a social institution that functions to support maximal development and protection of the young. However, under white supremacy, Blacks and other non-whites are not to be developed maximally; they are permitted to survive as functional inferiors, alienated from self and from their own kind. The non-white survival-unit is not permitted to defend itself or its young. The survival-unit functions accordingly.

The imposed internal dynamics of the survival-unit, as within the racist system in general, function to negate Black manhood, as fundamentally expressed in the relationship between breadwinning and true power potential. Even when high level income is allowed, there is no true power in its ultimate sense – meaning to support, protect and defend the lives of one's self, one's wife and one's children. Under any serious system of oppression, this right is denied the oppressed male, and with its denial there is a concomitant and proportionate loss of respect for manhood in the oppressed population. This attitude begins first within the oppressed man himself and radiates to all other members of the survival-unit. The resultant frustration of Black manhood potential – a pressure and grievance that cannot be redressed directly at its source under fear of death – forces behavior into dysfunctional, non-satisfying, circular, obsessive-compulsive patterns, in areas of people activity where greater degrees of maleness are permitted to be expressed (i.e., sex, sports and entertainment).

Under the white supremacy slavery system, the identity of "sex machines" was imposed upon Black males, especially as many hands were needed in the fields for toil and labor. The many babies that were produced gave Black males their most open avenue for at least a limited sense of manhood. Presently, with the birth control pills and with the pressure for population-zero for all non-whites, this major male ego-support also has been taken away. Without jobs, income, power or even babies, there is no proof of sexual functioning. When this reality is coupled with the awareness that many women can receive more from a welfare check than they can from their male partners, the reasons for women respecting men and staying with them steadily decline, and Black male/female alienation increases.

Recent statistics reveal that today (1974), 34% of Black families are headed by females as compared to 10% of white families, and this figure is increasing each year. In the metropolitan area of Washington, D.C., there are 61,000 Black male children growing up in homes without their fathers or other father surrogates, while 90% of their teachers in the public schools are also females. This produces a massive deficiency in adult males for role modeling and imprinting. Such role modeling and imprinting are essential for Black male children to understand adult male role functioning.

As Black males and females become more and more alienated, as our current rates of separation and divorce indicate, and as Black females are being left to rear Black male children alone, the alienation, hate and disgust felt towards adult males are visited upon their sons subtly. A female alienated from males is hard-pressed to reinforce patterns of conduct in a male child that remind her of unhappiness and pain. She is much more inclined to say, "There you go looking and acting like that no good nigger father of yours." The Black female teacher at school who also may be experiencing alienation from her Black man, if not inclined to make the same statement in such a direct manner, only says it more subtly, says nothing, or simply acts out her hate, disgust and distrust of Black males, achieving the same end result.

It is little wonder that 98% of all of the Black male children I talk with, who have reached the junior high school level, hate school. Schools and their personnel, like all other aspects of the racist system, do their share to alienate Black males from maximal functioning and thus further the ultimate alienation of Black males from themselves and their manhood. As a result of this pattern of socialization, Black males soon learn that it is easier to be a female child than a male child, and more promising to be an adult Black female than an adult Black male.

In childhood, male children learn – whether at home or at school – that they can make mothers and female teachers happy (and they will shower you with smiles and affection) when they act like "females" rather than like boys.

The dearth of adult Black males in the homes, schools and neighborhoods leaves Black male children no alternative models. Blindly they seek out one another as models, and in their blindness end up in trouble – in juvenile homes or prisons. But fate and the dynamics of racism again play a vicious trick because the young males only become more alienated from their manhood and more feminized in such settings. They are given orders by men to whom they must submit; they wait passively to be fed three meals a day by men; and finally, they have sexual intercourse with men. It is no wonder that they are unable to play the role of Black men when they leave.

One ex-prisoner patient told me, "It is easier to endure the life on the inside than to try to put up with the pressures of being a man, a husband and a father in the street." The intent of racist programming had been achieved: "Give up trying to be a Black man. Why not be a woman?"

Many Black males have answered unconsciously, "Why not!" The braided and curled hair, the earrings and bracelets, the midriff tops, the cinch waisted pants, the flowered underwear, the high-heeled shoes with platforms and the pocketbooks are all behavioral answers to the above. They say in loud and clear language, "White man, I will never come after you. I cannot run in my high-heels – you know that. And I may mess up my hair." The white-run clothing industry is all too pleased to provide the costumes of feminine disguise for Black male escape. However, they never would provide uniforms or combat gear if customers were willing to pay $1000 per outfit.

Television, which has become an important programmer of behavior in this social system and its culture, plays a further major role in alienating Black males (especially children) from Black manhood. Flip Wilson, the highest paid Black male on television maintains his high ratings by dressing in great detail as a tough and coarse Black female. One of my seven-year-old Black male patients told me, "My Mommy likes Geraldine, and I think Geraldine is cute." "Good Times," the latest media fare for indoctrinating the Black oppressed, shows a pitiful adult Black male who never can seem to find an adequate job and a Black adolescent male who is a criminal shoplifter and a complete clown. All of this takes place in the presence of a strong and powerful Black female, who periodically drops down on her knees to pray to a white Jesus whose miracles save the situation.

These weekly insults to Black manhood that we have been programmed to believe are entertainment and not direct racist warfare, further reinforce, perhaps in the unconscious thinking of Black people, a loss of respect for Black manhood while carrying that loss to ever deeper levels. One 12-year-old Black male summed it up in this manner when I questioned him about working hard and studying in school: "No, I do not want to study so I can help Black people. If you try to help Black people, you will be killed. Look at Martin Luther King, Malcolm X and George Jackson. I don't want to die."

This reality of white supremacy oppression must be approached either linearly (head-on) or with circular patterns of behavior to escape this horrendous reality of death. Sex, having been granted as the one (though limited) area wherein Black males could express manhood, became the area of behavior where circular patterns of escape were acted out. Symbolically speaking, attempts were made to hide in the dark Black vaginal orifice. When that closed down, the white vaginal orifice was tried. When that also proved unsatisfactory as a hiding place or passage to freedom, Black and white male anuses were tried. Or one might say, these became the hoped for "undercover" railroads to freedom – the underground railroads as escape from the white man no longer being operative.

Because Black men are forced into patterns of both conscious and unconscious logic, ever-increasing incidents of Black male passivity, effeminization, bisexuality and homosexuality can be understood logically and accurately predicted. There is only one solution – that Black males collectively face the horrendous presence of white males and conquer the accompanying fear engendered by this act. After the white man is faced, he must be resisted steadfastly and fought if he continues to wage war on Black people – as he has demonstrated historically that he intends to do. And it is Black males and not females who must do the fighting.

Black male homosexuality and bisexuality are only the long-run by-products of males submitting in fear to other males in the social arena; they fail to resist because death is the result of resistance. The large number of Black male homosexuals and bisexuals who report that they had and have little or no respect for their fathers might have had completely different life histories had they grown up with the knowledge that their fathers died while in defense of their manhood when it was attacked and challenged by the oppressor. This is especially true if their mothers also admired and respected the fathers' manhood. Then, manhood would have been viewed as something so precious that one dies in defense of it. This is a quite different input into the child's brain-computer than "He was a no good, trifling, lazy nigger, and you should never want to be like him."

That the social/political dynamic of racism, itself predicated upon the white male's alienation from his own genetic status, should in turn cause others to be alienated from their own genetic status, determining color or sexual orientation, should not cause surprise. It should put the victims of such a dynamic on the alert so that they efficiently and effectively can counter this destructive assault against the appreciation of their own total genetic status.

All Black children should be protected by Black people from being alienated against any of their genes – be those genes of color, sexual gender or sickle cell anemia. Racists will attempt to bring about such genetic alienation, but Black people should be prepared to counter it.

Black psychiatrists must understand that whites may condone homosexuality for themselves, but we as Blacks, must see it as a strategy for destroying Black people that must be countered. Homosexuals or bisexuals should neither be condemned nor degraded, as they did not decide that they would be so programmed in childhood. The racist system should be held responsible. Our task is to treat and prevent its continuing and increasing occurrence.

One method I have been using with all Black male patients – whether their particular disorder be passivity, effeminization, bisexuality, homosexuality or other – is to have them relax and envision themselves approaching and opposing, in actual combat, the collective of white males and females (without apology or giving up in the crunch). The fear of such a confrontation is at the basis of most of today's Black male pathologies in patterns of logic, thought, speech, action and emotional response as they participate in all areas of human activity.

I have been working with Black mothers of Black male children, attempting to help them rid themselves of the fear of their sons and their men dying, which pushes them unconsciously to make babies of their sons and their husbands in an effort to try to protect and defend them. This response is the exact reverse of what is needed under the conditions of racism. Black women must learn to rear sons who will learn from the cradle that their major function as men is not to get a good job and a fine car, but to defend, protect and support their people (in that order), even should death be the consequence. That the Black male is not a sex machine but a protector and developer of Black people must be learned during the rearing process. There will be good jobs and self-respect (if not fine cars) once the people are liberated. There will be no true self-respect until that task is completed.

As a people, we will need increasingly strong men because we can expect that white males, driven into homosexuality from their sense of weakness compared to the world's majority of colored men, also will move towards others (non-whites), which is always an attempt to compensate for the awareness of true weakness. Black male bisexuality and homosexuality has been used by the white collective in its effort to survive genetically in a world dominated by colored people, and Black acceptance of this imposition does not solve the major problem of our oppression but only further retards its ultimate solution.

7

What Freud Was Really Talking About...
The Concept of "Penis Envy"
(February 1975)

Every social system (including its reflected culture) has a priority objective whether that objective is articulated clearly or disguised hypocritically. In the final analysis, a social system is a behavioral system consisting of specifically designed patterns of behavior – patterns of logic, thought, speech, action and emotional response, structured both consciously and unconsciously, which are used as social tools to achieve the priority objective of a people. These behavior patterns are carried forth in all areas of people activity: economics, education, entertainment, labor, law, politics, religion, sex and war.

White supremacy is the single priority objective of the world's dominant social system. This system has been functioning for the past several hundred years. In discussing the psychogenetic motivations for the white supremacy system's origin in Chapter 1, I fully realize how presumptuous it may seem to some (in the context of the white supremacy system/culture) that I – a Black female psychiatrist – should presume to critique the thinking of Sigmund Freud, one of the acknowledged major thinkers of the white supremacy system.

However, having been taught and having read Freudian theory, I decided long ago that most of Freud's analysis made little, if any, real sense. After studying history and carefully analyzing what I see happening about me daily, I have concluded that I have every right, indeed every obligation and responsibility as a being on this planet, to set forth my thinking on the furor that has been made on the subject of Freud's work and thought. If I should need further justification for my activity, I offer the following for whatever it is worth: 1) many white psychiatrists already are concluding and stating aloud that (their) psychiatry is dead, a psychiatry that for the past 50 years has been based on Freudian theses (apparently they are recognizing from experience that the theory has little practical use); and 2) if Sigmund Freud was really an astute behavioral analyst and scientist, why was he unable to decode or predict the behavior of those in the environment in which he (as a Jew) found himself – an environment in which a full one-third of the world's total Jewish population would be destroyed?

Certainly if Freud, as a Jew, was going to spend most of his energy thinking about and decoding behavior, he should have thought in greatest detail about why his people (the Semites) historically had been under attack throughout the whole of their European experience. That Freud should tell others what to do with their behavior while he failed to provide answers for himself and for his entire group suggests that one can only take his ideas with the proverbial grain of salt. But as I demonstrate, Freud – perhaps feebly and unconsciously – was struggling to discuss the major issue of his existence as an oppressed "non-white" victim in a white supremacy culture. Therefore, his discussion, coming forth in the language of abstraction and displacement, has remained completely obscure and, in the final analysis, useless.

It is my view that the word *Semite* is derived from the Latin prefix "semi," which means "half". Semites of the Jewish religion are persons from Africa who were half black and half white. Black plus white always equals "colored," meaning persons carrying in their genetic makeup some capacity to produce melanin pigmentation and, in some instances, a genetic capacity to produce kinky hair. Jews who left Africa and went to Europe were colored people when they arrived there hundreds of years ago. Europeans (whites) never have forgotten the Semite capacity for genetic dominance of the Aryan (white) population. Although after much intermixing many Jews lost much of their skin color, they have continued to be identified as a colored people from Africa by the whites! This is the fundamental reason for the historic oppression of Semites within the white supremacy system/culture. Hitler articulated this most clearly when, on the one hand, he insisted the Jews were genetically inferior to the Aryans, but on the other hand he continued to speak of their genetic dominance over the Aryans (whites).

Freud could not focus fully on this because he desired acceptance in the white supremacy culture and did not want his science of psychoanalysis looked upon as a "Jewish (degraded) science." Thus, he could not come to terms with his own identity, nor the dynamic affecting those so identified by the surrounding social system. Instead of focusing on the dynamic of "self-repression," a very convenient displacement for the brain-computer that has a natural, uninterrupted linkage between "sex" and "self" (as sex is the act responsible for the existence of the "self" and the only act through which the "self" can be reproduced), as a Semite, Freud found himself focusing on "sex-repression." Sex-repression indeed did occur in the white supremacy culture, as demonstrated by the historic alienation from the condition of albinism and the act of "original sin" (sex) – which was viewed as responsible for that appearance of whiteness in a world of colored people.

My concentration here is the topic of "penis envy," a major cornerstone of the Freudian edifice. (In other chapters, I discuss the "Oedipal complex" and "castration anxiety.")   In brief, according to Freudian psychological theory, the little (white) girl is struck with an intense sense of loss and injury and with envy of the (white) male when she realizes that her clitoris is an inferior organ to the male's penis (wishing that she too had such a fine penis). Presumably, she is not satisfied until she has a penis of her own or some symbolic form of a penis. A major segment of the female's personality is presumed to be predicated on this traumatic realization.

As previously mentioned, Freud was a Semitic victim in a white supremacy culture, a culture that had its true genesis not in Greece but in Africa. The first albino mutations (whites) were produced from Blacks in Africa. These albinos, I suggest, were chased north by the Blacks or wandered north away from the intense sun so that they could survive. (See

Chapter 2.) They ended their trek in Europe, directly north of Africa. From the very first experiences of the mutant albino population, with the recognition that the condition of skin albinism (whiteness) could be annihilated genetically by those with black and brown skins (a phenomenon that is now known as genetic dominance over a genetic recessive state, such as albinism), there had been white fear of Black genetic power or white male fear and envy of the Black (penis) phallus and entire genital apparatus. This fear, in turn, produced a sense of inadequacy and inferiority in the white male as he compared himself to males of color.

The total white group's conscious or unconscious awareness of their genetic weakness and potential annihilation became even more pronounced – as a cultural theme – as Europeans (whites) began circum-navigating the globe in the 15th century on. At this time, whites discovered that they were a tiny minority on a planet wherein all others had colored skins. It did not take long for the group to realize that both colored males and females could annihilate the whites genetically. Thus, the white male felt genetically weaker, not only in comparison to the Black male but also to the Black female. The Black male had to be feared more because it is males who initiate the act of reproduction.

The above genetic dynamics are, of course, never discussed directly and overtly within the white supremacy system/culture. Most overt discussions on genetics center around analysis of the "inferiority" of Black and other non-white peoples, which of course is a projective compensation. The full discussion, however, that continues covertly and unconsciously permeates the logic sequences within the culture. Perhaps it will be fair to state that true awareness of the fundamental genetic issue is repressed.

White envy of the black phallus is addressed unconsciously when whites constantly concern themselves with the comparative size of the black phallus versus the size of the white phallus. This concern is raised in the form of the following question: "Is the Black male's penis really greater in size than that of the white male?" Any school child could suggest that a simple tape measure can settle the question once and for all, unless the questioners and "researchers" are afraid to measure.

In my practice, a Black mother informed me that her six-year-old son, attending a predominantly white elementary school, reported to her that one of his white male classmates had told him that he (the Black child) had a large penis. The mother stated that she asked her son what his response was. Her son told the white boy that all Black boys had large penises.

It is obvious that in the above situation, in a school with a majority of white children, at shower or bathroom time, the white male child would have had ample opportunity to see the size of white penises. He would have had the same opportunity at home. His need to comment on the size of the Black child's penis indicates that this Black penis must have stood out by all of his other comparisons, even at this tender age. It is also certainly clear that the Black male child had no concerns or fears about the adequacy of the Black male's penis.

Furthermore, it is my interpretation that the major concern is with the power of the genetic material in the black testicles and that the concern is displaced to a less threatening object (the phallus) and its size. To appreciate my analysis, remember that the major percentage of Black males who have been lynched by white males have had their genitals attacked, removed and taken away by white males (i.e., carried with them on their person). This behavior is peculiar to white males in their relationship to men of color. I interpret this behavior as fear of the Black male genitalia. Thus, it must be attacked and destroyed, but also there is envy and a desire for possession of same.

This should help to explain why white males who wish others to view them or wish to view themselves as strong, powerful and important, puff and suck on huge *black* cigars. Indeed, the more important they wish others to believe they are, the longer the cigar. Perhaps the foul odor is to draw the attention of others to themselves with their long black cigars (their symbolic phallus).

Also, the more powerful and important the white male perceives himself, the longer is his *black* limousine. Both the car and cigar can be viewed as phallic symbols. Perhaps black and dark brown pipes also should be included as similar symbols. (See Chapter 11.) It is again little wonder that white men build missiles shaped in the form of phalluses, paint them white and use them to annihilate peoples of color around the globe.

I have said all of the above to state that, yes, there is "penis envy" in the white supremacy culture, but it began with the white male's envy of the genetic power residing in the Black male's testicles and phallus. Perhaps there was also envy of the comparative longer length of the Black phallus. The sense of his relative genetic weakness or inferiority compared to Black males (because Black is always genetically dominant to white) caused the white male to attempt to project "inferiority" on white females as well. (See Chapter 6.) The white male's insistence that he is superior to the white female and his forcing this psychological dynamic in white family life has caused the white female, in turn, to wish that she could share his power and his status and symbolically, to have a penis of her own. The extent to which white females as mothers play a role in helping to turn their sons into effeminate homosexuals (female-acting men with penises) is again an attempt to resolve an aspect of the conflict.

Some white females react to this imposed sense of their genital inferiority by seeking to "liberate" themselves and secure black penises of their own, penises white males consider more powerful than their own. This is the dialogue that increasing numbers of white females covertly and perhaps unconsciously conduct *with white males* as they (white females) parade in front of white males with the Black male (black penis) they have captured for their own. The silent dialogue between the white male and white female in these social confrontations goes something like this, "Now I have one (a penis) that is bigger and stronger than yours, one that I know that you envy."

As the mothers, wives and sisters of white males, white females consciously or unconsciously always have understood white males' envy of Black males, even though the envy was expressed in terms of white male hysteria over white women being "raped" by Black males. White males knew or suspected that the white female desired the black penis more than the white one because white men themselves desired the black penis more than their own (why else cut off the black genitals and take them home). Thus, it is not surprising that there is increased white female/Black male activity (initiated in most instances by white females who have signaled to Black males that they are available). At the same time, other white females are saying they are going to be "policemen," "firemen" and "football players" – "just like men" – and are discussing their lesbian inclinations openly.

White males, with Freud's help, have projected their own intense sense of loss, injury, inadequacy and envy as genetically recessive albino mutants who are being annihilated genetically by both Black (non-white) males and females. It is they (white males) who have the *primary penis envy,* which is manifested in their envy of Black males' penises. They then project their sense of inferiority onto white females, causing them, in turn, to develop *secondary penis envy.* The accuser now stands himself accused!

These dynamics are at the root of the fear of all true competition white males feel towards Black males, thus preventing true competition in all areas of people activity: economics, education, entertainment, labor, law, politics, religion, sex and war. The obscurity of Freud's ideas can be clarified only if the system and cultural dynamics of white supremacy are analyzed and understood fully, for this is the context in which Freud wrote, suffered and died. Freud, attempting to escape his own reality as a Semite (in the full meaning of that term), was unable to face fully what he was seeing and experiencing about him, which was anti-Semitism (a dynamic of white supremacy). He felt it, but could not accurately describe it – perhaps because he feared for his life. Thus, his life experience came forth from his brain-computer as abstracted and displaced concepts.

To see clearly, Freud would have had to recognize that he was viewed as a "non-white" (a Semite – i.e., "mulatto") and not an "Austrian" which, like "German" and "American," means pure white. Freud was attempting too desperately, like the other Semites in Europe and America, to be integrated and accepted as "white." Therefore, he ended by seeing only "through a glass darkly," or really not seeing at all. Then again, perhaps

Freud sensed that offending the Aryans (whites) by making a fully accurate analysis would have brought disaster before it finally did come – in the Nazi holocaust. Personally, I see no need to repeat his fear nor his folly, even though the same danger exists.

REFERENCES

Cirlot, J.E.. *A Dictionary of Symbols*. New York: Philosophical Library, 1962.

Freedman, A.M.. and Kaplan, H.I.. *Comprehensive Textbook of Psychiatry*. Baltimore: Williams and Wilkins Company, 1967.

Hitler, A.. *Mein Kampf*. Costa Mesa: Noon Tide Press, 1986.

Memmi, A.. *Dominated Man*. Boston: Beacon Press, 1968.

8

Guns As Symbols
(1975-1977)

Anthony Sampson, in his book*The Arms Bazaar: From Lebanon to Lockheed* (1977), informs us that the word "...weapon was until the fourteenth century synonymous with penis..."

There are now 25,000 handgun deaths per year in the United States of America. The President of the U.S., in 1975, was subjected to two assassination attempts in a time span of three weeks. Handguns were the instrument used in each assassination attempt. The same President was against handgun control.

The above statements are laden with highly significant meaning, which is not immediately apparent and which can be understood fully only when the underlying psychodynamics of the collective white psyche and of the white supremacy power system and its culture are probed, dissected and revealed.

Joseph Kraft, writing in the September 25, 1975 issue of *The Washington Post* stated,

> The starting point for analysis is the recognition that, for better or for worse, the United States is a country with a thing about guns. Prowess with firearms was critical to survival in the frontier days. The right to bear arms is guaranteed in the Constitution. Millions of Americans regard hunting as a favorite recreation. Thousands collect guns as souvenirs. I once visited the home in Mechanicsburg, Ohio of a prominent official. In this home no wall was uncovered by some kind of rifle, shotgun, pistol or musket. The owner, William Saxbe, eventually became Attorney General.

Mr. Kraft later used the term "pro-gun culture" to describe American culture and society, as he cited that there have been no fewer than five different Presidential commissions that have recommended more stringent forms of gun control.

While recognizing along with Mr. Kraft the predominant use of guns in the American frontier days, I strongly disagree that guns were needed for survival in the simple terms of the continuation of life. After all, the Native Americans taught the Europeans how to grow corn to feed themselves and survive. Guns were needed, however, if Native (non-white) Americans were going to be removed successfully from the land that the Europeans (whites) wished to dominate and control.

This essay is being written neither in review nor in protest of the horrendous carnage of Native American life in particular, nor in protest of the general path of carnage that has been tread in this area of the world. It is being written in hopes of shedding light on the seeming dilemma that, in spite of the past and present potential carnage from handguns, there is tremendous resistance amongst the dominant population to have guns as well as all other instruments of life destruction (including atomic, hydrogen and neutron bombs) brought under control.

In my view, the gun is a critical symbol in the subconscious mind of white peoples everywhere. This symbol is primarily operative, as are all true symbols at the unconscious level of brain activity.

Increasing numbers of Black behavioral scientists are beginning to understand that the dominant thrust in what has become known as "Western civilization" is racism.

Once we become aware of the deep humiliation that is apparently felt by whites *because of their skin whiteness* (due to the genetic mutation to albinism) and because of their genetic vulnerability when compared to non-whites (black, brown, red and yellow peoples), it is possible to understand the historically degraded status of sex in the white supremacy system/culture. Sex is "the act of self-reproduction" and the act responsible for "the production of the self" and "the appearance of the self." In the white brain-computer, if the white, pale, genetically vulnerable self is degraded, then the act that produced that self will be degraded in that same brain-computer.

An example by a famous "Western" author of what whites have thought consciously about white skin is presented by Mark Twain who, in his essay "Skin Deep" from *On The Damned Human Race*, stated:

> ...Then there would have been the added disadvantage of the white complexion. It is not an unbearably unpleasant complexion when it keeps to itself, but when it comes into competition with masses of brown and black the fact is betrayed that it is endurable only because we are used to it....Nearly all black and brown skins are beautiful but a beautiful white skin is rare. How rare, one may learn by walking down a street in Paris, New York or London on a weekday – particularly an unfashionable street – and keeping count of the satisfactory complexions encountered in the course of a mile. Where dark complexions are massed, they make the white look bleached out, unwholesome, and sometimes frankly ghastly.

The acts of self-production and self-reproduction are not the only targets of degradation in the white psyche (brain-computer). Within the thought and logic processes of the white psyche, the genitals themselves are degraded – both male and female genitals – those parts of the anatomy and physiology that are responsible for self-production and self-reproduction. Especially, the white male sexual apparatus is seen as inferior and inadequate when compared to the sexual apparatus of the Black male. (See Chapter 7.)

In the May 1977 issue of *Medical Aspects of Human Sexuality*, in an article entitled "Men's Fear of Having Too Small A Penis," Povl W. Toussieng, M.D., writes, "A surprisingly large number of men fear that their penises are not of adequate size." Although Toussieng makes no reference to the race or color of the men he interviewed, it is known in clinical practice that this is not a major fear of Black men. However, he does state,

> It is hard to determine the exact origin of the myth of the big penis. In many cultures such as ancient Egypt the penis did become a fertility symbol and was, consequently, pictured with enormous dimensions. In classic Greece, however, small genitals were considered more

beautiful than larger ones. Romans reversed this concept and Western culture appears by and large to have followed them.

It is interesting that Toussieng makes no mention of any attempt to measure the penis size of white and Black men in a culture heavily laden with this specific white male preoccupation – a culture in which large numbers of white males are daily in close proximity to Black males and aware of their presence in the society, especially in the arena of sports (games symbolic of special male prowess and virility), where Black males dominate.

Interestingly, Clyde Keeler, writing on albinism in an article entitled "Cuna Moon-Child Albinism, 1950-1970," (*Journal of Heredity*, No. 61, 1970) states,

> The voice quality of albino males is soft and higher pitched than in moreno males. In addition, they appear to be deficient in sex hormone, and while they may be fertile, they have a lower phallic posture, due to flaccidity. Albinos usually have flabby muscles and reduced muscular strength as shown by manumometer readings.

This is of interest because, in my view, all skin whiteness is related to albinism or a variant thereof. Keeler's observation implies that there may be a genetic association between albino or white skin color and the appearance and posture of the penis (albinism influencing small penis size or lack of penis posture causing its appearance to be small). Also, it is known that in comparison to the Black population, whites have less muscle definition – thus, muscular flabbiness – compared to Blacks.

It may be said that most fundamentally there is a genetic basis and secondarily an anatomic and physiologic basis for the white fear of white genetic annihilation. This, in turn, became the basis for the global system of white supremacy domination and its attendant culture – a system and culture evolved and structured to prevent white genetic annihilation and to ensure white genetic survival.

Indeed, if the understood threat to white genetic survival was the Black male's genital apparatus, consciously or unconsciously, the white psyche would be compelled to produce a weapon of defense, of comparable or greater power than that of the Black male's penis and testicles.

It should be made clear here that Black males' genital apparatus is the most feared relative to the genital apparatus of other non-white males because in possessing the greatest potential to produce melanin – the pigment responsible for all true skin coloration – Black males have the greatest genetic potential to annihilate the global white minority.

The individual and collective white brain-computer, given that task of solving the global problem of white genetic survival, eventually evolved a solution in the form of a technology that would address the specific issue of white genetic and genital weakness or inadequacy.

Technology always is developed to take over at the point of the human organism's anatomical and physiological limitation. Thus, the white brain-computer printout was a *weapon* that would be the exact symbolic replica of the male genitalia – a weapon that would take over at the point of limitation of the white male genital apparatus, an apparatus that had the very specific limitation of being unable to annihilate Blacks and other people of color genetically. Diagrams I-IV illustrate what I am stating.

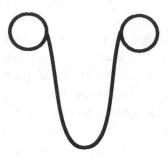

Diagram I
The Male Genitalia (diagrammatic sketch)
Penis and Testicles
Front View

Diagram II
The Male Genitalia (diagrammatic sketch)
Penis and Testicle
Lateral View

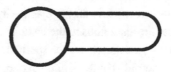

Diagram III
The Male Genitalia (diagrammatic sketch)
Penis and Testicle
Erect State

Diagram IV
The Gun (diagrammatic sketch)

From the above four drawings, it is clear that the gun, in its essential shape and functioning, is the exact counterpart to the functioning genital apparatus and to the erect penis that is ejaculating. In other words, the handle and chamber are analogous to the testicles; the barrel of the gun is analogous to the penis; the bullets are the sperm contained in the ejaculate with their genetic material. (In the white psyche, white genetic annihilation by Blacks or other non-whites is experienced as the destruction of life by the Black genital apparatus.) The firing gun in function achieves for the whites the destruction of the lives of Blacks and other non-white peoples.

Thus, to the extent that the guns manufactured and made by the white collective in the context of the white supremacy system/culture were used against Blacks and other genetically dominant colored people on Earth, they became the answer (at least, a temporarily comforting answer) to the great fear of white genetic annihilation. The gun became not only the weapon, the developed technology to ensure white genetic survival, but it also became the symbolic white penis. Thus, it is no accident that white males often refer to one another as "son-of-a gun." This is a symbolically determined pattern of speech, and I am certain that white males who use it have not understood in depth why such a phrase entered and remains in their brain-computers. This phrase deprecates the white male genital apparatus that "fathers" white people with their genetically deficient state of albinism. It says instead that the white male prefers the gun to be his phallus and the phallus of his father. The gun then becomes the desired all-powerful phallus of the white male, which he conceives of as being an equalizer to the phallus of Black and other non-white males.

This symbolism underlying the production of the gun in the white psyche and the white supremacy system/culture also explains the Western expression "God did not create all men equal but Colonel Colt did," referring to the creator of the Colt revolver. Apparently white males were thinking, at an unconscious level to be sure, that God did not create them to be genetically equal to men of color, but their technology of compensation was the gun.

Understanding this gun symbolism also clarifies the observation of Anthony Sampson in the opening paragraph of this essay – that the word "...weapon was up till the fourteenth century synonymous with penis..." in Western (white) civilization.

The gun is not the only weapon in the white supremacy system/culture that in form and function is symbolic of the functioning male genital apparatus. The cannon – with its cannon wheels and long black nozzle or tube and big black cannon balls shot out as projectiles – is one example. Similarly, bullets and bombs are dark-colored and resemble individual sperm in general shape and form. And it is of further importance that the gun and these other weapons usually are painted black or are at least dark in color.

In contrast to these dark-colored weapons are the more recently developed missiles that are often painted white, but again shaped as gigantic white penises. These white phallic symbols are now the super weapons of the "superman" and the "superior" race.

It is of great interest that these modern, large, white missiles surround the vast majority of non-white peoples on the planet and when used can counter the threat of white genetic annihilation.

Knowledge and understanding of these symbols will make clear the meaning of the Washington Monument and, in addition, its proximity to the domed Jefferson Memorial in Washington, D.C. When these two architectural structures are viewed at a distance, they look like Diagram V.

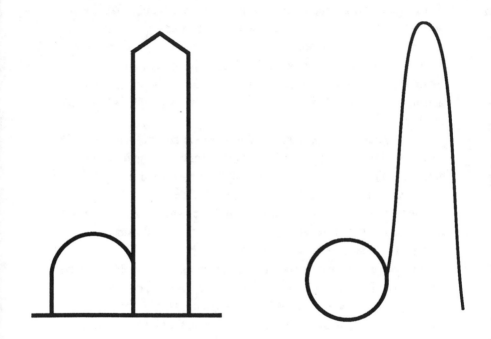

Diagram V
The Washington Monument and
The Jefferson Memorial
View from a distance
(diagrammatic sketch)

Is it not apparent that this is the same side view of the penis and the testicles that are the basis for the form and structure of the gun? This same lateral view, in abstract form, of the penis and testicles was the symbol for the World Fair held in New York, 1941-1942.

With all of the above in mind, let us again return to the gun. Upon brief reflection it will be noted that traditionally in the white supremacy culture guns were/are worn on one or both hips of the male, at the exact level of the male genitals. It is no accident that in this culture the act of ejaculating is often referred to as "shooting off."

When the man wearing a gun in a holster is viewed laterally, the gun appears exactly as the side view of the penis and testicles. If guns are worn on both hips and brought together centrally on the belt to the vertical midline of the body, they present the full face view of the penis and both testicles. (See Diagram VI.)

In the U.S., the most popular hero has been the gunfighter, now the present-day detective or lawman. The first chapter of Paul Trachtman's book *The Gunfighters* is entitled "The Deadly Brotherhood of the Gun." The "gunfighters" came into prominence following the close of the Civil War. Most of the gunfighters were Southerners who felt humiliated by the loss of their slaves and the war and by the temporary appearance of power held by Blacks who were their former Black slaves.

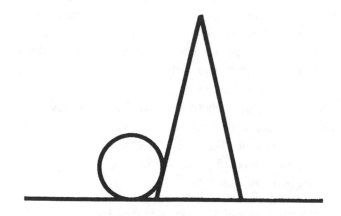

Diagram VI
Symbol for the World Fair
New York, 1941-1942

The resulting deep sense of white male insecurity and inadequacy was compensated for by the obsessive use of the gun. This was the era of Frank and Jesse James, Billy the Kid and a host of others for whom the gun made up for a sense of profound and deep inadequacy hidden by a thorough and ruthless exterior. That the lives of others were treated with little value merely reflected the failed sense of adequacy and diminished sense of importance in their own lives.

During this same period, the gory sport of "cockfighting" was highly popular and important as a diversion among ranchers in the West. Thus, It is not surprising that the white male also referred to his penis as a "cock," or that when a gun (the symbol of the white male phallus) is prepared for firing it is first "cocked." In this area of the world in the white supremacy system, a detective who *always* carries a gun is a most important hero. The detective with his gun has been referred to as a "dick." From this came the long-time comic strip hero detective, *"Dick Tracy."* The white male also has referred to his penis as a "dick." And it cannot be ignored that the first child all American children still meet in primary public school is a white male child named *"Dick"* along with his sister "Jane." In effect, at this early age, the white male child is being instructed to recognize that his *identity* is synonymous with *penis (gun)*. These symbolic reinforcements continue until his death. That is why there is a continuing necessity for gun violence via television for American (white) children.

All of the above has been stated not only to point out a basic preoccupation of the white supremacy system/culture with the threat of white genetic annihilation, but more importantly, to shed light on why there cannot and will not be gun control or weapon control in the global white supremacy system/culture.

With the gun being the symbolic genitalia of the white male (his answer to the threat to white genetic survival), gun control would represent white male (genital) castration. Such gun control would spell the immediate end of white genetic survival on Earth. John Ellis, in his book *The Social History of the Machine Gun*, states,

> In Africa small parties of Europeans, soldiers and armed settlers often had to face the resistance of large numbers of poorly armed natives.

The odds were so in favor of the natives that the white men were obliged to adopt all weapons that would help to maximize their firepower....In all parts of the continent, against Zulus, Dervishes, Hereros, Matabele and many other peoples, Gatlings, Gardners and Maxims scythed down anyone who dared to stand in the way of the imperialist advance....Without the handful of machine guns, the British South Africa Company might have lost Rhodesia; Lugard might have been driven out of Uganda and the Germans out of Tanganyika. Without Hiram Maxim much of subsequent world history might have been very different.

Ellis remarks further:

In Africa automatic weapons were used to support the seizure of millions of square miles of land and to discipline those unfortunates who wished to eschew the benefits of European civilization. With machine guns in their armory, mere handfuls of white men, plunderers and visionaries, civilians and soldiers were able to scoff at the objections of the Africans themselves and impose their rule on a whole continent.

Thus, in this area of the white supremacy system where in 1975 there were 25,000 deaths caused by guns, there cannot be gun control. Guns and missiles are viewed as essential aspects of white male anatomy and physiology. Is it an accident that in the U.S. white male children learn to use guns before they learn to use their penises, while Black male children learn to use their penises before they learn to use guns?

I will close with further observations. Following a lecture that I presented in Los Angeles, California in May, 1977 in which I included a discussion on the symbolism of the gun in the white male psyche, a white male in the audience pointed out the parallel symbolism in the large black umbrella often carried by white males in the white supremacy culture. I agreed that his observation seemed to be a valid one. The long black umbrella, carried everywhere, became a part of the standard dress of the well-to-do Englishman at a time when it was said that "the sun never sets on the British Empire." Of course this great empire consisted of control over vast numbers of non-white men and their genitals that had the power to annihilate whites. The white man's traditional long black umbrella said, in effect, "I also have a large black phallus or at least a phallic symbol that denotes my importance and power – and a power over the Black male genital apparatus. "

The same symbolism explains a recent murder in Washington, D.C. A white male shot a white female companion in the mouth, as she was in bed with two other white females engaged in sexual activity that all four had been involved in earlier. As the white female victim was engaged in being sexually "pleasured" by two white females, the white male who was left out – feeling genitally rejected and inadequate compared to two females – pulled out and used (consciously or unconsciously) his preferred symbolic penis, the gun.

REFERENCES

Ellis, John, *The Social History of the Machine Gun.* New York: Pantheon, 1975.

Keeler, Clyde. "Cuna Moon-Child Albinism, 1950-1970," *Journal of Heredity.* No. 61, 1970.

Sampson, Anthony. *The Arms Bazaar: From Lebanon to Lockheed.* New York: Viking, 1977.

Toussieng, Povl. "Men's Fear of Having Too Small a Penis," *Medical Aspects of Human Sexuality.* May, 1977.

Trachtman, Paul. *The Gunfighters.* Virginia: Time-Life, 1975.

9

The Mother Fucker and the Original Mother Fucker (June 1976)

I have defined racism as the behavioral power system of logic, thought, speech, action, emotional response and perception – whether consciously or unconsciously determined – in persons who classify themselves as "white." The goal of racism is white domination over the vast majority of the world's people whom the whites have classified as "non-whites" (black, brown, red and yellow) in order to ensure white genetic survival.

My interest in the phenomenon of racism has resulted from my awareness of the negative impact this destructive system has on the lives and behavior of the vast majority of people on this planet who are non-white, and who are the victims of this power system.

The specific nature of the destructiveness of racism was set forth by the Caucus of Black Psychiatrists at the 1969 Annual Meeting of the American Psychiatric Association (Miami Beach, Florida). The Black Caucus stated that racism was not only the number one mental health problem in this nation, but additionally was the number one cause of all other mental health problems.

Racism is carried out in all areas of people activity: economics, education, entertainment, labor, law, politics, religion, sex and war (as explained by Neely Fuller in his book *The United Independent Compensatory Code/System/Concept*). From the above, it follows that if the basic underlying psychodynamic motivations in the individual and collective white psyche are understood, that is, to survive as a mutant, genetic deficient minority (which includes the evolution of a power system to ensure that survival), then all patterns of white behavior eventually can be decoded and fully understood – whether they are patterns of logic, thought, speech, action, emotional response and/or perception in any of the nine areas of people activity. Similarly, because all non-white peoples on the planet Earth are now subject to and affected by the global white supremacy system, if the white psyche is decoded and understood fully, it is possible to decode and understand the present behavioral manifestations of all of those who are victims of white supremacy domination and oppression, the total non-white majority as a collective and as individuals.

The term "mother fucker" is a pattern of speech used with extremely high frequency amongst Black people, specifically Black males in the U.S. In my attempt to decode and understand this particular pattern of high frequency behavior or language use, it was necessary to begin with the knowledge that all Black peoples, like all other non-white peoples, are relatively powerless victims of the white supremacy system, irrespective of their income levels.

I then examined certain other specific patterns of language used by Black males within the white supremacy culture. To begin with, Black males in particular, but also Black females, refer to the white male as "The Man." Once this term "The Man" is thought or uttered, the brain computes that inasmuch as there are only five major categories of people ("man," "woman," "boy," "girl" and "baby"), if the white male is "*The* Man," meaning logically "The *only* Man," then any other male must be one of the four remaining people categories – "boy," "girl," "woman" or "baby."

Historically, Black males have fought being referred to as "boy" by white males and females. Only recently has the use of this degrading appellation ceased to some extent, although there is a current television series called "Chico and The Man." The title implies "the boy" and "The Man." "The Man," of course, is white and "Chico" is a non-white male.

Because the use of the word "boy" in reference to Black males ceased, it only meant that Black males could then refer to themselves as any one of the remaining three categories of people: "baby," "woman" or "girl." It certainly did not imply that Black males would be referred to as equals of white males. This never could occur under the system of white supremacy domination.

When the use of the word "boy" was no longer the term of common reference for Black males by whites, Black males began referring to themselves as "baby." For until most recently, with the changes in dress and clothing styles, most Black males deeply resented any reference to themselves as "girl" or "woman." But the recent style changes towards high-heeled shoes, curled hair, hair curlers, braids, earrings, bracelets, necklaces, pocketbooks, midriff tops, cinch waisted pants etc., that many Black males have adopted now suggest that there is a developing tendency, widespread amongst Black males, to not mind (consciously or unconsciously) being mistaken for a "girl" or a "woman."

However, at present, the term "baby" is a fully accepted appellation for Black males in reference to one another. It is thus not uncommon to hear one Black male say to another, "Hey 'baby,' what's happening?" In addition to Black males frequently referring to one another as "baby," many Black females often refer to their Black male peers and companions as "baby." While Black adult females refer to Black adult males as "baby," Black adult males often refer to Black adult female peers and companions as "momma," often expecting those "mommas" to provide food, clothes and shelter for them. It is not uncommon to hear "Hey momma, can I ride with you?" Further, Black adult males also refer to the place where they sleep as a "crib." The brain thus computes: an adult male who refers to another adult male as "The Man" (meaning, the only man), to himself as "baby," to the woman that he sleeps with as "momma," and to the place where he sleeps as a "crib," will call himself or any Black male reflection of himself a "mother fucker."

Thus it is clear that the origin of this specific pattern of speech begins with the perhaps unconscious recognition that within the framework of the white supremacy power system and its reflecting culture, power rests only in the hands of whites, more specifically, in the hands of the white male. And relative to the white male, the Black male is a powerless "baby." All babies everywhere are powerless compared to adult males or men. "Mother fucker" is therefore a profound political statement, as it addresses itself to an existing and specific set of power relationships – namely, the white male's continuing dominance over the Black male.

It is the confrontation with the stated fact of his social and functional powerlessness in the total context of the white supremacy system that causes one Black male to explosively challenge and fight another Black male when called "mother fucker" with the proper negative vocal intonation. This is true because Black males are totally uncomfortable with the reality of their relative powerlessness compared to white males, even though this awareness of powerlessness is more often unconsciously repressed than consciously dealt with in the Black male psyche. It is my estimate that 70% of the Black male on Black male homicides follow the use of the term "mother fucker" said in the specific tone that implies, at the unconscious gut level, "You are a powerless baby."

The reality and awareness of Black male powerlessness in the context of the white supremacy system causes such gut and psychic pain for the Black male that the brain-computer switches over to the very deep levels of the unconscious mind, to the realm and region of symbolic word formation and thinking. Here the brain pieces together, in coded symbolic language, the phraseology that hides from the conscious mind the continuing existence and activity of a totally unacceptable reality. Indeed, there is no single term that is more emotionally charged nor a phrase that is used more often by Black males in the U.S. than "mother fucker." This suggests that the most obvious of all realities for Black males is their powerlessness relative to the power of the white male in the system and culture of racism.

But, it is not sufficient to have decoded this particular word pattern in the white supremacy culture. The question indeed arises, why is *this* particular word formation and combination used to denote Black powerlessness? This more fundamental question can be answered. Again, however, it is necessary to begin with the psyche of those who organized the white supremacy power system as well as the fundamental reasons and motivations behind its origin.

The total world white collective has been involved in the establishment and maintenance of the white supremacy power system. It is, however, the white male who has been involved most specifically in the system's establishment and maintenance. The system's major characteristics thus reflect more of the projections of his psyche than those of his female counterpart.

I stated in the beginning of this book that whites are undoubtedly a genetic mutant albino population. They are albino mutants from the original Black (hue-man) beings, causing the formation of a mankind and a huemankind. This statement is given strong support by the work of the anthropologist Louis Leakey who stated in his book *By The Evidence (Memoirs, 1932-1951)* that human life began in Africa and that the first human beings were Black.

From the modern science of genetics, we know that it is possible for all pigmented population groups to produce white (albino) mutants. We also know that it is impossible for albino mutants to produce Black offsprings.

As reported in *National Geographic* and *Natural History* magazines (see references), recently found in Africa was the first known albino gorilla infant who was the offspring of its coal black gorilla mother and father. This evidence strongly supports the extrapolation that if a higher primate (in this instance, a coal black gorilla pair) can produce a platinum blond, blue-eyed, pink-skinned (albino) then certainly this could also be the pattern by which blond, blue-eyed, pink-skinned (white) men and women also were produced – as genetic mutants or albino mutants from the Black norm. That the norm for the entire human family is to possess melanin–pigmented skins supports that extrapolation.

The albino mutants that easily could have evolved in Africa either could have been chased northward by their pigmented parents and kinsmen, or they could have migrated northward on their own, away from the intensely sunny environment of Africa where their non-pigmented, defective skins would not be damaged by the less intense sun rays. Moving directly northward from Africa, one lands in Europe, the now recognized home of the whites.

The main point of this perhaps seemingly discursive discussion is that white-skinned (albino) persons were most probably the genetic mutant offspring from Black parents. In other words, Black males and Black females were the parents, the original mothers and fathers, of the albino or white population. The marriage of albinos with one another subsequently produced what is now known as the white race. If this description of the origin of whites is accurate, as this writer strongly believes, then deep within the unconscious psyche of the white collective is an awareness of their origin amongst Blacks, that Blacks were their parents and that they (whites) were the defective offsprings of Blacks.

The white male, the prime organizer of the white supremacy system/culture, is thus aware (although perhaps at deep unconscious levels) that his original mother was a Black woman (just as his original father was a Black man). Therefore, in spite of the overt psychological need to repress this fundamental knowledge of origin, the conscious recognition of which would necessitate a confrontation with the genetic mutant and genetic defective status of skin whiteness, white males have exposed their unconscious awareness by referring to Black women in this world area as "mammy," and "aunt" or "auntie" and referring to Black males as "pappy" and "uncle." These terms cannot reflect true simple endearment as they occur in the presence of degradation, enslavement, oppression and Black destruction.

Further, white males strongly supported Black females suckling white babies and also endorsed Black men and women caring for white children (the extension of the white male himself). This close contact of the white child particularly with the Black female was supported by the white male in spite of the degraded slave and oppressed status the white collective imposed upon the Black collective. Thus, as the white baby suckled the breast of the Black woman, the white adult male, as he watched the Black slave "mammy" suckle his white baby, could unconsciously fantasize himself as being at the breast of his original Black mother.

Even more significant is the fact that the white male could not abstain from making sexual aggressions toward the Black female. Indeed, some of the most important founding fathers of the so-called United States of America were involved actively and continuously in relationships with Black women (i.e., George Washington and Thomas Jefferson). This pattern of sexual aggression of the white male towards the Black female continues unabated to this day. Ultimately, it is little wonder that *black* stockings, *black* underwear and *black* sleepwear are items of sexual stimulation for the white male collective.

It should be noted that the term sexual aggression is used to imply a sexual relationship between political unequals. The white male has power, and the Black female, like the Black male, is powerless. Sexual favors are thus directly and/or indirectly forced from the powerless partner. Each time the white male imposed (imposes) himself sexually upon the Black female, at the deep levels of symbolic thought he can be viewed as having intercourse with the reflection of his original Black mother. Thus, within the deep and fundamental psychodynamics of the white supremacy system/culture, the white male becomes *"the original mother fucker."*

Thus, through the subtle and intricate dynamics and the unconscious underweavings of the white supremacy system/culture, the white male has projected *his* image of himself as "mother fucker" on to the total Black collective throughout the world. Indeed, each time one Black male even utters the term "mother fucker" to another Black male, there is probably some white male on the planet who is having sexual intercourse with a Black or other non-white female – the symbolic representation of the white male's original Black mother. Even the white male's pornographic magazines are filled with pictures of white males having intercourse with Black females.

This need to return to and to have intercourse with the Black mother is undoubtedly the true basis for the Greek myth, Oedipus Rex. It also explains why this symbolic story (myth) continues to have major significance in the white supremacy system/culture. The myth of Oedipus tells of Oedipus sleeping with his mother (the Black female) and slaying his father (the Black male). The myth of Oedipus parallels, in importance, the biblical myth of Adam and Eve, which in coded language depicts the origin of the first whites (albinos) from Black parents.

At yet another level, the white male's desire to return to the Black female in a sexual encounter also can be viewed as a symbolic attempt to re-enter her womb, in hopes of coming out again (being born again) non-defective. In other words, the white male harbors an unconscious desire to be born again but without the genetic defect of melanin pigment deficiency or albinism. It must be noted here that "being born again" is a major concept in the most important religion in the white supremacy system/culture – Christianity. An extension of the concept of "being born again" without genetic defect is to be born without "sin" and to rid one's self of "the original sin". The original sin in white supremacy's Christianity, on close examination, is the act of sex that produced the appearance of nakedness or the genetic mutation of albinism or white skin.

That the concept of sin, shame and guilt are related to the naked white body as perhaps an unconscious association was made manifest when a significant number of white males began to run about naked (body whiteness fully exposed) at the height of the Watergate scandal, when the evil doings of the highest ranked men in the global white supremacy system became *exposed* to the world. This behavioral phenomenon of white men running naked in public and the hiding in shame were called "streaking." It has been laughed at and discussed but never fully explained before now. It should be noted also in this context that the "good book" in the white supremacy system/culture (the Bible) is most often itself covered in black, almost never in white!

But let's return from these asides to the main point of discussion: the white male as the original "mother fucker" and his sexual return to the Black female as an expression of his unconscious desire to be reborn with Black skin.

Within the context of the American segment of the white supremacy system/culture, one of the most popular white male entertainers was Al Jolson. Jolson became famous singing as a white male in *black face*, pretending that he was Black or having a fantasy that he was Black while the white audiences that enjoyed him, one can suspect, similarly were engrossed in the same fantasy.

One of the most popular songs sung by Jolson was "Mammy." He was pretending to be the Black offspring of a Black woman, while singing about how much he loved his dear old mammy. Today, that song continues to stir the hearts (the unconscious) of many white males and, I suppose, also some white females. Had Jolson and any of the other white males in black face been simply thinking of a "Black mammy" who had nursed and cared for them, there would be little need to color their own faces black, leaving bare their white lips to reveal that the color defect was yet present.

The unconscious need for the white male to return to the Black woman in the fantasy of being born again without genetic defect, more often than not, is performed in the context of degrading the non-white female. This powerful need to degrade the Black female who symbolically represents his original Black mother is primarily a result of the genetic dominance of the Black (and other non-white females) over the white male; she is able to cause his genetic annihilation because all of her offspring by the white male are non-white, like herself.

Thus, the white male, with each and every encounter with the non-white female, is confronted forcefully with the deficiency of his genetic status and is reminded of his true status as a recessive genetic mutant. He feels degraded in the encounter with the Black female because of her genetic dominance and so must, in turn, seek to degrade her. Ultimately, the white male views the Black female as a threat to his survival on the planet.

A secondary factor causing the white male to feel the need to degrade the Black female in sexual encounters is the white male's (and female's) anger towards the original Black mother. Whites blame the original Black mother for giving birth to them with a genetic deficiency (albinism). That anger is still being acted out by the white male against the Black female. This anger is reflected in the reports of many Black females who have had sexual encounters with white males and report that white males often want not only to ejaculate in their faces and over their bodies, but they also want to urinate and to defecate on them as a part of the sexual encounter. (It is certainly clear that many white males relate to white females in this manner, but it is known to all that white males look down upon and degrade white females. This degradation of the white female by the white male is the basis for the white female's current women's liberation movement.)

The very high, perhaps unconscious, level of psychic pain experienced by the white male because of his genetic deficiency as an albino variant and his neurotic desire to be born again from the original Black mother is perhaps the reason why the phrase "mother fucker" is such an awesome phrase for the white male to utter. It is a phrase that the white male is almost unable to bring his vocal apparatus to form. This is in stark contrast to the frequent uttering of the phrase "mother fucker" by Black males. When translated, the term means functional powerlessness for the Black male in the context of the white supremacy system/culture; however, it is an externally imposed powerlessness. For the white male, on the other hand, the same phrase has an even more disturbing, frightening and devastating meaning in the same systemic and cultural context. For the white male, the term translates into, not functional powerlessness that is externally imposed, but his own "genetic powerlessness." Such a consideration is totally unthinkable at the conscious level and even the unconscious level for the white male psyche.

The basis for certain specific patterns of word usage in the white supremacy system/culture is impossible to fully comprehend without an understanding of the origin of that system/culture. White supremacy (racism) began with the production of the first albino mutants from Black mothers and fathers in Africa. Once isolated, these recessive genetic mutants began to mate with one another and multiply, producing what is now known as the white race. The white race historically has sought to hide its genetic origins in Africa amongst Blacks, just as it has sought to deny the origins of the white civilization from the culture of Blacks in Africa, seeking instead to proclaim an origin amongst the Greeks. Historically, whites also have sought to degrade Africa and everything Black. By doing so, whites can avoid confronting the true meaning of skin whiteness as a mutation and genetic deficiency state from the Black norm – the "hue-man" norm.

REFERENCES

[1] Fuller, N.. *The United Independent Compensatory Code/System/Concept.* Published by author, 1969.

Leakey, L.S.B.. *By The Evidence (Memoirs,* 1932-1951). San Diego: Harcourt Brace Jovanovich, 1974.

Riopelle, A.J.. Kuh, M.. "Growing Up With Snowflake," *National Geographic.* October 1970. Vol. 138, No. 4.

Riopelle, A.J.. Zahl, P.A.. "'Snowflake,' The World's First White Gorilla," *National Geographic,* March 1967. Vol. 131, No. 3.

Witkop, C.J. Jr.. "Albinism," *Natural History.* October 1975. Vol. LXXXIV, No. 8.

10

Ball Games As Symbols:
The War of the Balls
(August 1976)

Dedication

This chapter is dedicated to all of the Black men who, through sports and through ball games in particular, symbolically are recapturing "the balls" – for that is also a part of the struggle. They are forcing the oppressors of Black people up against the psychological wall and, thereby, heightening the contradiction.

Sometimes, during certain periods, there is conscious focusing on certain segments of reality data, and later – due to the dynamics within the total environment – the same body of data slips into the realm of unconsciousness for individuals as well as for the total collective. For example, in the framework of the white supremacy system/culture, in its current phase of "refinement," it is no longer in vogue to lynch Black men, hang them on trees and castrate them. It is no longer the style to speak overtly in terms of "killing niggers." Thus, there are many who believe that these activities – these thoughts and acts – have ceased to be a part of reality within the culture. However, these modes of thought and behavior were handled consciously and overtly in the recent past only until "ball games" became fully established as the major national (indeed global) pastime in the "Western civilization."

Genetic Annihilation and the White Psyche

The global white supremacy system/culture is the sum total of the conscious as well as the unconscious tactics, strategies and methodologies evolved in all areas of people activity. Additionally, these manuevers seek to prevent white genetic annihilation and attempt to resolve the psychological anxiety and tension related to that ever-present threat. Thus, the tasks of white supremacy domination require constant vigilance.

The deep pervading fear of *white genetic annihilation* in the white psyche has caused a neurotic (unconscious) preoccupation with genes, genetic material, and those aspects of the human anatomy that either contain or transport the genetic material in the sexual act (the act of self-reproduction or self-annihilation as is a possibility in the case of the whites). Since Black or other *males* of color are the only ones who actually can initiate and carry forth the act of white genetic annihilation through sexual intercourse, the white preoccupation was/is specifically with male genetalia (as opposed to female), namely the testicles ("the balls") and the penis. The testicles contain the genetic material, and the penis transports the genetic material in the act of ejaculation. Thus, in the white brain-computer there is a dominant association between "balls" (testicles) and contests of power. Because this white genetic survival conflict is not handled overtly and consciously, there is a neurotic preoccupation in the white psyche with genes, genetic material, testicles and penises. Yet at another level, the preoccupation was/is actually with "warfare." Continuous warfare is requried to prevent the genetic annihilation of the global white minority. Warfare in this sense refers to the domination and destruction of all people of color, particularly Black males and their "balls," by every necessary means, which have included the initiation of "infertility epidemics" in Africa.

Games

Although there are commonly held views that games are merely a form of play and entertainment even when they are played professionally and that for most people the permanent fascination of games lies simply in the pure joy of playing them, the child psychiatrist realizes that for the young, games and play are the "work of children." It is one of the means by which, through the handling of toys and objects in a symbolic way, children master adult role expectations and attempt to resolve unconscious conflicts brought about by the dynamics and interplay of factors in their surrounding environment. Play and games then become the child's unconscious attempt to master the environment, its conflicts and threats to the child's sense of security.

Those who have taken the trouble to study games throughout the world realize that not only the play and games of children but most specifically the games in adult life, as participated in by a given people, reflect their history, folklore, traditions and conflicts. Frederick V. Grunfeld, in his book *Games of the World*, has stated,

> Though the modes of gamesplay tend to remain constant, their symbolism is often influenced by contemporary events, particularly by the politics of the day. During the Napoleonic Wars, for example, chess sets were made showing Napoleon as General, Napoleon as First Counsel, Napoleon as Emperor – always, of course, with the Corsican assuming the position of the white King.

The suggestion here is that all ball games in the white supremacy system/culture similarly play out, at an unconscious level, dominant political (i.e., power) concerns. The fundamental power concern in the white supremacy system/culture is white genetic survival through white supremacy domination. Such domination can be established and maintained only if white *males* and *females* (the total white collective) control all of the "balls" (testicles) of non-white men, off and on the playing fields and ball courts. In other words, the name of the real game – the power game – is continuous world-wide control of the testicles of all non-white men by white males and females as the only means of ensuring white genetic survival in a world where the melanin-producing genetic material of non-whites is dominant. Without control of the non-white genetic material, whites will be annihilated genetically.

Since these facts of genetic reality can be neither denied nor discussed at the conscious level of brain activity, this dominant theme is manifested daily at the symbolic level via games with symbolic balls: footballs, baseballs, soccer balls, hand balls, golf balls, ping pong balls, earth balls, hockey pucks, etc. These symbolic ball games have a highly important role to play at the unconscious level, informing all white males especially – but also females – to keep their attention and their eyes constantly fixed on the balls as a matter of life and death.

The high level anxiety and fear associated with the continuous threat to white genetic survival must be played out symbolically through the numerous forms of "ball games." All of these games are played mainly by men, are centered on who has the ball and are concerned with who finally controls the ball when the game (of power) ends. The anxiety and tension that accompanies ball games is parallel to the anxiety and tension experienced at the thought, in the white psyche, of white genetic annihilation. Similarly, the increasing violence that accompanies ball games parallels the increasing level of violence needed to maintain global white supremacy, as the entire non-white world seeks its liberation from white domination.

Some of these highly symbolic "ball games" are played with white balls and others are played with colored balls, usually black or brown. Generally, the white balls are small in size, whereas the colored balls are much larger in size, paralleling the respective genetic power in the white and colored testicles. Currently, the most popular games, those that attract most male attention, are played with big brown balls (footballs and basketballs). This rise in popularity of colored balls parallels the rise in power, at the global level, of the Third World or non-white nations.

Also, as white females demand their liberation from white males in order to become co-equals in running the global system of white supremacy, they simultaneously seek expression of this equality by participating in all of the "ball games," including football and basketball. At the same time, white females step up their sexual aggression toward Black and other non-white males, greatly increasing the incidence of white female/Black male marriages. In these arrangements, the white female obtains control of the Black and other non-white male "balls." (Non-white males and females are powerless under the global system of white supremacy domination.)

As the threat to white domination and, thus, the threat to white genetic survival increase at the global level, a mass hysteria develops over playing with "balls" until the entire society and social system is either watching or playing ball games. It is of little wonder that violence is becoming an increasingly dominant aspect of ball games when it is understood that behind the symbolism of the ball games is the very survival of the white race. When war is in progress, the top priority is always the status of the war. White supremacy (racism) is war against all persons classified as non-white. In the meantime, the balls are passed, hit, bounced, dribbled, batted, punted, kicked, thrown, shot, rolled, struck, driven, caught and captured to see who is the final possessor of the balls, or to see who is the most agile, astute or strongest in mastering and controlling the balls.

Another point that effectively reveals the relationship of ball games to the white psyche and emphasizes the extent to which balls are a symbolic preoccupation is the reference in the white supremacy system/culture to the act of sexual intercourse as "balling." The "ball" fantasy in the white psyche can best be stated as, "If the 'balls' can be controlled on the court or the playing field or through ownership, they can also be owned and controlled in real life." It is little wonder that in contrast to Black males, white males play ball games as though they are a matter of "life and death" and not as though they are simply to be enjoyed. When whites lose control of the balls, whiteness becomes extinct.

It is no accident that the phrase "to blackball," in the language of the white supremacy culture, means to "exclude" and to have the power to exclude. Similarly, the genetic material in the Black testicles (black balls) has the power to genetically "exclude" or annihilate the recessive genetic material in the white testicles. Hence, "one drop of Black blood (Black genetic material) makes you Black," a highly familiar expression in the white supremacy culture.

Specific Ball Games

Close examination of specific phenomena in ball games that are popular in the white supremacy culture will support the preceding discussion. In the game of billiards or pool, there are eight colored balls, a white ball and a long dark stick placed on a table. The object of the game is to use the long stick in causing the white ball to knock all of the colored balls under the table. The last colored ball knocked under the table is the black ball. When the game is over, the white ball is the only ball that remains on top of the table with the long dark stick. Then the game starts again.

Bowling is also an interesting ball game in the white supremacy culture. Usually, this game is played with a large black ball being rolled forcefully down an alley where it is expected to knock down 10 white pins; the central pin is referred to as the "kingpin." Clearly, the bowling pins are white and, in shape, are phallic symbols. In other words, the pins are white phallic symbols that are knocked asunder by a heavy black ball, over which the bowler attempts to gain mastery. In symbolic fantasy, the bowler sees himself as master and possessor of the larger black ball and thereby in control of the harm it can bring to the white male genital apparatus (the white pins).

Bowling was introduced to America by Dutch colonists in the 18th century. It is a derivative of the French game *guilles* that was brought to England in the 19th century and later to Germany. Games that consist of throwing balls of various sizes date back to ancient Rome and Greece, early cultures that had extensive contact with Black men in Africa. A modern French derivative of that ancient game is jen de boules. F.V. Grunfeld states, "The French (whites) play boules with what has been described as a mild fanaticism." It is well to recall that a considerable period of French history was spent controlling Black and brown men in Africa and Asia.

Earth ball is a modern American version of an ancient game. It is played as a struggle between two teams or "tribes" who jostle, rush, push and elbow one another to move the large dark (colored) ball in the desired direction and to gain possession of it. The game attempts to develop a sense of common purpose amongst the members of the tribe or team. This game was started in California, with most, if not all, players being white. (See Grunfield's *Games of The World*.)

The importance of games utilizing large brown balls in the white supremacy culture is of special interest. The most important of these games are football and basketball. Is it only an accident that Black males, now that they have been allowed to play, have become the most outstanding players in these sports, nationally and internationally? Is it only an accident that in the game of football, the "field general" (the quarterback) almost always must be white, no matter the color of the other players? And, of course, the owners always must be white so that no matter who wins or who is the star, the white owners control the big brown balls and who gets to play with them.

It is of symbolic importance that the large brown basketball is thrown into a circular opening (the basket – usually a white net) that can be viewed as a symbol of the white female vaginal orifice. Similarly, the large brown football is kicked through a white upright opening (the goal posts) that can be viewed, again symbolically, as the uplifted legs of a white female in the act of sexual intercourse.

Perhaps unconsciously the white male psyche considers here that the white female's preferred sexual choice is "tall, *dark* and handsome." In tossing or kicking the large brown balls into the white net or the white goal posts, the white male is able to fantasize that he is satisfying the white female maximally via an identification with the Black male and the brown balls, which the white male – in play – believes he now possesses or controls.

This writer is reminded here that a common "underground" thought and saying of white men is that they are not really *men* until they have had sexual intercourse with a Black female. This again is a demonstration of white males fantasizing that they are in the customary role of the Black males, whose genitals they apparently admire and envy. Thus, the Black male is their true standard of real manhood and genetic power – the ultimate controller of the Black "ball." As white males attempt to master the placement of these large brown "playing" balls in "openings," their activity can be viewed as attempts to resolve the dilemma of their self-questioned manhood. Their manhood is always in question because of their genetic recessive status compared to the genetic dominance of the world's majority.

In this regard, it is not surprising that large numbers of white females hang around Black basketball and football players and that these Black males often are trapped into sexual involvement by these white females. The Black male ball players, in turn, also are conditioned under white supremacy domination to want to place brown balls in white nets (white vaginal orifices) as a mark of supposed true Black manhood, since Black males refer to white males as "The Man." In placing brown balls in white nets and between white goal posts, the Black males in fantasy become "The Man."

Hockey, a sport that Black men are not allowed to play in the white supremacy culture, also consists of attempting to place a round black object (the hockey puck) into a white net opening (symbolic of the white vaginal orifice). The object that is used to place the black puck in the opening is a long colored stick (symbolic of the black phallus). White males, fight ferociously among themselves to get the black round object in the white net opening (as a test of their strength or their manhood). Apparently, for the white male psyche, it is anathema to have to compete with a Black male (the possessor of real black balls and stick) in this challenge: controlling a black ball and a black stick and getting the black object into the symbolic white net opening on the white ice field.

Soccer, or European football, traditionally is played with a white ball, smaller than the large brown football and basketball. This sport is less popular in the United States, but it is very popular in Central and South America. The white soccer ball is not to be touched with the hands; it is knocked and kicked. The kicking of the white ball becomes a very violent and vicious activity. Again, however, the greatest player, the master of the large white ball, turned out to be the Black Brazilian, Pele, who married a *white* female. The owners of the professional soccer teams also remain white, of course.

Another popular ball game played with a smaller white ball is baseball. Baseball was the great all-time American (a.k.a., white) sport until a Black man, Hank Aaron, became the world's greatest hitter (controller) of that white ball, hitting it with a brown or black bat. It is little wonder that as he moved ever closer to taking the title of control away from the white

Babe Ruth, Aaron began to receive letters from white people threatening his life. This behavior remains incomprehensible (after all, it's only a game!) unless one is aware that the white ball is symbolic of the white testicles that a Black man had knocked out of the ball park. The Black man, in this manner, controls the symbolic small white testicles. This is not psychologically tolerable in the white supremacy culture – as it represents white genetic annihilation for which whites traditionally have killed to prevent.

This unconscious response to non-whites controlling white balls clarifies the reason that a couple of years ago the American Little League Team (white), which consistently was being beaten by non-white children in Taiwan, was prevented from competing further with these non-white children. And now the American children are prohibited from playing with the Taiwanese teams. White male children must not be confronted (in the white supremacy culture) with non-white children controlling white balls (testicles). Such a continuing experience is totally inconsistent with the optimal development of the white supremacy psyche, as well as with the white male's survival need to control all of the "balls" on the planet Earth.

Next smaller in diameter in the "white ball" series is the tennis ball. To date, there has been only one Black male world champion controller of that small white ball – Arthur Ashe, although amongst Blacks, Althea Gibson became a master of the white ball before Ashe. Is it only a coincidence that when Ashe began to play tennis with champion force, the game then allowed the introduction of colored tennis balls in major tournaments? A Black male is just not supposed to bat a small white ball into total submission. Ashe became the number one world tennis champion in 1975, but he did not sustain that position in 1976. Ashe has been quoted as saying that he does not play just "to win," but for the enjoyment of the sport. This attitude is in stark contrast to that of Jimmy Conners (white), who has stated that he plays only to win and has described his approach to the game as a *killer instinct*. I can imagine the psychological pressure put on Arthur Ashe as long as he remained in the position of champion controlling the small white tennis "balls." I am certain that he could be liked better, in the context of the white supremacy culture, as long as he held any position other than number one controller of the prestigious small white tennis "ball."

The smallest ball in the popular "white ball" series is the golf ball. Like tennis, golf has been the ball game of the most powerful males in the white supremacy system/culture. However, like tennis, it is spreading slowly throughout the white supremacy culture to include large numbers of white and non-white females.

Interestingly, golf, the most "elite" of all of the ball games in the white supremacy culture, is played with a long dark-colored stick or "iron" held between the legs. This iron is smashed against the side of a very small white ball. The object is to knock this small white ball into a hole in the black earth (black mother earth – the Black female?). By attempting to place his small white ball in the black earth, using a long dark stick, again the white male is attempting to identify with the possession of the genital equipment and privilege of the Black male, whose rightful partner is the Black female. If this pattern of play in golf does not qualify as the very essence of male genital symbolism and neurotic conflict in the white male psyche, as formulated in this specific discussion, then nothing does. Again, is it only a coincidence that the major event in golf competition should be called the *Master's Tournament*? Is this not a fitting title for the most elite of all ball games played by the masters of the "master race"?

One final question: Is it a reflection of white male self-hate and self-rejection and rejection of the inadequacy of the white testicles ("balls") that the games played with small white balls involve the balls being attacked, hit, struck and knocked far away from the body – in an act of masochism; whereas by contrast, the games played with large brown balls involve holding on to and possessing the balls? No large brown balls are struck with objects in the white supremacy culture's popular ball games. There is indeed significance in these facts. And even though the large black bowling ball is rolled away from the body, its aim is to knock down symbols of the white phallus.

Further, is there parallel significance in the fact that the most powerful man in the global white supremacy system (Gerald Ford), on the day of his departure from office after losing the presidential election, left immediately to play golf – to beat the small white balls masochistically across the fairway in his hour of defeat and humiliation? It is of further note that his predecessor, who was forced from office in absolute disgrace, also spends much of his time on the golf course beating small white balls.

It seems of interest that the more powerful the white male becomes in the context of the white supremacy culture, the smaller the ball that becomes his focus of attention. Is this because the more the white male achieves what he wanted to believe was real power, the greater the realization that his perception was only an inadequate compensation for a fundamental lack of true power – *genetic* power?

Is it not also curious that when white males are young and vigorous, they attempt to master the large brown balls, but as they become older and wiser, they psychologically resign themselves to their inability to master the large brown balls? Their focus then shifts masochistically to hitting the tiny white golf balls in disgust and resignation – in full final realization of white genetic recessiveness. It would be of further interest to ascertain the number of army generals in the white supremacy system who play golf (demean white genetic material) while planning for race war or the destruction of non-white genetic material. After the Chinese, a non-white people under white supremacy domination for many decades, were able to chase the whites out their country, the most popular ball game in China became ping-pong. The object of this ball game is to smash a tiny white ball back and forth across a table, perhaps in unconscious retaliation for the humiliation imposed upon the Chinese people by the whites. The Chinese finally mastered (beat) the white "balls."

Similarly, golf and baseball, two "white ball" games, have become the most popular ball games in Japan, a country of non-white people conquered, attacked and humiliated in atomic war by white people. Perhaps at the conscious level, the Japanese (non-white) people believe they are imitating their conquerors, whom they admire. At the unconscious level, however, they are, in turn, humiliating the inadequacy of the white testicles or "balls." The dynamics that motivate the conquered and the conquerors are never the same.

Is there also a connection between the defeat of highly armed Americans (whites) in the Vietnam War, wherein white males were beaten by a tiny nation of non-white people, and the fantastic increase in the popularity of tennis throughout the U.S.? The entire U.S. nation, since the close of the Vietnam War, has begun to beat the small white tennis balls, the symbolic white testicles, following a humiliating defeat (loss of power) for the American (white) nation. Or did tennis just become popular after *Watergate*?

Furthermore, is it just a coincidence that there was a greatly increased interest of white females in tennis at the same time that they began their women's liberation movement, a movement that attacks white males and their sense of superiority, a movement that has referred to white males as "male chauvinist pigs"? Through the game of tennis, white females symbolically can attack the white testicles – the part of the anatomy that is supposed to make the white male superior to the white female. Is this also why tennis is becoming increasingly popular among Blacks in America?

Also, is there a relationship among the number of white males seeking sex change operations (to remove their hated male genitalia), the number of white male physicians willing to perform this surgery, and the white male's loss of the Vietnam War to non-white men, as well as the rise in power of non-white men in general on the planet?

I wish an ever-increasing success to all Black males who participate in ball games, and I look forward to the day when the majority of quarterbacks are Black or at least in proportion to the number of Black football players. Still, the most important message in this essay is that in the last 100 years, the white collective simply has moved from the overt sport and entertainment of lynching and castrating Black men (removing their testicles), thereby controlling their "balls," to a more highly refined series of symbolic representations of the same act: ball games. And, whether through lynching and castration or modern ball games, the object and neurotic preoccupation is the same: the white male seeks to prevent non-white males from ever controlling white "balls," and therefore they must control the anatomical balls and the contents of the colored anatomical balls – the genes of non-white men – that threaten white genetic survival. Ball games merely reflect the white collective's admiration and fear of Black testicles, their contempt for white testicles, and their willingness to fight – no matter how violently – to maintain control of the balls on all fields and courts, which symbolize every place on Earth. This neurotic preoccupation of whites is, of course, essential for the genetic survival of their race.

The rules may change, but the real game is always the same. This deep significance of "balls" in the context of the white supremacy system/culture cannot be discussed overtly without causing the collapse of the entire political and psychological white supremacy edifice. Events in the world of symbolism are far ahead of events in the world of conscious reality because the former represents a more complete recording of the totality of reality data in the brain-computer. Thus, through the world of symbolism, perhaps we can gain insight into the world of reality that must be mastered. By decoding and translating symbols, we can confront those aspects of reality that generally we would prefer to ignore. Norman O. Brown's statement in *Love's Body* sums it up: "The axis on which world history turns is symbolism – The axis of world history is making conscious the unconscious."

Ball games = war of the balls = war of the testicles = war of the genes = race war.

11

The Symbolism of Smoking Objects
(March 1977)

As a psychiatrist and behavior analyst, I take the position that all major patterns of people behavior, within an evolved system of behavior, can be decoded and understood once the *ultimate goal objective* of the evolved system of behavior is decoded and understood. The failure to decode and comprehend the ultimate goal objective only permits behavioral units to be dealt with and described as isolated abstractions without in-depth meaning and certainly without function within the system/culture as a whole. Furthermore, this failure makes it impossible to perceive the logical coherence and interconnectedness between all of the major patterns of behavior in the behavioral system.

To use an analogy in the physical sciences, the failure to decode and comprehend the ultimate goal objective of an evolved behavioral system is tantamount to present-day physicists attempting to analyze the physical universe without Einstein's equation $E = MC^2$, the Theory of Relativity.

Indeed, in the final analysis, an evolved behavioral system is also a system of energy and specific energy pattern configurations, no less than the "physical" universe is a system of energy and specific energy pattern configurations.

Once the concept of a "unified field theory" of behavior (or evolved system of behavior) is understood adequately, all major behavioral patterns that develop within the total behavioral system context are seen as having both meaning and function within the total behavioral system. Thus, these behavioral patterns partially express and eventually achieve the ultimate goal objective.

Today smoking, or the oral use of smoking objects, is a major pattern of people behavior in the dominant behavioral system on Earth. Six hundred eighty-eight billion cigarettes were manufactured in the U.S. alone in 1976. Fifty-three million American adults smoke some form of tobacco. Eighty-nine thousand Americans *die* annually from lung cancer, which is approximately 244 persons dying each day from this ravaging disease. Yet, since 1964, when the surgeon general's report first linked cigarette smoking with disease, there has been a smoking controversy among Americans – for and against smoking.

The above facts and health statistics alone, which do not include the number of deaths caused by fire through the mishandling of smoking objects, should make everyone alert to and curious about the behavioral pattern of smoking and the causes of this behavioral pattern. This essay seeks to pinpoint the perhaps unconscious, but major, underlying determinants of this behavioral pattern that heretofore have not been understood or probed adequately. By elevating the level of insight into the behavioral pattern and its causes, conscious control over the behavioral pattern may be enhanced, and the incidence of smoking may decrease.

As I have stated previously, the existing global behavioral system/culture of racism (white supremacy) is the sum total of the conscious and unconscious patterns of symbols, logic, thought, speech, action, dreams, emotional response and perception. It includes the tactics, strategies and methodologies evolved by the global white collective in all areas of people activity (economics, education, entertainment, labor, law, politics, religion, sex and war) to resolve the psychological anxiety and tensions related to the threat to white genetic survival.

Beyond the resolution of this anxiety and tension is the ultimate goal objective of preventing the ever present threat to white genetic survival from ever becoming a reality; this task requires constant and continuous vigilance by all members of the white collective.

However, because of the minority status of the white collective on the planet and because of its genetic recessive status relative to the skin-melaninated global majority, there exists in the collective white psyche a profound sense of *genetic* and, therefore, *genital* weakness and inadequacy.

Because it is males who are physically and physiologically responsible for the initiation of the act of self-production and self-reproduction, it is the white male in the white collective who most greatly senses (consciously or unconsciously) and experiences genetic and genital inadequacy. This is attested to strongly by the white male's and, indeed, the total white collective's continuously prevailing concern with "Who has the largest penis, the Black male or the white male?" Indeed, large numbers of white males today are preoccupied and concerned that their penises are too small, such a concern being reflective of the sense of genital and genetic inadequacy. Black males are not preoccupied similarly. (See Chapter 7.)

That the darker male is viewed as more powerful and more substantially virile and masculine in the white supremacy system/culture is again attested to by the fact that the white female's idealized male is described by the white collective as "tall, *dark* and handsome!" The word *dark* does indeed refer to a high(er) level of melanin skin-pigmentation and hair-pigmentation.

The importance of the dark man as a symbol of genital and genetic *adequacy* in the white supremacy system/culture was the basis for the crowd-drawing power and significance of two of the most important movie heroes of the last century in the U.S. – Rudolph Valentino and Elvis Presley. The case of Presley removes all doubt from my thesis because his style of singing and of moving his genital area was strictly copied, *as best he could*, from Black male singers. In the case of Valentino, two of his most important roles were in the movies *The Shiek* and *Son of the Shiek*, wherein he played *non-white*, North African men (Arabs). Subsequently, a very popular condom was brand-named *Shiek*. Valentino also portrayed the Moor. His great appeal to the white female (and male) was that he was dark and made up to appear even darker. Supposedly, he was also a master lover.

Yet another instance of the importance of black as a symbol of male genital and genetic adequacy is the fact that the standard wedding attire for the white male in Western (white) culture is *black* (and in the most formal weddings, males wear black tails), while the bride wears white.

When dressed for most other important social occasions, the white male similarily dresses in black 'tails' and black tie. Although the "tails" hang in the back, they remain phallic symbols. Similarly ties (also usually dark colored) are phallic symbols in a behavioral system/culture that believes that "clothes make the man." The implication is that mother nature (in the case of the albinos) failed in some respect.

White males also believe that they look more virile and attractive when suntanned (brown and bronzed). This belief is maintained despite the fact that each year in the U.S. alone, there are 300,000 new cases of skin cancer caused primarily by whites attempting to tan their pale skin into greater attractiveness.

In this area of the world, white males also have had a long nefarious history of lynching and castrating Black males and taking their genitals, as well as other parts, home as prized and desired souvenirs to be possessed – symbolically making them their own.

Just as the important ball games fall into two series (large black and brown and small white), all major smoking objects in the white supremacy culture fall into the same two series: large brown (cigars and pipes) and small white (cigarettes).

Furthermore, the ball games played by the supposedly more virile men entail the use of large brown balls, while the smoking objects chosen by those men who wish to view themselves and be viewed as powerful, virile and important are large *brown* smoking objects (cigars mainly, but also pipes).

The late British Prime Minister, Winston Churchill, was estimated to have smoked 300,000 eight or nine inch double coronas. John F. Kennedy also is reported to have loved Havana cigars. And Fidel Castro, who considers himself to be white, is never seen without a long cigar in his mouth.

Whereas I maintain that the brown and white "balls" used in the ball games in the white supremacy culture are symbols of the black and white testicles, respectively, I maintain further that the brown and white smoking objects are similarly symbols of the black and white phallus (penis). Together, the balls in the ball games and the smoking objects constitute a highly important symbol package of the complete male genitalia – the penis and the testicles.

The white supremacy system/culture is preoccupied most fundamentally *not with profit,* but with its genital and genetic status and survival on the planet. It is only logical that since this great survival concern is not discussed at the culture's conscious level, it manifests in other major behavior activity within the system/culture, albeit largely at an unconscious level. Thus, it is not surprising that these two important black and white symbol series (balls and smoking objects) should be a central preoccupation that cannot be curtailed in spite of the violence in ball games and the cancer associated with smoking.

The white supremacy system/culture is dominated by white males. However, white males still experience a deep sense of male genital and genetic deficiency and inadequacy. This is due to the fact that white males fear genetic annihilation by men of color. Thus, major activity on the part of white males (via the system/culture they established) consists of the unconscious drive and desire to boost or supplement the level of one's maleness or masculinity and to internalize more male principle, element or substance by any means possible. This sense of deficiency in male principle also may be expressed in terms of sensed inadequacy and, therefore, dependency and male-principle dependency need gratification. In other words, in a culture and behavioral system where the most dominant feature is a sense of male genital and genetic inadequacy (on the part of albino males), the attempt to compensate for this sensed deficiency most certainly will be manifested in some manner and patterns of behavior.

The habitual pattern of placing the symbolic phallus (penis) in the oral cavity is one example of symbolic compensation for sensed male genetic and genital inadequacy. Smoking, as previously stated, is placing a symbolic phallus in the oral cavity as a means of, again, internalizing more masculinity (as the penis is that which most obviously makes the male a male).

Male homosexual acts of placing the penis in the rectum or in the oral cavity also achieve symbolically the results of internalizing and ingesting, through a gastrointestinal tract opening, male substance. In this instance, what is internalized is the ejaculate, which parallels the inhalation of smoke and the swallowing of saliva when mouthing a cigar or pipe.

It should be noted here that in the 1960s when Black people, behind Black male leadership, began to challenge the white supremacy status quo with cries of "Black Power," there was an increase in the number of cigars imported to the U.S. Cigar imports more than doubled from 30 million to 80 million per year between 1967 and 1974. Large numbers of people also began to smoke small, long, dark brown cigarettes (e.g., *Mores*).

An interesting mythology surrounds the cigar: During their manufacture, these smoking objects are hand-wrapped while held between the legs of Cuban (non-white) women. This reference to the proximity of the cigar (the brown smoking object and phallic symbol) to the non-white female's genital anatomy supports my contention of the symbolic function the cigar plays in the fantasy of the white male psyche. Here, one is also reminded of the underground saying in the white male culture that one is not a man until he has had sexual intercourse with a Black female, meaning, until he has demonstrated that his white phallus is as adequate as that of the Black male.

Understanding the above symbolism will explain further an advertisement for *More* cigarettes printed in the December 19, 1976 issue of *The New York Times Magazine* which read as follows:

> Why isn't More white? Because More is burnished brown. To make its longer, leaner design look as good as it tastes. And when it comes to the taste of More, you can enjoy its smooth mildness longer. Because More burns slower. So More doesn't end with just good looks. There's lots of good taste as well. It's like any really good cigarette. Only it's More."

This ad carries an even greater significance because of the great emphasis placed on oral sex by the white supremacy system/culture, in contrast to the behaviors of non-white peoples. This ad also must be seen in the context of the epidemic of pornographic magazines that place heavy emphasis on Black males as objects of oral sex for both white males and females. The above ad also allows the following question to be raised: Is the brand name *More* a substitute for "Moor"?

With the above interpretation of symbols in the context of the white supremacy system/culture, it becomes increasingly apparent that there cannot be a ban on cigarette smoking in spite of its cancer causing potential. If indeed the basic dilemma in the white supremacy system and culture is genital and genetic inadequacy and the objects and acts symbolic of ingesting more phallus were banned, what behavioral substitutes would be suggested that could solve the basic anxiety-provoking dilemma of white genetic annihilation? Perhaps genital transplant surgery from Black males to white males? Hopefully, not frank cannibalism!

In Chapter 8, I discussed the gun as a symbol in the white supremacy system/culture. I demonstrated that the gun similarly cannot be banned because it is the symbolic phallus substitute for the white male. The white male's penis and testicles genetically cannot annihilate Black and other non-white males, but his gun can. Therefore, to ban the gun for the white male is to castrate him symbolically, to remove his defense mechanism for the ever present threat of white genetic annihilation.

We are now in a position to understand the inadequately explained and inadequately understood concepts of penis envy, castration anxiety and the castration complex, all key concepts in the Freudian psychoanalytic edifice. These concepts take on valid applicability in the context of the white supremacy system/culture, in that they all relate to anxieties, fears and tensions of the dominant members of the white supremacy culture – the white males, who then project these tensions and fears in their various and sundry forms onto others (white females and Black and other non-white males and females).

In reality, it is the white male who basically envies the genital power and genetic status of Black and other non-white males. And without his guns or other weapons, the white male feels castrated in the presence of Black males and females and all other non-white peoples.

Castration anxiety, which Freud inadequately assumed had meaning only in the family context, now can be understood as the basic fear in the global white supremacy system of white genetic annihilation.

This fear has been evolving in magnitude since albinos (whites) were first developed as genetic mutants from Blacks in Africa many thousands of years ago – only a short period of time in the context of the 3.5 million years that Black people have been on Earth.

The global white supremacy system is the evolved methodology of compensation for white male castration fears and anxiety of the fear of white genetic annihilation based upon white genetic insufficiency.

This essay illuminates the major fallacy in the Western pattern of perception and thought – the failure to be able to recognize and decode the whole. Western perceptions are unfortunately limited and fragmented, tending towards ever higher levels of abstraction and isolation of what has been abstracted, but never fully and consciously perceiving what has been abstracted in relationship to the whole (e.g., guns are always seen in their isolated abstraction, as are balls and smoking objects.)

This failure (if not refusal) to perceive the whole is a result of the repressed conceptualization of the white self as the albino mutant (fragment of whole) offspring from Black (whole) progenitors. Thus, there is an inability to place the "white self" in the total perspective of the *hue-man* family and the totality of the universe, without the admission of the genetic defective status of skin whiteness. The white collective, therefore, must deny the meaning and reality of Africa as its own birth place and the point of origin of its own civilization.

12

Black Fear and the Failure of Black Analytical (Ideological) Commitment (June 1979)

It is known that an extremely high level of fear and a profound sense of vulnerability of existence can lead the human brain-computer into ineffectual patterns of circular thought. In such cases, problems perceived are avoided and *never* solved. This is in direct contrast to effective patterns of direct linear thought that move continuously forward in straight line progress, from problem perception and depth analysis to proposed conclusive modes of problem solution. This holds for individuals as well as collectives. The sense of powerlessness evolves out of fear and vulnerability and, with its imposed patterns of circular (as opposed to linear) thought, sets the stage for mental (behavioral and emotional) illness, which is always seen at levels of increased incidence amongst oppressed populations.

Circular thought means moving from problem perception, *away* from problem solution (down a diversionary path), and back again to problem perception. This may then be followed by worrying and obsessive complaining. There is never consistent motion towards problem *solution* because to do so would challenge and alter the power dynamic of oppression. Thus, high-level fear is set in motion.

Circular thought describes the short-circuiting of logic networks in the brain-computer, an organ which has evolved by nature as a problem-solving instrument.

Linear thought suggests movement from problem perception progressively *towards* problem solution, changing step-by-step whatever needs to be altered to achieve total problem solution – utilizing whatever means necessary to achieve this end. This form of thought is consistent with the function and structure of the brain as a problem-solving organ in the human organism.

Black people throughout the world, live under the power of the white supremacy system of total oppression and domination, implying the absence of any true power to determine ultimately what happens to their individual and collective lives. This is the major and only *problem* facing Black and all other non-white peoples throughout the world. This is precisely why they are called and classified as *Black* and *non-white*, to set them specifically in oppositional contrast to, and in conflict with, the genetic reality of *white*. But because this is a frightening and painful reality upon which to focus Black and other non-white attention, we as Blacks, particularly in the U.S., succumb to circular thought. Likewise, there is not only a failure to approach problem solution, but there is a stubborn refusal even to look directly at *the problem*. Ultimately, there is a disturbance in problem perception. Therefore, Black people in the U.S. reject the conscious recognition of the global white supremacy system, its absolute necessity of non-white oppression and its very specific implications of a continuing powerlessness and potential destruction – as opposed to a natural death – for Blacks and other designated non-whites.

Jonestown, Guyana is an outstanding example of the destruction that Blacks fear under the existing white supremacy system. In 1979, close to *1,000* Blacks from the U.S. were relocated to Jonestown and then murdered under Nazi concentration camp conditions through a process controlled by white people. This extermination center was set up with the full knowledge of segments of the U.S. government. It is, thus, no accident that the year 1979 gives further witness to the near total *collapse and loss* amongst Blacks – individually as well as collectively – of the ability to effectively perceive, analyze and propose solutions to the problem of white supremacy and its implications for continuing Black powerlessness and social disintegration. In brief, it is clear in 1979, 21 short years before the year 2000, that there is no commitment by Blacks to analyze of the problem of white supremacy comprehensively. Blacks are without a perception or analysis of racism, or of a scientific counter-racism. Blacks, therefore do not know what to do with themselves.

Thus, we are witnessing a collective Black floundering and an *ideological* vacuum and disorientation. All that remains is for Blacks to escalate tragically their activity of powerless arguing and squabbling amongst themselves and to compete with one another for white supremacy jobs and grant crumbs. Or, Blacks can pretend, as a diversionary thought strategy, that the "real" struggle exists between imagined Black "classes" or between Black males and females. Every energy and psychological effort is expended, at both the individual and collective levels, to "black out" and avoid focusing on the true problem of white/Black confrontation – white supremacy. All Blacks realize, consciously and/or unconsciously, that to engage in such a realistic focus can mean certain death at the hands of white supremacists.

The total Black collective in the U.S. has yet to confront consciously the "mind-blowing" logic and thought-distorting shock and fear that set in following the assassinations of practically all courageous Black male leaders: Malcolm X, Martin Luther King, Jr., Whitney Young, Medgar Evers and Fred Hampton, and then the holocaust of Jonestown, Guyana, which many conscious Blacks accept as a planned government action. Since all of these deliberate deaths have occurred, there has been a profound *disinclination* by surviving Blacks to confront the awesome and murderous *reality of white supremacy* directly. The struggle for justice and true Black power now is perceived "through a glass darkly" and not face-to-face because there is overwhelming fear. In spite of their super-ficial differences, the various analyses of the Black problem by the afforementioned men, if carried through to their ultimate implications, all lead ultimately to an eventual neutralization of white power control.

Since the demise of these Black men, who all were aware of the necessity to resist and destroy white supremacy, the remaining rhetoric coming from our Black collective is consistent with *submission to* and/or *cooperation with* the racist oppressive dynamic – albeit with an historical and continuing chorus of complaints. This behavior of submission to and cooperation with white supremacy is consistent with the illusion that there can be a complete *integration* of non-whites into the white supremacy system. In contrast to these modes of thought and action, the Black men cited above are examples of *resistance to* and *destruction of* white supremacy as an absolute form of injustice. These latter forms of behavior require high levels of self- and group-respect and can be sustained only when there is the willingness to give one's life for the achievement of justice, as each of these men demonstrated.

However, it has been demonstrated (by the aforementioned men) that the almost certain consequence of a pattern of consciously-determined resistance to and destruction of white supremacy is death at the hands of white supremacy advocates – those who see and understand white supremacy as necessary to white survival. Even young Black children are able to perceive and articulate that "If you try to help Black people, you will be killed." When I asked a 10-year-old Black boy, "Don't you want to study hard in school so that you can help Black people?" he immediately answered "No," giving the above explanation. The chill of this reality inherent in the maintenance of white supremacy does not escape Black children, and it most certainly does not escape their elders, although the latter are more sophisticated and know better than to admit the same openly.

This fear of death at the hands of the white supremacy collective – because it cannot be admitted aloud by the adult Black population – has been repressed. The result of covering the fear has been the emergence of the sick, protective logic that there is no longer a problem of white supremacy, except in England perhaps and in Southern Africa; for Blacks in the U.S., all of that has been solved. Additionally, there is the claim that the only remaining stresses are Blacks rejecting other Blacks, be it male versus female and female versus male, female versus female and male versus male, or the fantasized Black middle class versus the fantasized Black lower class. (Of course, the fact is that "class" does not refer to income alone but to actual existing *power*. And since Blacks across the board are oppressed and powerless under white supremacy, *none* of us have power. Therefore, there are no classes among Blacks.)

But to return to the issue of Black defensive logic, these patterns of logic, which emphasize that the existing problems are mainly between Blacks, are reflective of Black self-hate. This self-hatred is escalated and reinforced by increasing Black suicide, Black-on-Black homicide, child abuse and spouse abuse.

In addition to the aforementioned non-productive behaviors, there are also increasing patterns of behavior that can be described as inducing semi-trance states, such as rhythmic hand-clapping, singing, dancing, excessive "rock" music playing, listening to radio music and shouting in religious settings. These patterns of behavior are manifested continually by Black people to pitch themselves into possible altered cortical brain states. Likewise, such brain states seem to have the effect of dampening the sense of an overwhelming external pain or danger over which Blacks conceive we have no control. These practices, of course, avoid problem confrontation and thereby prevent problem solution.

Similarly, the increase in interracial marriages can be viewed as a means of escape and a means for Blacks to avoid the awareness of their continuing status as *permanent outsiders* – outside of the "white chalk circle" of white supremacy's numerical and genetic global necessity. It should be noted that in the white supremacy societal unit of Nazi Germany the highest incidence of interracial marriage between Semites (non-whites) and Germans (whites) occurred just prior to the ultimate destruction of the Semites in the Holocaust. The Semites of the Jewish religion were looked upon as non-whites because their ancestors were Black and resided in Africa prior to entering Europe. (See Chapter 18.)

Similarly, some Blacks have sought to escape the confrontation with white supremacy through Marxist doctrine, by attempting to conceive of themselves as members of the "working class." They fail to see that Marx, who was a Semite (a non-white), was a victim of anti-Semitism. One third of the world population of Semites of the Jewish religion were destroyed by German white supremacy – meaning that millions of Marx's own descendants were destroyed in this process. Still, not one word of Marx's doctrine addresses itself to this potential fate of his own group. He did not understand that he was being classified as non-white, nor did he understand white/non-white color confrontation. Thus, he was ill prepared to address it and its destructive implications. He too became confused in recognizing himself as a non-white, in the struggle that goes on between the *white* classes: the upper, middle and lower classes. He failed to realize that, irrespective of income, education and position, he and all other fellow Semites constituted the powerless, non-white, non-class victims in a white supremacy system. All non-whites, then as now, fall *outside* all three of the aforementioned *white* class groupings because the word "class" specifically refers to power – ultimately the power to protect one's life and the lives of one's group members in the framework of an existing power system.

This attempted escape into Marxist doctrine falsely comforts some Blacks (as it did many Semites in Europe). In accepting this doctrine, they are convinced that there are some whites (the workers) who wish to unite with non-whites out of a supposed common interest. They further believe that these whites do not function under the white supremacy *necessity* (the global fear of white genetic annihilation by the genetically dominant non-whites) that governs the survival psyche of all who accept classification as "white" people. Though they have no proof that a significant number of such whites exist, some Blacks persist in following the Marxist doctrine in order to avoid the fear-inducing awareness that Blacks and other non-whites are and always have been, weak and vulnerable in the context of the global white supremacy system.

Like the 10-year-old Black male child I mentioned earlier, all Black adults will have to learn how to admit openly and honestly their fear of dying in the process of actively trying to destroy the injustice of global white supremacy. Only then will Black brain-computers cease patterns of circular logic, the logic of fear and escape, such that a firm Black analysis of the white supremacy dynamic can develop. With this established, a long-term commitment to white supremacy neutralization can follow.

A prerequisite to overcoming fear is the growth of self- and group-respect. This respect cannot develop as Blacks strive to the blame one another for the symptoms of their common oppression. This respect cannot flourish in the presence of a belief that Blacks cannot develop their own analysis of and provide their own solutions to Black problems without the leadership, approval and/or funding of non-Blacks. In keeping with this goal, I recommend to the Black collective that we need not have any conferences other than to announce the existence of our fear of white supremacy and to share with one another all possible solutions for overcoming these fears.

Solving the problem of political and social oppression of a people is fundamentally no different than solving a problem of illness in the human body. What is essential in the latter instance is an accurate diagnosis of the problem through observation, examination and various clinical tests and studies. The diagnosis represents a summarized statement of the specific pattern of physiologic derangement and a statement of the major and minor causal factors. A program of treatment and cure is based upon producing the specific measures to counteract the causal factor(s) efficiently and to alter any potential for the return of those factors permanently. Finally, the test of diagnostic accuracy is the effectiveness of the treatment and cure.

The physician functions as a scientist to the extent that he or she bases the plan of treatment and cure on concrete observation, examination and analysis of the problem. This physician/scientist is more dependent upon his or her current observations and analysis than upon some previously written descriptions of "similar" disease states found in some valued textbook written by learned and respected ancient authorities. The physician/scientist is ever-cognizant of the possibility of new disease states that never existed previously or of old disease states that never were described accurately and thus for which there are no established plans for treatment and cure.

Physicians who lack fundamental self-respect and self-confidence are unable to make their own observations and analyses because they do not trust their own sensory apparatus, nor do they trust the ability of their own brain-computers to make accurate correlations of the incoming sensory data. Therefore, they will be incompetent in observing and treating new problems, and they will be unable to perform adequately in the management of new variations seen in previously recognized disease processes.

External environmental dynamics, which affect the body in health and disease, are changing constantly, causing new and differing pictures of disease states. The major factor in diagnosis is the ability of the physician/scientist to make his or her own observations and for the brain to make critical analyses of the data of observation, which is experience. This series of acts, observation, experience and analysis then becomes the basis for all follow-up activity in treatment and problem solution.

In summary, the physician/scientist, beginning with his or her observations, works to uncover the courses of disease. Through knowledge of the specific disease process, he or she works to affect treatment and cure. Just as the physician/scientist has to face the problem of physical disease, Black people and their scientists have to face and solve the problem of Black oppression under white supremacy. In fact, Black people seeking a scientific approach to the problem similarly must begin acting as scientists, observing their situation, recording their own data and following up with their own analysis of their observations, experience and data. Their own analysis will then inform them of what it is that they, as Black people, need to do to achieve their goal objectives.

To the extent that we fail to make our own fundamental observations and to validate our own sensory experience, we can conclude that Blacks lack the necessary levels of self-respect and self-confidence needed for independent functioning. To the extent that we believe we cannot depend 100% upon our own sensory apparatus, we fail to have confidence in our ability to make encompassing analyses; and to that same extent, we are forced into dependency upon those whose brain-computers we believe to be *superior* to our own.

If we do not have confidence in our ability to make independent Black observations, Black analyses and Black plans for Black action, why should we talk about or seek Black liberation? One never should seek independence from those upon whom one feels permanently dependent, for that would be an act of suicide. And, indeed, if that independence were won, it soon would be returned to the former state of dependence. Furthermore, if we believe that we are intellectually inferior to white people, as our distrust of our capacity to observe and make correlations would strongly imply, we simply should say this out loud for all the world to hear: "Blacks are genetically inferior in terms of their intellectual capacity as compared to their white counterparts." Then we should content ourselves quietly and politely to be totally and permanently dependent upon the white collective for all that we need, do, think and say.

If Black behavioral, social and political scientists are supposed to be incapable of making accurate analyses of behavioral, social and political situations (local and worldwide), then Black physicians are also incapable of making accurate medical diagnoses, and all Black patients should seek white doctors. This would imply similarly that Black lawyers are incapable of successfully handling legal cases, and all Black law clients should seek white lawyers. Likewise, all Black students should seek white teachers. Furthermore, all Black women seeking husbands should seek white husbands, and all Black men seeking wives should seek white wives. This activity would carry such reasoning to its logical though absurd conclusions. If we do not wish to imply all of the above, let us get about the business of Black problem-solving, beginning with the problem of Black oppression under white supremacy. First and foremost, let it be the responsibility of every Black person to know and understand how the dynamic of white supremacy domination is expressed in all areas of people activity: economics, education, entertainment, labor, law, politics, religion, sex and war.

13

The Concept and the Color of God and Black Mental Health (November 1979)

Agnostics doubt and question the existence of God. Atheists deny the existence of God. These two groups combined constitute a tiny minority of the world's people. The vast and overwhelming majority of the peoples on Earth have a conceptualization of, and a belief in, the existence of God (no matter how named or defined) as the supreme force or supreme being responsible for the creation of the universe. Therefore, this supreme being constitutes the highest and ultimate focus of their worship, devotion and obedience.

In all but the agnostic and atheistic groups, the training and teaching of children about the concept of God, in a given culture, begin at the earliest possible age of comprehension and understanding. Customarily, long before children are capable of understanding any philosophical and abstract consideration of God, they are exposed to the system of rituals that the given people have evolved over thousands of years. The rituals form a part of their recognition of, worship of and obedience to their concepts of God. Thus, long before there is true cognitive understanding, there is participation in the practice of recognizing God. This participation and practice becomes a part of children's (and ultimately adults') concept and image of self in relationship to the total environment, but also in relationship to the highest and ultimate focus of their worship, devotion and obedience to *the God of the people.*

For it is the totality of experience in the environment from the moment of birth that forms the self-image and self-concept in the brain-computer of each human being. From this self-image and self-concept, all patterns of behavior evolve. Likewise, from the entire constellation of behavior in the individual, the determination of mental health or mental illness is made.

As a practicing general and child psychiatrist, my definition of mental health is as follows: patterns of logic, thought, speech, action and emotional response, in all areas of people activity, that simultaneously reflect self- and group-respect and respect for harmony in the universe. The *critical* question that arises now is, "What does the 'concept and color of God' have to do with Black 'self- and group-respect and respect for harmony in the universe'?"

The oppression of Black and other non-white people means that there is no non-white self-determination. It also means, most fundamentally, that there can be no true and *functional* Black self-respect. More specifically, this means that the existing levels of non-white functional self-respect, as manifested in all areas of people activity, are extremely low. These low levels of functional self-respect imply that the self-image and self-concept are more *negative* than positive. Likewise, the impact of non-white individual and collective behavior in and on the total environment is more *negative* than positive.

To have a negative impact on the total environment is a manifestation of behavioral powerlessness. To have a negative impact on the total environment is a manifestation of the self-image and self-concept as *powerless*. To have a negative impact on the total environment is a manifestation of having been shaped and molded by the total environment into a functional inferior through the process of *inferiorization*. (See Chapter 20.) The process of oppression is to mold the victims of oppression into functional inferiors. (See Diagrams I and II.)

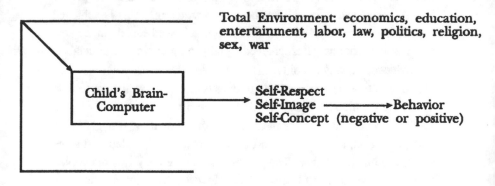

Total Environment: economics, education, entertainment, labor, law, politics, religion, sex, war

Child's Brain-Computer

Self-Respect
Self-Image ⟶ Behavior
Self-Concept (negative or positive)

Diagram #I

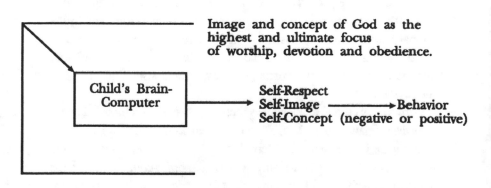

Image and concept of God as the highest and ultimate focus of worship, devotion and obedience.

Child's Brain-Computer

Self-Respect
Self-Image ⟶ Behavior
Self-Concept (negative or positive)

Diagram #II

As previously stated, the global system of white supremacy oppression functions through all areas of people activity. The ultimate thrust (towards the victims of oppression), in all of the nine areas of people activity, is to cause and affect their *universalizing*. This is achieved equally in the area of religion as in sex. It is achieved equally in the area of war as in economics. It is achieved equally in entertainment as in labor. It is achieved equally in politics as in law. In other words, all nine areas of people activity are used equally in the system of non-white oppression to achieve the ultimate goal of non-white inferiorization.

The concept and the color of God are focused on most strongly in the area of religion, although all areas of people activity overlap, influence and fuse with one another. The global white supremacy system evolved a religion referred to as Christianity. However, it is referred to most appropriately as the dominant pattern of religious thought generated by the white supremacy system. Similarly, all forms of economics within the global white supremacy system – whether referred to as *capitalism, multi-nationalism, communism* or *socialism* – are identified more appropriately as the patterns of economic thought and practice generated by that system. Further, all forms of political organization within the global white supremacy system – whether referred to as *democracy, nazism, Soviet hegemony, fascism* or *nationalism* – are referred to more appropriately as the various patterns of power relationships generated by that system.

Absolutely critical to the white supremacy system of religious thought was the formation of the image of a *white man* as the "son" of God. This white male image then was referred to as "Christ" – no matter that the prophet Jesus was a Black man. Because the brain-computer functions most fundamentally on logic circuits, at deep unconscious levels it automatically computes that God, the father, is also a white male. If God is other than white, he would have produced a Black (or other non-white) son. (See Diagram III.)

Thus, any person *programmed* to accept the Christian religion, whether conscious of it or not, *has* the image and concept of God *as a white man* in the logic network of his/her brain-computer.

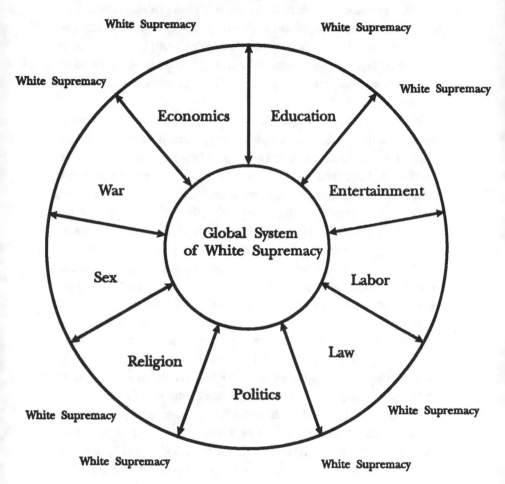

White Supremacy

White Supremacy

White Supremacy

White Supremacy

White Supremacy

Economics

Education

War

Entertainment

Global System
of White Supremacy

Sex

Labor

Religion

Law

Politics

White Supremacy

White Supremacy

White Supremacy

White Supremacy

White Supremacy

White Supremacy

Diagram #III

Areas of people activity in the global
system of white supremacy domination
that reflect and carry forth white
supremacy domination

Couple this image and concept of God *as a white man* with the white supremacy system's formal definition of God as "the supreme or ultimate reality; the Being perfect in power, wisdom and goodness whom men worship as creator and ruler of the universe." Then of absolute necessity, the logic circuits of the human brain-computer have to print out "The white man (as God, the father of the white male Christ) is the supreme or ultimate reality; the white man is the Being, perfect in power, wisdom and goodness whom all men should worship as creator and ruler of the universe."

With this unconscious logic circuit of "God is a white man" firmly in place, white domination over non-white people could last for one trillion years. This would be true if this critical and essential logic connection could be implanted and plugged into the brain-computers of a sufficient number of black, brown, red and yellow peoples, who constitute the vast majority of the peoples on the planet. With the white man as God, the non-white global collective would be obedient to the white man always.

It was the necessary duty of the vast army of white supremacy (Christian) missionaries sent out around the world, following the guns of white supremacy conquest, to implant – deep within the unconscious logic networks of non-white brain-computers – the critical image and concept of God *as a white man*. This unconscious implantation has been success-ful to the extent that many non-white people on the planet conceive of themselves as members of the Christian (white supremacy) religion. In the U.S., the overwhelming majority of Black people, as well as a large portion of other non-white peoples, consider themselves Christian.

Thus, all Black and other non-white peoples who profess to be members of the Christian (white supremacy) religion, whether they are conscious of it or not, worship the white man as God (not as "a" god, but as "the" God). And, in the unconscious logic networks of their individual brain-computers lies the logic that *the white man* is the supreme or ultimate reality – the Being perfect in power, wisdom and goodness whom men worship as creator and ruler of the universe. Although Black and other non-white peoples may understand that they are oppressed by the global white collective, of which the white males are the dominant members, the brain-computer's cold logic circuits also unconsciously inform the non-white (Christian) victim that it is *impossible* to free or liberate one's self from the *supreme being* who has *created the universe!*

In other words, if in the deep, unconscious recesses of my brain-computer rests the fundamental logic that God is a white man and that I should worship "God," all of my attempts at liberation will move me only in a circle. Indeed, the circumference of my "liberation movement circle" could be so wide that it really appears to me that I am moving in a straight line of progress. But moving in a circle, no matter how big the circle, is tantamount to standing absolutely still, marking time. Many Black people in the U.S. now are beginning to feel as though our liberation efforts (in spite of loss of life and whipped heads) have left us still standing on the same spot of white oppression.

For the vast majority of Black and other non-white peoples today, the arrival of these ice cold facts of brain-computer logic at the conscious level will be experienced initially as shattering and self-disintegrating – primarily because it is God the protector and the creator upon whom the self is taught (programmed) ultimately to depend. If the concept of God is removed from my brain-computer, upon whom or what am I to lean, especially if I am feeling oppressed, depressed and overwhelmed? If there is nothing or no one to provide support, then I believe that I will collapse and disintegrate.

Nonetheless, as a general and child psychiatrist, I am fully aware of the destruction spawned by the unconscious logic implant "God is a white man." However, no matter what the level of initial trauma felt when this logic circuit is brought to conscious awareness, it must come fully to light and be *yanked out*. Indeed, there can be no mental health, self-respect or positive self-concept for Black or other non-white peoples as long as this specious and destructive logic circuit remains in place.

It might be instructive at this juncture to recall that Christianity was based upon the life and activity of an African (Black) prophet named Jesus. That the white Romans recognized this fact is reflected in the early portrayals of Jesus and his mother as the Black madonna and Black child. To this day, a picture of the Black madonna and Black child secretly is cherished as one of the most holy icons of the original Christian church, the Catholic church.

What then necessitated changing the image of Black Jesus and Black Mary to white Christ and white Mary? To answer this question, we must return to the most fundamental fact in the existence of the global white collective: White-skinned peoples initially were the mutant albino of Black peoples in Africa. These white-skinned peoples were recognized as having a disease, just as today's modern science of genetics refers to the condition of albinism (the lack of melanin pigmentation) as a genetic deficiency disease. The white-skinned early albinos were rejected by the normal pigmented majority. They were chased out and isolated from the normal Black genetic groupings. Eventually, they had to migrate northward to remove themselves from the intense African sun rays. Migrating northward from Africa, the albino populations eventually settled in the area of the world now referred to as *Europe*. There, they increased in number and eventually returned to conquer the peoples of color in Africa, Asia and the rest of the world. They returned with the idea that they would conquer and no longer think of themselves as the rejected and diseased population; instead, they would think of themselves, in compensation, as the superior and supreme supermen and look upon all skin-pigmented peoples as the "genetic inferiors."

With the necessity for such a *compensatory* ideology and concept of self as superior, the white psyche could tolerate no concept of anything *higher* than the white self – not even God. Thus, when the concept of the son of God was formulated, in their thinking, the "son" eventually took the form of a white man, which by brain-computer logic would mean that God himself had to be a white man. Thus, the white collective, *in logical reality*, is not in worship of any force beyond itself.

Further, it is apparent that the collective white psyche felt anger towards God for bequeathing them what is now understood as a genetic defect – namely, white skin. In turn, they have spawned the thinking that doubts and denies the existence of God. Thus, they have conceived of themselves as being at war with nature, which is the reflection of God. They function as though they are in a contest with God and try to out-create God. Presently they are in a quest to produce genes and life itself. In fact, their dominant occupation is the destruction of the universe. And it is no accident that within the language system of the most highly evolved white supremacy unit, the word *God* is the exact mirror image of the word dog, and within the same language system, the dog – not God – is said to be man's best friend.

Blacks and all other non-white peoples who have operated under the concept of God *as a white man* for the past 2,000 years, should begin an immediate return to the fundamental concept of God as originally understood in Africa before the input of the albino (white) collective. The African understanding of God was that it was the only and all-in-one energy force that created and simultaneously *was* all energy in the universe. This understanding recognized the God force as the source of all, the being responsible for all and the *multiplicity* of energy configurations in the universe. Furthermore, the belief held that there are no energy configurations in the universe that are not from God and that are not God.

It was the African way to respect completely this source of all energy manifest in and responsible for all things. This is African *spirituality*. Spirit is energy. Spirituality is the ability to get in touch with, not only the ultimate source of all energy, but also the various multiplicity of energy configurations, which include matter, plants, animals, etc. This was, for Africans, the essential cosmic connection – the power connection.

Since *melanin* is a superior absorber of all energy, it is essential to establish this understanding of God and "all energy." The fact that the albinos (whites) lack melanin may also help to explain why they have quite a different concept and understanding of God (all energy or all spirit), why they conceive of a trinity and why, in the view of many non-white peoples, they (whites) lack "spirituality" and the capacity to tune in to, and thereby establish harmony and justice in, the universe. Further, because they lack the melanin sensory system, they cannot intuit that all is one.

However, at some unconscious level, there must be within the collective white psyche the awareness that the color *black* is essential to be in touch with the God force, justice and wisdom, and that is why they clothe their men who are supposed to have knowledge of justice in black; and they clothe their scholars at the point of their scholastic (wisdom) achievement in *black* academic robes. Of course, one might cite a few exceptions, but black for ministers, priests, judges and scholars is the norm in the white supremacy system/culture worldwide.

I recommend that Black and other non-white peoples begin to practice consciously removing the white image of the son of God from their brain-computers and, thus, removing the corollary logic that God is a white man. Secondly, Blacks and other non-white peoples must practice utilizing our particular energy crystalizations (bodies) as *direct* connections with the God force. (See Diagram IV.) This means we must learn to use our energy crystalization antennae to connect with the source from which all energy flows. It is the same as plugging an electric cord into a wall socket. By so learning to tune in to the cosmic energy source, it is possible to find the cosmic purpose of one's particular energy configuration known as one's body. Then, it will be possible to use that cosmic energy for constructive purposes.

I can say no more about how it can be done, but only that it can be done, just as I am saying that it is possible to break the logic circuit "God is a white man" in the non-white brain-computer.

To be Black and accept consciously or unconsciously the image of God as a white man is the highest possible form of self-negation and lack of self-respect under the specific conditions of white domination. Such perception, emotional response and thought are therefore *insane*. This logic circuit ensures that Black people always will look up to white people and, therefore, down upon themselves. Only by breaking that logic circuit can the concept of Black and other non-white *liberation* become a reality. This is the direction in which we Blacks must propel ourselves as we enter the 21st century.

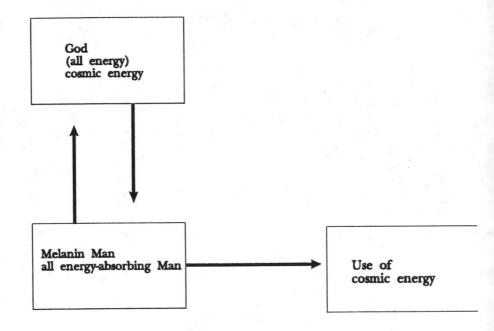

Diagram #IV

14

The Symbolism and Meaning of Rape (October 1980)

The *symbol* consists of multiple levels of energy data. The *hieroglyphs*, higher writings or writings concerning multiple levels of energy data, are written symbolic thought and language. Similarly, the *parable* is a statement of combined, multiple levels of energy data; it is also a statement of symbolic thought.

Part of our ancient heritage as Black (African) people is the knowledge of the symbol. This working knowledge includes the ability to speak, write and decode symbolic language and thought. Melanin is essential for having deep knowledge of the symbol because melanin is capable of absorbing a broad spectrum of energy frequencies or data.

Black is considered to be a *perfect* absorber of energy. There are inumerable facts that support this assertion. For example, Osiris, the great Egyptian (African) god, was referred to as "Lord of the Perfect Black"; Albert Einstein's great work on energy was based upon earlier knowledge in physics of the so-called "black box" energy absorption and mission experiments; black holes in cosmic space are so named because of their great power to absorb all forms of energy.

Persons *lacking* high levels of melanin pigmentation in the nervous system, which includes the skin as its outermost manifestation, have great difficulty in absorbing energy data from the universe at multiple frequencies deep energy levels. Therefore, these white-skinned peoples, the founders of Western civilization and culture, experience great difficulty in understanding and decoding the symbol. This is the most fundamental reason that "Westerners" have difficulty in *thinking* like "Easterners" (black and brown peoples – people with higher levels of melanin in their nervous systems), and vice versa. Melaninated peoples are functioning with a sixth sense, the additional sensory system being that of melanin pigmentation, while Westerners function with only five senses. Thus, the Western dictionaries define *hieroglyphs* as "difficult to decipher." Similarly, the Western dictionaries define *parable* as "an obscure or enigmatic saying."

Black and other non-white peoples who have been trained to think like Westerners now have to retrain their brains and nervous systems to function at full capacity through conscious effort to use their melanin networks. This can be achieved through the practice of *self-respect,* wherein Black and other non-white peoples respect and pay close attention to what *their own* six-sense nervous systems inform them of. This is quite contrary to focusing on what white-skinned peoples are able to focus on and what they train non-white peoples to focus on. Melanin-deficient "educators" can train non-white peoples to use only a portion of their nervous systems at best. Thus, it is the responsibility of non-white peoples to take charge of developing the full use of their melanin potential.

Familiarity with these issues are necessary for an examination of rape as a *symbol* in the white supremacy system/culture. Rape is an unjust and sick pattern of behavior. It is a behavior pattern reflective of very low levels of self-respect and, therefore, of mental illness. Simultaneously, rape manifests very low levels of respect towards others. It is a horrendous violation of the selfhood of another.

The most frequent form of rape is that in which a male aggressively and abusively imposes his genitals onto a female with the threat of destruction. This conduct is seen most frequently in situations of male confinement: in penal institutions, juvenile corrective institutions or psychiatric institutions – which are staffed and supervised inadequately. A fundamental aspect of rape is the imposition of the male genitals upon someone considered physically weaker or vulnerable by someone who (at least superficially) looks upon himself as being more powerful and capable of subduing another. Condensed to the least common denominator, rape is an act in which the genitals become a weapon. A weapon is most fundamentally an instrument of aggression and is conceived of as an aide to the human body when the body alone is considered inadequate for the task of subduing and conquering.

In today's world, rape is common. In the U.S., it is reported in highest incidence amongst members of the Black population, with Black males raping Black females. There is said to be an approximately equal incidence of white males raping Black females as Black males raping white females. The incidence of white males raping white females is lowest. In past decades, white male rape of Black females was of highest incidence.

Instead of breaking into the hysteria of the women's liberation movement regarding the issue of rape, I prefer to examine the meaning of this behavior, commencing with male use of male genitalia. As I have stated in all of my writings during the past 10 years, there is no behavior that can be adequately understood and decoded outside the context of the power relationships that exist amongst peoples. In today's world, the most fundamental of all power relationships is that of white power versus non-white (black, brown, red and yellow) powerlessness. The underlying factors and forces that have led to the evolution of this specific power system are 1) the numerical minority status of white-skinned peoples globally, and 2) the fact that white skin is genetically recessive to the dominant genetic potential to produce melanin. If white-skinned peoples had not evolved a global system in which they established power over the world's non-white majority, the white collective would run the risk of white genetic annihilation.

The fear of such annihilation has influenced the white collective to evolve, over the centuries, massive weapon systems – from simple to gross and horrible instruments of destruction and annihilation. This was done, most fundamentally, to "equalize" the genetic power for white collective destruction, power possessed by the planet's men of color.

The ability to decode symbols is essential to obtain an accurate understanding of exactly what is happening in the surrounding environment. For example, the ability to decode helps us to understand deeper meanings inherent in the major instruments evolved by the global white collective (to prevent white genetic annihilation) and the shaping of such instruments after the form of male genitalia: guns, bombs, cannons, cannon balls, airplanes and nuclear missiles. (See Diagram I.) It is little wonder, then, that the gun has been called "the great equalizer," or that a white male who is really supposed to be "something" is referred to as a "pistol."

At the same time, the highest percentage of money expenditure is going towards the "arms race" – the race for accumulating sufficient weapons by both white superpowers, hopefully sufficient to prevent global white genetic annihilation. These weapons surround all of the world's non-white peoples. Of course, this is not what is said overtly. Overtly, whites claim that the white superpowers are arming *against one another*. But this is the language of the *white* lie, the *great* lie, the super or superior lie.

In the depths of the language itself, it is possible to understand the exact meaning of the arms race. The arms race also means the "race" (genetic group) of people whose genetic existence is tied to weapons of violence (arms). Just as hidden within the word "America" (AMERICA), is the phrase, "I am race." Thus, it is a symbolic anagram. The whites are the only group on the planet to develop the word "race," and they have given this word maximum meaning.

Clearly, in the global white supremacy system/culture, the highest percentage of energy is directed towards the construction of weapons out of a sense of genetic and genital weakness and inadequacy. Of all of the cultures in the world, Western (white supremacy) has the highest level of sensed male inadequacy and male awareness of genetic and genital vulnerability, thus the need for weapons of attack. This culture clearly has equated the male genitals with *weapons and aggression*.

As mentioned in Chapter 10, the white collective looks upon the Black male specifically as the possessor of the genitals most capable of causing white genetic annihilation. This explains the expression, "to black ball," which means, "to exclude from social life."

Thus, in the white supremacy system/culture, white females have been taught to focus on all Black males as potential rapists. At the same time,

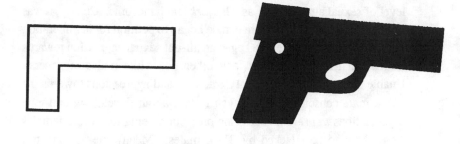

The Gun (diagrammatic sketch)
(The gun - a symbol of male genitalia)
Diagram IV

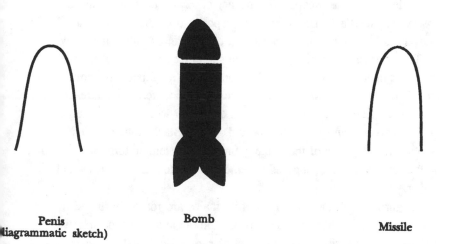

Penis
(diagrammatic sketch)

Bomb

Missile

Weapons as Symbols of the Phallus
Diagram I

white females are taught to describe the males that they have the greatest level of sexual attraction for as tall, *dark* and handsome. Clearly, it was no accident that once the white female began to petition for her liberation from the white male, she also began an all-out sexual aggression towards the Black male in particular, and other non-white males in general. Unable to admit her own sexual attractions and aggressions towards the Black male consciously, she began to talk about developing anti-rape organizations *to prevent rape* – the projection being that white females were about to be attacked by Black males. Meanwhile, the greatest incidence of rape was being conducted by Black males against Black females.

The above discussion is the best explanation for the white collective's (most specifically, the white male collective's) production of massive numbers and kinds of weapons of destruction (which land on Black mother Earth) that are symbolic substitutes for a genetic and genital apparatus perceived as inadequate. Simultaneously, it explains the use of the male genitals as weapons in the act of *rape*, most pronouncedly observed in the Black male population – a population forced into political (power) and functional inadequacy by the oppression of white supremacy.

The weapons produced by the white supremacy system are the truly respected male genetic and genital apparatus of the global white collective. These symbolic weapons are perceived as countering the threat of white genetic annihilation by Black and other non-white male genitalia. These weapons then are used to rape and destroy Black mother earth, just as other technologies of the white supremacy system/culture rape and pollute the planet as a supposed statement of white male adequacy and power.

In turn, Black and other non-white males are forced by the same environment into thinking of their genital apparatus as destructive weapons of aggression through the act of *rape*. Black males engage in this activity out of their imposed frustration and sense of political power-lessness and inadequacy. Non-white male genitals are used as destructive weapons primarily against Black and other non-white females.

This behavior also can be viewed as paralleling white male collective's sexual attacks on non-white women in the global white collective's wars of domination against non-white peoples. The white male's sense of genetic inadequacy contributed to the white male collective's need to continue to debase non-white women through rape and other forms of sexual abuse. Such abuse was necessary because the white male collective felt debased by the dominant genetic power of non-white women.

Similarly, because within the context of white supremacy more stress and pressure is placed on the Black male than on the Black female, the Black male often perceives that the Black female has more power than himself and that she therefore does not respect his manhood. In his sense of inadequacy, he strikes out in the rape of the Black female, seeking to debase her to the level to which he feels debased under the power system of white domination.

Although there is no overt discussion of these dominating logic and thought sequences, they nonetheless act as powerful determiners of behavior patterns as seen in white and Black male populations. However, because there is no overt discussion of them, these behaviors have not come under conscious control wherein people consciously can think through their impulses to balance disturbing concepts and images of the male as inadequate.

Likewise, the global white collective and all of its non-white victims in the world, see no connection between the increased incidence of rape and the popularity of a singing group that calls itself the "Sex Pistols," thus associating sex with violence. The same culture does not see any connection between the numbers and shape of its missiles, bombs, guns and male genital apparatus and the ever increasing incidence of sexual violence – the highest level of violence being expressed in the act of rape.

In the magazine *India Today* (Vol. 2 No. 7, August 1-15, 1980, North American edition), on one page there was an article on the epidemic of rape in India and on the very next page there was an article on the development of missiles and other nuclear weapons of destruction by the subcontinent of India. The latter article was entitled "Soaring Into the

Space Age." Consciously, this page and subject association may be accidental, but unconsciously it is logical.

India is one of the poorest countries in the world, with mass levels of unemployment and starvation. Those black and brown men are feeling debased and powerless under global white supremacy, which they still fail to understand after centuries of colonization. In India, there is a massive mental disease of people hating their skin color and wishing themselves to be as white as their early white (Aryan) invaders. They are obsessed with a caste system based on skin color, with the blackest people looked upon as "untouchables." They hate themselves and feel debased under white supremacy. Also, these non-white men have not discovered yet how to feed their people. Therefore, because of this debased view of self, they rape, just as the global white collective has raped the non-white women of the world and continues its rape of black mother Earth with weapons and pollution.

Since the white supremacy system is predicated on the white collective's (most specifically, the white male collective's) sense of genetic and genital inadequacy and vulnerability, it reflects this sense of inadequacy and vulnerability in the raping of women, weaker men, and black mother Earth. Rape is most fundamentally a symptom in the entire syndrome of sensed male inadequacy. Therefore, those who wish to combat the world's epidemic of rape must wage counter-struggle against the global white supremacy system.

Rape will cease as a dominant behavior amongst Black males once they begin to respect themselves fully as men, cease reacting unconsciously to the white supremacy system's attack against them, and learn to struggle efficiently and effectively to neutralize and destroy this grave global injustice.

15

The Symbolism, Logic and Meaning of "Justifiable Homicide" in the 1980s

Where there is no vision the people will perish
— Proverbs 22:1

Black people are afraid, but Black people are going to have to get over their fear. Black people do not know what is happening, but Black people are going to have to learn and understand what is happening. Black people are not thinking, but Black people are going to have to begin thinking. Black people are not being quiet, but Black people are going to have to start getting quiet so they can think. Black people are not analyzing and planning, but Black people are going to have to begin analyzing and planning. Black people do not understand deep self-respect, but Black people are going to have to learn the meaning and practice of deep self-respect. Black people are going to have to stop permitting Black children to play with parenthood. Black people are going to have to stop moaning, rocking, crying, complaining and begging. Black people are going to have to stop thinking that rhyme and rhetoric will solve problems. Black people are going to have to stop finger-popping and singing. Black people are going to have to stop dancing and clowning. Black people are going to have to stop laughing and and listening to loud radios. All of these behaviors, and many more, have absolutely nothing to do with addressing the challenges and conditions of the open warfare continuously being waged against the Black collective.

We Black people do not see the war being waged against us because we don't want to and because we are afraid. We are engaging in behavior designed specifically to *block out* any awareness of the war – our true reality. Our behavior thus forces us into the *insanity* of hoping and begging – as opposed to the *sanity* of analysis, specific behavioral pattern design and specific conduct in all areas of people activity: economics, education, entertainment, labor, law, politics, religion, sex and war.

A major strategy in the war against the Black collective is the killing of Black males. Black males are being killed daily, in ever-increasing numbers, across the country. Other as non-white males also are being killed in ever-increasing numbers. These Black and other non-white males are being killed by white males in uniforms who have been authorized to carry guns. This particular form of murder and slaughter is called *justifiable homicide*.

Our Black collective today has no greater understanding of this war and the phenomenon of justifiable homicide than it did when Black males were being lynched and castrated daily, 100 years ago in the period of "Reconstruction," or reestablishment of white supremacy following the Civil War. Nor does the Black collective have a greater understanding of the current "open hunting season" on Black males than it did two and three decades ago.

Because we really do not understand what is going on, in our impotence and ignorance, in our powerlessness and frustration, we start getting mad, fussing, crying, rhyming, begging with picket signs, rioting in misdirection, hooping and hollering, moaning in our churches and preparing again to vote for any white man who smiles at us even though he lies to us. These behaviors are all absolutely useless. Such behaviors are in vain and will take us nowhere. They will all come to naught and the problem – the war – will simply continue and intensify.

The stage has been reached in our experience of captivity out of Africa wherein we are being challenged to demonstrate a deep self-respect, requiring us to use our whole brain-computers – not just the right side, which permits us to engage in rhetoric, rhythm and rhyme. Now we must begin to exercise and use the left side of our brain-computers, the left cerebral hemisphere, which permits us to analyze critically and decode what is happening daily in front of our eyes and to organize a self- and group-respecting behavioral response to that which the environment is presenting us. We must have a *disciplined,* self- and group-respecting response to the specific war being waged against us.

Without critical thinking, however, there is no self-respect. Without self-respect, there is no courage, no self-defense, no justice, no peace and no progress.

In his struggle against white supremacy, the great leader of the Chinese-speaking non-white people, Chairman Mao Tse-Tung, accurately stated as recorded in *The Collected Works of Mao Tse-Tung,* "It is well known that when you do anything, unless you understand its actual circumstances, its nature and its relations to other things, you will not know the laws governing it, or know how to do it, or be able to do it well."

With this in mind, all Black people everywhere must begin to understand the exact and specific nature of the war that is being waged against the Black collective. All Black people must begin to understand in depth *why* we are witnessing Black males being shot dead almost daily by white males in uniforms and why it will soon escalate to more than one per day. Without the specific understanding of why we are seeing this behavior, we are unable to organize behaviors to meet this war strategy effectively.

Furthermore, Black people everywhere must begin to understand why the Black collective, and Black males in particular, have been under intensive attack for the past 2,000 years. Indeed, Jesus was a Black male who was lynched by uniformed white male Roman soldiers 2,000 years ago, as a result of the same war that has continued into the present day extension of the *same* Roman (white) empire.

Whenever there is a sense of increased vulnerability within the local and/or global white collective – as, for example, caused by inflation (currency devaluation), unemployment, loss of a war or counter-struggle by non-white peoples (e.g., Arabs controlling and limiting oil supplies, Iranians taking white hostages, Black guerillas struggling in southern Africa and the loss of the Vietnam War) – there will be an increase of the ever-present "normal" daily slaughter and murder of Black and other non-white males by those both legally and illegally authorized to do so. This murder and slaughter will be *logically* viewed as justified within the specific logic framework of the fear of white genetic annihilation.

Within the historic framework of Western civilization and culture (the civilization and culture organized to prevent white genetic annihilation), *all* white peoples have the spoken or unspoken *mandate* to participate actively in their collective struggle for global white genetic *survival*. This specifically means, of necessity, the murder and slaughter of Black and other non-white males whenever it is felt within the white collective to be necessary and, therefore, justified.

Because Black males, of all non-white males, have the greatest potential to genetically annihilate the white collective, Black males will experience the greatest ferocity of white supremacy's attack through justifiable homicide. Because Black and other non-white males have the potential to produce white genetic annihilation through the use of their genitalia and because genetic annihilation is the most fundamental fear of the global white collective, this collective (consciously or unconsciously) evolved a "counter" *weapon* or system of weapons, that theoretically could achieve *non-white genetic annihilation.*

The sport of hunting animals (in most instances they have black or dark brown fur) in the white supremacy system/culture, wherein there is thrill, excitement and pleasure associated with the killing, is the way in which the white collective (most specifically, the white male collective), stays in physical and psychological readiness for killing Black and other non-white males (justifiable homicide), albeit that this obsessive practice may be functioning at unconscious levels of brain-computer activity. Unlike Black and other non-white peoples who killed animals for food and shelter purposes, the white collective engages in this activity as obsessive sport and play. By using the gun (the great equalizer) against helpless animals, they attempt to achieve a sense of manhood and security. A fleeting sense of manhood can be achieved by the white male sports hunter because in killing the large black or brown animal (the symbolic non-white male) there has been a symbolic destruction of the major threat to white genetic survival. Since the achievement, however, is only symbolic, it must be repeated, and so as soon as the hunting season opens, it is time to hunt again.

In the same period in which there has been an increasing incidence of justifiable homicide, there has also been an increasing enthusiasm for killing helpless animals, making such hunting locations as Potters County, Pennsylvania world famous. White adult males have been taught by their fathers to kill and destroy helpless animals for sport, and in turn, the next generation of white males is taught the means by which to ensure white genetic survival.

Non-white males may say that they also hunt and enjoy hunting, but obviously hunting does not carry the same unconscious meaning for the non-white male as it does for the white male in the context of the global white supremacy. Furthermore, Black males never have gotten a thrill from hunting down white males with dogs and rifles, as has so frequently been practiced by white males against Black males.

It is absolutely critical that all Black people examine and think through the meaning of the following facts: at the very same time Black males are being shot down in the street in ever increasing numbers, The August 31, 1980 *Washington Post* has reported that Poland, a so-called communist country already is asking the United States to increase credits for grain purchases from $550 million in the current fiscal year to $670 million in the fiscal year that begins October 1 in order to finance the feed grain it needs to build up meat production. Do "enemies" provide finance for feed grain to build up meat production for one another?

> On August 12, the press reported a West German loan of $672 million designed 'to help bail Poland out of its economic difficulties' (Dusko Doder, *The Washington Post*.) On August 22 a consortium led by the Bank of America granted Poland an additional $325 million.

> A recent unclassified CIA study reveals that the West has lent Poland a total of $21 billion, the bulk of it in the last five years. The same study reports that the West has lent the Soviet block as a whole an astronomical $78 billion – an amount equal to the total assets of Exxon and General Motors combined. Other experts put the total debt figure well above $100 billion.

Why are we bailing Poland and the Soviet Union out of their economic difficulties, feeding them massive transfusions of hard currency to buy bread for their restive masses and technology to boost their obsolescent centralized economies? Why are Western banks relieving the USSR of the expensive burden of propping up the Polish economy and regime?

The answer lies in a terse banker's paradox: Make a small loan and you have created a debtor; make a large loan and you have created a partner.

...The $1 billion which Western banks have funneled to Poland during the current crisis is a startling political intervention on behalf of that country's communist regime...

The critical question for Black people is "who is the real enemy?" While massive numbers of Black males are unemployed and increasing numbers are being shot down in the streets in a presumably capitalist country, that same capitalist country is helping white communist countries and their workers return to their jobs and have sufficient meats and other foods on their tables. Basically, the U.S. is supporting the whole white, so-called communist block. This does not include the Chinese-speaking non-white peoples.

What is starkly illustrated here is that "capitalism" and "communism" are not two enemies, but simply the two extreme ends of the total spectrum of *economic* practices *under* the system of *white supremacy*, wherein it is of priority that all whites (males in particular) have jobs whether they are at the right or left *economic* ends of the white supremacy spectrum. The same would be true of the Democratic party/Republican party political spectrum, which in this area of the world is the total political spectrum of *politics* under white supremacy.

Also, it must be noted that while Black males are being shot down in increasing numbers and experiencing high unemployment, white Cuban communists, in mass numbers, are being admitted to find their places, jobs and housing in this capitalist country and are referred to as "political refugees." Black Haitians, however, are not admitted and treated similarly.

In the global white supremacy system, *all* persons classified as non-white are outside the white power spectrum and are, in effect, the *real enemy*. Thus, they are manipulated and/or eliminated at the will of that power system. In the context of global white supremacy, the only *permanent enemies* are those persons capable of white genetic annihilation, meaning Black and all other non-white peoples (most specifically males).

In the most narrow perspective, justifiable homicide refers to the overt shooting murder of a Black male or Black males by white uniformed male(s). In a broader perspective, "justifiable homicide" also can refer to the numerous more subtle tactics of Black male control and destruction. To deny Black males jobs and genuine upward mobility is to deny them the functional roles of husband and father. To deny Black family units functional husbands and fathers on a mass level is to deny these families stability and to deny male children models for adult male functioning. Deprivation of male models for male functioning means permanent Black male social disfunctioning, affecting all areas of people activity for multiple generations.

The massive increase of Black male bisexuality and homosexuality to epidemic proportions can be correlated directly to the debased functioning of adult Black males in Black family units by the racist system. The large number of Black males engaging in drug use and abuse, including alcohol, also is tied directly to the severely crippled Black family structure, brought about through systematically denying Black males functional roles as husbands and fathers. The massive numbers of Black males trapped in the juvenile justice system and the penal system also are related directly to the absence of truly functional fathers and husbands in the homes from which these victimized males have come. Current statistics (1980) indicate that among Blacks, the proportion of one-parent families is a staggering 49% (1.8 million families). This is 83% higher than a decade ago. Poverty rates among one-parent units are enormously higher than among two-parent units.

The television media also play a major role in reinforcing the debasement of the Black male. Bill Cosby is debased by always being depicted conversing at the level of infants. Muhammed Ali is debased by always being shown clowning, chasing roaches and biting into sandwiches instead of watermelons. Sherman Helmsley's character "Mr. Jefferson" in *The Jeffersons* is always clowning, acting like a monkey and climbing over furniture, inspite of supposed superior economic attainment. Mr. Jefferson is contrasted to a more intelligent, manly white male who is married to a Black female (who in real life is married to a white male).

With the massive failure and absence of Black adult male models in family constellations in real life, television provides Black male youths with the white father model of *The White Shadow*, conditioning these children to get used to the absence of Black adult male models and to look up to the white adult male as "the man." This theme is advanced further in *Fantasy Island* (starring Herve Vellaichaise) and *Different Strokes* (starring Gary Coleman). Most Black people will look particularly at Gary Coleman and say, "He's a millionaire." However, both Gary Coleman and Herve Vellaichaise are *non-white males*, with constitutional and/or genetic deficiencies, causing their physical stature to be abnormally short. Yes, they are indeed excellent actors, but it is their genetic or constitutional abnormality, playing opposite adult white males of normal physical height, that is the core white supremacy presentation in both of these *popular* television series.

The profoundly destructive statement that Black and other non-white males are genetically and constitutionally defective compared to white males is the subtle core message that is being propagated over the airways. This image of non-white male genetic and constitutional abnormality is set forth weekly, while as background, newspapers and radios give continuous coverage on the discussion of Nobel Prize winner Dr. William Shockley about the supposed genetic inferiority of Black people and the need for their sterilization. Several years ago, the weekly television presentation and promotion of the Black male as a female and a transvestite, as portrayed in Flip Wilson's role of "Geraldine," was a similar undermining of the Black male's genetic makeup and masculinity. There was/is no such similar weekly television portrayal of a well-dressed white male as a female and transvestite in the white supremacy system and culture.

Blacks and other non-white people do not perceive these messages because they are blind to the context of the white supremacy power structure that surrounds them. They look at such programs and are pleased; they smile and laugh. Nonetheless, this continued presentation of Black genetic inferiority makes the final destruction of Blacks appear to Blacks themselves as a relief from the burden of their own genetic inadequacy. One can be assured that there will *never* be a weekly television presentation of a constitutionally and genetically deformed blue-eyed, blond *white male,* playing opposite an intelligently behaving Black male of normal stature, as long as the white supremacy system remains intact.

These more subtle means of achieving justifiable homicide all serve to advance the ultimate goal of white genetic survival. For, with Black adult males unable to function as men (on drugs, in prison, as clowns and buffoons, as infants and perceived as genetic defectives, transvestites and homosexuals), there will not be a major threat of white genetic annihilation, and white genetic survival is assured. The white collective cannot be asked to cease their drive for justifiable homicide in its gross and subtle forms. To do so would mean white suicide.

It is therefore the self-respecting task of Blacks and all other non-whites to understand the war and the behavioral dynamic of white supremacy, in which they are presently trapped. Through this understanding, we must evolve our own behavior (in all areas of people activity) that will eventually checkmate this global white necessity and injustice.

Black people may begin by educating all Black male children to understand white supremacy and by putting increased pressure on Black males to recognize their role as husbands and fathers. This understanding means that Black men must work and provide support for their families, which the white collective attempts to prevent them from doing. Males who do not demand and fight, if necessary, to have jobs cannot become husbands or fathers. Most certainly, teenage male children cannot become parents, which means that Black females will have to learn when and under what circumstances they should relate to Black males in the act of sexual intercourse and self-reproduction.

This internal pressure to preserve the role of Black manhood becomes a means by which the concept of Black manhood is developed and preserved by Black peoples themselves. This activity will counter the thrust of the Black male as female, clown, infant, buffoon, transvestite, homosexual. Black males who are unwilling to fight for their manhood are thereby indicating that they debase Black manhood and will not be able to teach it to the next generation. These males do not deserve the privilege of procreating themselves, and this should be enforced by all Black females who are self-respecting.

White supremacy is war against Black people in general and against Black males in particular, as embodied in such tactics and strategies as justifiable homicide. It will require a total commitment and counter war effort on the part of all Black peoples to neutralize, by every means at their disposal, this war of racist injustice.

As Black people, we also can adopt the definition that under the conditions of white supremacy, Black manhood does not mean macho or money, but instead it means *warrior* or *soldier* against white supremacy, embracing everything that the words warrior or soldier imply. Those who do not wish to be warriors or soldiers should not procreate themselves, as their offspring can be expected to be destroyed by white supremacy anyway. This is by no means a definitive statement on Black response to justifiable homicide, but it is an attempt to elevate the discussion on this specific white supremacy war strategy. Further discussion amongst Black people will help to define all necessary Black behavioral response.

16

Paper Money and Gold As Symbols
(1980)

The image or concept of the *self* in the deep recesses of the brain-computer, as programmed through the total environment interacting with the genetic and constitutional base, determines all patterns of *symbols*, logic, thought, speech, action, emotional response and perception in all areas of people activity. As such, the self-image is the core from which all else evolves in the brain-computer. Thus, the deep self-image is the key concern of the psychiatrist.

Why should one focus on deep symbols? What do we achieve through symbol analysis and understanding? Truth cannot be concealed. Truth is "that which is." It is specific energy in the universe. It literally begs to be revealed, especially when hypocrisy and deceit – distorted statements of "that which is" – move towards domination. Truth then reveals itself, speaks and surfaces through the *symbol*. The symbol is the form through which a highly dynamic idea or concept can "tunnel" underground through the unconscious to be expressed. The symbol is the product of environmental energy condensation.

R.A. Schwaller de Lubicz in his book, *Symbol and the Symbolic*, explains:

> ...that true progress in human thought can be made only if we call upon the 'symbolizing' faculty of human intelligence, the faculty developed and refined in the Temple Culture of ancient Egypt and reflected in the hieroglyphics that have come down to us undisturbed. The mentality of ancient Egypt helps to free us from our present intellectual impasse, while 'symbolism' must be recognized for what it is: the

intuitive means of overcoming the limitations of reason and achieving
a higher humanism.

Schwaller de Lubicz also indicates...

> Egypt and other cultures grounded in the symbolic method, were
> indeed, through symbols, educating the neurological structures of the
> brain to maintain an active, conscious connection not only between
> the bilateral lobes of the cerebral cortex, but also with the impulses
> and subliminal information received from the ancient and deeper
> limbic and reptilian centers, so that these aspects of our nature could
> be integrated into the activity of our reasoning mind.

Symbols and the decoding of symbols has yet to become a major area
of interest and study in Western civilization. This is regrettable at one
level, yet very understandable at a deeper level. *Decoding* the symbol is
an activity not unlike that of the physical scientist who places matter or
living substance under the lens of a light microscope or an electromicro-
scope for the purpose of gaining deeper insight into and understanding of
the structure and function of that matter. In both instances (decoding the
symbol and examining matter under a microscope), the process of investigation serves to refine our knowledge and influence our behavior in the
universe. Decoding the symbol also leads to a deeper understanding of
the self, and so frees the self. There are few who would argue that in-depth
knowledge is not superior to knowledge of the surface alone.

The process of decoding and visualizing the symbol does not require
the aid of a device beyond the human body, such as the microscope. Such
a process requires first and foremost the activity of the right cerebral
hemisphere and those sensory, neuro-chemical channels that feed primarily into this area of the human brain-computer. As a theoretical extension,
I am convinced that the neuropigment *melanin* plays a crucial role in this
right cerebral hemisphere sensory, neurochemical system.

Melanin acts as an energy-data absorbing biological pigment in the
nervous system leading specifically to the right cerebral hemisphere.
Melanin as a neuropigment has the capacity to absorb levels of energy
activity outside the spectrum of energy frequencies processed by the five

traditional senses (sight, hearing, touch, taste and smell) recognized in Western civilization, the civilization evolved by the white skinned collective who *lacks* any substantial quality of melanin skin and nervous system pigmentation and likewise, who has a lesser energy-data gathering capacity.

Let us now examine some views on money.

> For the love of money is the root of all evils; it is through this craving that some have wandered away from the faith and pierced their hearts with many fangs. (Holy Bible, Timothy 6:11)

Ernest Becker in *Escape From Evil* states:

> One of the fascinating chapters in history is the evolution of money – all the more so since it has yet to be written.... One of the reasons it isn't written is that the origin of money is shrouded in prehistory; another is that its development must have varied, must not have followed a single universal line. Still a third reason touches closer to home: modern man seems to have trouble understanding money; it is too close to him, too much a part of his life. As someone once remarked, the last thing a fish would discover is water, since it is so unconsciously and naturally a part of its life. But beyond all of this, [money]....is still sacred, still a magical object on which we rely for our entrance to immortality. Or, put another way, money is obscure to analysis because it is still a living myth, a religion.... How else explain that we do not yet have a single history of money, despite the massive collection of anthropological and historical monographs, the observations by Plato and Aristotle themselves, those by Augustine on money fetishism...the insights of Marx, and now, finally of modern psychoanalysis?

Becker also writes:

> ...Death is overcome by accumulating time-defying monuments. These accumulations of stone and gold make possible the discovery of the immortal sourl...Death is overcome on condition that the real actuality of life pass into these immortal and dead things; money is the man; the immortality of the estate or a corporation resides in the dead things which alone endure."[5]

In *Life Against Death*, Norman O. Brown asserts:

> No wonder economic quality is beyond the endurance of modern democratic man: the house, the car, the bank balance are his immortality symbols. Or, put another way, if a black man moves next door, it is not merely that your house diminishes in real estate value, but that *you* diminish in fullness on the level of visible immortality – and so you die.

, In his essay "The Ontogenesis of the Interest in Money" (*The Psychology of Gambling*, edited by Jon Halliday and Peter Fuller), Sandor Ferenczi states,

> Every psychoanalyst is familiar with the symbolic meaning of money that was discovered by Freud. Whenever the archaic way of thinking has prevailed or still prevails, in the old civilizations, in myths, fairytales, superstitions, in unconscious thinking, in dreams and in neuroses, money has been brought into the closest connection with filth!

Ferenczi outlines in some detail his own view of the transformation of anal-erotic interest into monetary interest, wherein the individual ends by being able to possess something of color that has value, is hard (and not soft), it neither has odor nor causes the person who touches it to be soiled or dirty.

Edmund Bergler, author of *Money and Emotional Conflict*, states,

> Money neurosis can be found in every country, every culture, every group of any given society; therefore it cannot be used to prove anything against our system of free enterprise. For money neurosis is a by-product arising independently of any external system.

In sharp contrast to the above quotations and viewpoints on money, Ernest Becker, in his work *Escape From Evil*, relates an African view of money:

> Recently I have heard *Bantu* of the old school say, with reference to our modern products, the Europeanized *evolves*, 'These are men of

lupeto (money)'. They have explained to me that the Europeanized young men of ours know nothing but money, that it is the only thing possessing any value for them. They...give up their Bantu philosophy...for a philosophy of money. Money is their one and only ideal, their end and the supreme ultimate norm...regulating their actions....Everything has been destroyed by this new value, this modern universal rule of conduct: lupeto (money).

These intriguing remarks can be understood only when we probe deep beneath the surface to comprehend what money (paper money) represents at the unconscious level of the symbol – a level far deeper than ever suspected by Sigmund Freud. To fully understand, one must examine the depth of the Western self-image and its origin.

No clearer statement of the Western self-concept need be found than that expressed by essayist Samuel Langhorn Clemmens, known to all as Mark Twain. In "Skin Deep," one of a collection of essays entitled *The Damned Human Race*, Twain described a gathering of people in India, commenting on their costumes and complexions as follows:

...The company present...made a fine show, an exhibition of human fireworks, so to speak, in the matters of costumes and cominglings of brilliant color....

I could have wished to start a rival exhibition there, of Christian hats and clothes. It would have been a hideous exhibition, a thoroughly devilish spectacle. Then there would not have been the added disadvantage of the white complexion. It is not an unbearably unpleasant complexion when it keeps to itself, but when it comes into competition with masses of brown and black the fact is betrayed that it is endurable only because we are used to it. Nearly all black and brown skins are beautiful but a beautiful white skin is rare....Where dark complexions are massed they make the whites look bleached out, unwholesome, and sometimes frankly ghastly. I could notice this down South in the slavery days before the war. The splendid black satin skin of the South African Zulus of Durban seemed to me to come very close to perfection.

Having heard from a 19th century American essayist, let us now listen to a similar statement published in the final quarter of the 20th century

(June 1979). Roger C. Sharpe, in *How to Get a Great Tan (Without Frying)* explains:

> It's time to feel alive again. To shake off winter's draining hold and get out into the reviving glow of the summer sun. It's also the season when there are two kinds of people: those who tan and those who wish they could. This summer, don't be left out in the shade. It's time for *you* to glow with a healthy tan. From Memorial Day to Labor Day, you'll be on display. That means trimming off those excess pounds, and donning a new skin you'll be proud of. Let's face it: a great tan makes you look younger, sexier, more relaxed. A bit of color can take you a long way. It will make you feel better about yourself. And it will make others look at you twice, especially when there's more of you that can be seen. Yet, as with most good things in life, getting a great tan is a double-edged sword. For most of us, who have only weekends or a brief summer vacation, there is never enough time to spend in the sun. So when we do get out there, we tend to overdo a good thing. The consequenses are rapidly felt. We stumble back to our homes and offices, burned to a crisp. What promised to be a gorgeous tan looks more like a patchwork or streaks and splotches. Our earlobes are tender (another too short haircut) and the backs of our knees are sore. For the next week, we are plagued with flaking skin in the bedsheets. We itch. We don't feel young and we don't feel sexy. We wanted a great tan and we come home a mess. Surely there's a better way! There is. In the pages that follow, we've tried to give you some good, practical advice, based on on-the-spot research and talks with medical experts. We openly discuss the positive aspects of tanning, as well as the dangers. So this summer, be smart. Find out what happens to you in the sun before you go out there. You can get a great tan, more effectively. If you're a natural for tanning, you'll pick up pointers that will help you get – and keep – a better tan. And if you're the type who never seems to be able to catch the rays, this summer could be your turning point.

The same author continues in the chapter "Getting the Perfect Overall Tan":

> Something you should keep in mind if you decide to go nude this summer is that there may be parts of your body that have never been exposed to anything stronger than the bathroom light. You don't want to rue the day you went back to basics, so some commonsense advice

is in order. Don't try to overdo your time in the sun; keep your initial tanning time down to a minimum. Gently break in those formerly unexposed parts of your body to the idea that this is their year in the sun. Extra sunscreening for these areas are also in order to prevent any drying and unnecessary burning. After all, what's the point of sunning all over if one part of you gets golden brown and another bright red? So be careful. Take things a day at a time.

Melanin is the black pigment which permits skins to appear other than white (black, brown, red and yellow). Melanin pigment coloration is the norm for the hue-man family. If there are non-white readers who disagree with this presentation of white rejection of the white-skinned self, may I refer you to the literature on the currently developing sun-tanning parlors. In a *Newsweek* (December, 1979) article entitled, "90-Second Suntans," there is a picture of a heavily tanned girl clad in a bikini swimsuit. Under the picture the caption reads, "Los Angeles tanning booth: Brown at any price." The article concludes:

> For growing hordes of sunlamp worshippers, however, it seems to be a tan at any cost. 'Something is going to get all of us one day, so why worry about it?' rationalizes Robert Duncan, Manager of a fast-food restaurant in Costa Mesa, Calif. 'If tanning is going to kill me at least I'll be a good-looking corpse.'

The above testimonies, from white persons writing perhaps a century apart, manifest the white collective's dissatisfaction with the white complexion. Likewise, a pervasive and strong desire on the part of the white global collective to have skin that looks otherwise – skin that shines, skin that is satin black or golden brown in color, skin that does not exhibit a melanin pigment deficiency – is articulated clearly.

In addition, Western culture has a folk saying, "Clothes make the man," the implication being that the worth of the person is established only after his/her body (shamefully white) is covered. This same symbolism was expressed unconsciously at a mass level at the height of the Watergate Scandal – the only time in the history of America (the major unit in the global white organization) when a President was forced to resign because of *shameful* behavior. At the peak of this period of national *shame*, white males began to dart about naked, running across open spaces, exposing their naked white bodies, and then *hiding*. This behavior, which was never decoded at deep levels, was called *streaking*. The behavior symbolically represented that in the white collective brain-computer the *naked white body* is equated with *shame*. Thus, when deep national shame is exposed to the world, there is a compulsion to expose the naked white body.

There is also a parallel with the present increase in the practice of nudism in this area of the world, when America is experiencing a loss of power and prestige at national and international levels. At the time, America begins to reveal more and more of the naked white body. This pattern of increased white body exposure also includes the topless and bottomless bars that came into prominence following America's great shame in the loss of the Vietnam War.

Now examine a dollar bill. Note that the original paper is basically white. On one side, the printing and engraving is done with *green* ink on white paper. On the other side, the printing and engraving is done with *black* ink on white paper. A major symbol on the dollar bill is also the African pyramid and the symbol of Osiris, the divine eye. Osiris was referred to as "Lord of the Perfect Black." Now recall the familiar expression, "Money does not grow on trees." The surface implication is that money is not so readily available. At a deeper level in the Western psyche, the statement likens paper money to tree leaves. One side of that paper money is green, and the money is in turn referred to as *"green backs."*

To further decode the symbolism of paper money, one must understand that all paper money in Western culture is the symbolic equivalent of the proverbial fig leaves. Western artists always depict fig leaves as the objects used to cover the genitals of the white bodies of Adam and Eve – covering their nakedness, their bodily shame.

The side of American paper money engraved and printed in *black* symbolically (and unconsciously) represents the black (melanin pigmented) skin that the albinos or whites should have possessed, were it not for their genetic defect of albinism (the reason for which they were originally cast out of Africa by their Black mothers and fathers).

Further, it is no accident in the present day capital of the global white supremacy system – Washington, D.C – that the vast majority of the people in the city are Black and that the paper money is printed by a large majority of Black workers. In other words, Black backs are producing "green backs," which could equally be referred to as "black backs." For in the minds of the white collective, whites should have black backs instead of white backs and they should not need green backs to cover white backs. A similiar realization causes whites to tan, as though the hue achieved through tanning is "supposed" to be their true color.

This decoding allows the slang (in this sense, symbolic) expression, frequently used by Blacks in America, "Give me some skin," to be placed in a more meaningful perspective. On the surface level this expression means, give me your hand – skin touching skin – to shake, as a greeting. At yet another level the implication is: "Give me some money."

Blacks living amongst the white collective have internalized unconsciously the symbolic equation of paper money with the covering for the degraded white skin. In fact, albinism is the origin for the unconscious development of this white equation of paper money with skin.

In their book, *Money Madness*, Herb Goldberg and Robert T. Lewis state:

> Studies of self-made wealthy men, for example, show an extremely high incidence of parental death and parental divorce, which resulted in a high degree of insecurity early in life. Many of these men, as young boys, apparently set out to amass so much money that they would never be left stranded again. They also were faced with assuming adult responsibility while still children, and they tried to prove to themselves and others they didn't really need to depend on parents.

Does this not parallel the experience of the rejected albino mutants who created Western civilization and culture?

With the symbolism of money in the white supremacy culture decoded, the phenomena of gambling, monetary inflation cycles and other behaviors present in all areas of the Western civilization can be better understood.

Money, like the fig leaves, is the symbolic covering of white bodily shame and is designed to give a sense of value when no *value* is present. Its *immersion* in shame and valuelessness operates at a level unavailable to conscious thought. Money is considered at surface levels of the white or Western psyche to have *high* value (which is like saying that white is genetically superior). However, because in *deep reality* money is designed to cover white body shame and represents shame, the real value of the money will always *rise* and then *fall*. The latter means that in reality money is worthless and debased (which is the same as tanning the white skin after saying that white is superior). This reflects the fact that while whites are saying they are superior, they unconsciously feel inferior to the melanin pigmented global majority. The concept of white skin superiority is the same as inflated money, worthless.

Similarly, in the highly symbolic phenomenon of *gambling* there is the attempt to get money because it presumably has high value. Yet the most common reality of gambling is not winning money, but *losing* money and being disgraced – revealing white body shame, literally and figuratively. By placing gambling in the the context of the decoded symbolism of money, the suicides committed by whites who lost their money during the recent depressions can be explained: they had lost, albeit at unconscious levels, the covering for white body shame. Blacks and other peoples of color were not similarly affected, and not simply because they may not have had that much money to lose in the first instance. Psychologically, Blacks and other persons with permanent skin melanin could handle better being without money because they have no fundamental body shame to cover.

Decoding the symbolism of money also makes it possible to understand why Sigmund Freud and his followers associated money with fecal matter and filth, which are usually *brown* or *black*. The white psyche then (as now) could not confront self-negation and the sense of white body shame consciously. Therefore, it is not possible for the white psyche to probe deeply enough to see that paper money is the cover for white body shame.

That same white psyche then displaces the association of money with *melanin pigment* to associate money with the only other brown and black pigment manufactured in the human body, the pigment responsible for the color of fecal material, *coprobilirubins.*

This discussion brings to mind a seminar I attended while training to become a child psychiatrist. The esteemed "father of child psychiatry" and the program director of the seminar, Dr. Reginald Lourie concluded, while evaluating the case of a Black child, that the reason this child hated himself (and the reason Black people in general hated themselves) was because he was the color of feces. Of course, my strong objections at the time did not change the basic logic of Freudian psychoanalytic theory, which many Black professionals have learned by rote, internalized and projected onto their Black patients. What Dr. Lourie, following Dr. Freud, had done was state that *melanin* pigment was the equivalent of the *coprobilirubins.* It was easier for the white pysche to state consciously that it desired to be tan like fecal matter than to admit consciously a desire to have melanin pigment and to be like black people, whom whites in psychological compensation, had to debase.

Decoding the symbolism theory further explains the reason why some whites in their sexual practices like to be smeared with human excrement. And likewise, this decoding illuminates the meaning behind one of the most common forms of expression in the white culture, which is "SHIT," or to refer to someone as a "SHITHEAD." Also, it now should be more than crystal clear why, at unconscious levels in the white psyche, it is perceived that Black and other skin-pigmented peoples do not need money like white people do. White people need paper money to cover white body shame while Black and other skin-pigmented peoples do not have the need of such covering.

When Blacks and other non-whites are struggling to obtain equal pay for work done equal to that of whites, they are struggling against this unconscious symbolism. As long as the system and culture of white supremacy remains intact, non-whites will *not* have the same money to work with as whites and their money will *not* be able to do what money in the hands of whites is able to do.

Because Blacks and others with permanent melanin skin pigmentation do not feel a sense of white body shame, they do not have the same anxious motivation to acquire money as does the white-skinned global collective. Although some have sought to attribute this lesser general motivation to "genetic inferiority," "a lack of intelligence" or "laziness," these rationalizations cannot withstand deep analysis.

The symbolism of gold in the white supremacy system is quite similar. Previously, I mentioned Mark Twain's reference to "The splendid black satin skin of the South African Zulus..." as well as Roger C. Sharpe's question, "After all, what's the point of sunning all over if one part of you gets *golden* brown and another bright red?" And, everyone in this culture is familiar with the many suntan lotions and creams that advertise their ability to help one acquire a *golden* tan. I therefore theorize that because: 1) black and brown skin (melanin pigmented skin), with its natural oils, glistening and gleaming in the sunlight, looks like gold (as is attested to in the white supremacy culture by the frequent references to a "golden tan," meaning a golden brown or black color), and 2) that which was deeply desired more than anything else by the albino mutants in their white psyche (no matter how deeply repressed), was to have melanin pigmented skin, then the metal gold (the only metal substance with lasting luster and a color that approximates the color tones of melanin pigment) became the deeply unconscious symbol of the most desired substance in the entire global white supremacy system/culture. Gold is then the symbol for melanin skin pigment in the white psyche. The possession of gold in the white psyche is the unconscious equalizer for the absence in whites of melanin. That is the reason mulatoes, or Semites, of the Jewish religion always were accused of having all of the money and gold.

The symbolism of gold explains the most fundamental reasons that, for a considerable period of time, Western paper money was backed by the *gold standard*, which prevented general fluctuations in the value of paper money. Symbolically, the gold standard meant that melanin was and is the norm and standard for human beings. Presently, the world monetary system is on the dollar standard, but there are many Western national units pressuring for the return to the *gold standard*.

The value of gold is tied unconsciously in the white collective brain-computer to the power of the peoples who possess melanin in the world – the black, brown, red and yellow peoples. When global events shift to indicate that white is not really superior – as in the Iranian hostage taking – the white-skinned collective experiences self-doubt and the deeply repressed sense of white genetic inadequacy begins to break through the apparatus of the white psyche. Then, the relative value of white skin and its symbolic cover (the dollar) drops and the value of the melanin equivalent, gold, escalates as expressed by the value and cost of gold on the world market. It should be noted that as the value of gold moves up, the value of the paper monies in the white supremacy system declines. In the white supremacy system/culture, white skin and melanin pigmented skin and their respective symbolic equivalents, *always* move *opposite* one another in value, when the paper money is not backed by the gold standard.

That gold has long been associated with black-skinned people in the collective white psyche is given further strong support in Greek mythology, specifically in Jason's search for the *Golden Fleece*. Jason hoped to obtain the *Golden Fleece* from the Colchians, whom the Greek historian Herodotus (425? B.C. - 484? B.C.), according to Robert Temple's *The Sirius Mystery* discussed.

> My own idea on the subject was based first on the fact that they (the Colchians) have black skins and wooly hair (not that that amounts to much, as other nations have the same), and secondly, and more especially, on the fact that the Colchians, the Egyptians, and the Ethiopians are the only races which from ancient times have practiced circumcision....

The phrase "Golden Fleece" is made up of two words associated with Black people: "gold," denoting black or brown skin and "fleece," denoting lamb's wool or kinky hair. The search for the Golden Fleece becomes the search for melanin.

J.E. Cirlot's Dictionary of Symbols says that the Golden Fleece "is one of the symbols denoting the conquest of the impossible or the ultra-reasonable." For white-skinned peoples, it is impossible to produce melanin or golden brown or black.

Later, in the Middle Ages, Western man (the white collective) continued his perhaps unconscious search to make or acquire melanin (satin black and golden brown) through the higly symbolic process called alchemy. Israel Regardie reveals in *The Philiosopher's Stone* that the word *alchemy* is an Arabic term consisting of the article *al* and the noun *khemi*. The noun *khemi* refers to Egypt, whose Coptic or Ethiopian name is *Khem*. *Alchemy* would then be translated as, "the Egyptian matter" or "that which pertains to Egypt." The term *al Khemi* could also be translated and understood as "the Black matter," or "that which pertains to the Blacks" or "that which the Blacks are able to make or to do." Alchemy was essentially a symbolic process involving the endeavor to make gold, symbol of illumination and salvation. More specifically, the attempt was to convert lesser metals, such as silver and lead, into gold. The lesser metals can be translated as "a less desirable skin color or white skin color." These highly obsessive and fruitless laboratory experiments eventually led to the development of the science of *chemistry*, whose very name comes from *alchemy*. Chemistry later became the basis for the modern science of genetics, in which Western man continues his efforts to make new genetic material, hoping to create life (and possibly genes that can produce melanin).

Again, what is revealed is Western man's search for that which the Egyptians and the Colchians (the Blacks) were able to achieve. The real mystery to the white psyche was that Blacks were able, with their genetic material, to produce the gleaming satin black and shining golden brown skin color through the presence of melanin in their skin, a pigment whites were unable to produce. However, then as now, whites deeply desired the ability to produce melanin colored skin.

It is of even greater symbolic significance that the special wisdom, knowledge, power or abilities of the Eyptians, which the European alchemists had hoped to duplicate, was thought by Europeans to be associated with or contained in "the philosopher's stone." The alchemists desperately sought to find or get a fragment of "the philosopher's stone," as it was the prerequisite for turning lesser metals into gold.

The *Journal of Human Sexuality* reported in "Pelvic Congestion Syndrome in Men" that the word *stone* in the language of the ancients means "testicle." Testicles contain the genetic material. In the context of the decoded symbolism of gold, the alchemists' search for the "philosopher's stone" can be translated as the search for the testicles that contain the genetic potential to produce the satin black and golden brown skin color. The word *stone*, meaning testicle, even comes down to the present in such language expressions as "stone ache," which is a colloquial term used for "testicular ache."

The foregoing discussion is presented in the hope of increasing professional understanding and appreciation of the world of symbols, logic, thought and behavioral dynamics in which we presently find ourselves. This world creates the functional pathologies that our patients expect us to be able to solve.

The central pathology of logic and thought spawned by Western civilization is the lack of white self-appreciation, predicated upon the fundamental inadquacy of the white genetic makeup. This lack of self-respect has spread wherever Western civilization has gone and now infects all of the peoples on the planet. As we move through this period in which paper money and gold are increasingly difficult to obtain (even for many white-skinned people), it is now possible, with this symbolism decoded, to understand why Blacks and other non-whites will continue to experience difficulty obtaining paper money and gold.

The psychiatrists working with Black patients will have the task of helping those patients understand paper money and gold as symbols in the culture and, most importantly, increase their sense of self-respect and self-worth – even in the face of the declining value of paper money and decreasing availability of gold. Indeed, Blacks and other non-whites *already* possess that for which gold and paper monies have become the symbols. Psychiatrists working with white patients also will have the task of helping those patients understand paper money and gold as deep symbols in the historic Western culture and, further, as substitutes for white self-respect. Psychiatrists must help those white patients struggle to gain and maintain self-respect, despite their conditions as albino mutants in a world where the norm is to have skin coloration.

The price of gold, or the number of paper dollars that will have to be spent for gold, will *increase* as long as Black and other melanin pigmented peoples continue to exercise increasing self-respect and black, brown, red and yellow power on Earth, relative to the power of white-skinned peoples. The price of gold, in terms of the numbers of dollars spent per unit of gold, will *decrease* only if white-skinned peoples are able to force skin pigmented peoples back into "their place," as designated in the white power equation of white over non-white: W/NW.

17

The Symbolism of Boxing
and Black Leather
(July 1982)

The global practice of white supremacy encompasses all patterns of symbols, logic, thought, speech, action and emotional response in all areas of people activity, for those self-defined (individually or collectively) as "white." Therefore, the system of global white supremacy can be most readily understood as a survival system, a system based upon the facts of the global white numerical minority status, white genetic recessiveness and white genetic vulnerability. It is also important to comprehend that it is a "fear" system – a system that is consciously or unconsciously aware of its genetic vulnerability and fearful of its genetic annihilation.

Like the symbols discussed in preceding chapters, the sport of boxing, in the white supremacy system and culture, is yet another instance of specific behavioral and object symbolism that manifests the collective white concern of its genetic vulnerability. Much of the motivation to write this essay came from the heavyweight boxing championship fight between Larry Holmes, the undefeated Black champion, and Gerry Cooney, the number one white contender and subsequent loser. Race was the major and overriding concern in this contest, with Cooney portrayed as the "white hope." The real fight took place with the atmosphere created by the series of "Rocky" movies. In these fantasies, Sylvester Stallone plays the white fighter in the red, white and blue trunks who is always victorious over his Black challenger.

Encyclopedia Britannica (15th Edition) states,

> Boxing is the art of attack and defense with the fists in which the two
> contestants wear padded gloves, box bouts of three to 15 rounds (each
> round normally of three minutes duration), and generally observe the
> code set forth in the Marquess of Queensbury rules.... Contestants are
> matched in weight and ability, each trying to land hard and often with
> his own fists and to avoid the blows of his opponent.

> The term pugilism and prizefighting in 20th-century usage are
> practically synonymous with boxing, though the first indicates the
> ancient origins of the sport in its derivation from the Latin 'pugil', "a
> fighter with the cestus (a hand covering)," related to the Latin pignus,
> 'fist,' and derived in turn from the Greek 'pyx' 'with clenched fist';
> while 'prize-fighting' emphasizes the pursuit of the sport for gain.
> Samuel Johnson in his Dictionary (1975) defined a prizefighter as 'one
> that fights publicly for a reward.'

Of the history of boxing, *Encyclopedia Britannica* continues

> There is evidence that boxing existed in ancient Crete, where a
> civilization was established by about 1500 BC. Centuries before the
> arrival of the Greeks, boxing was known in the Aegean....In the early
> days, fighters wore thongs of soft leather bound around their fists and
> (often) two-thirds of the way up their forearms to protect hands and
> wrists. Beginning in the 4th century BC, harder leather was used for
> the thongs, with the result that they became weapons as well as
> protection. And finally, late in the history of the Roman Empire, the
> Greeks adopted the hand covering called cestus, which was studded
> with iron or brass nuggets and was used in battles to the death in the
> Roman arenas....The first Greek fighters were not paid; glory was the
> only reward they sought. Later, wealthy men trained their slaves as
> boxers and had them perform for special entertainments. In the 1st
> century AD, Romans forced cestus clad slaves to bludgeon one
> another to death in a gruesome perversion of sport for the
> entertainment of crowds who thronged to arenas to see the kill. With
> the rise of Christianity and the concurrent decline of the Roman
> Empire, pugilism as entertainment apparently ceased to exist. At least,
> there is no record of it.

In more modern times, with the rise of London as a major city in the 17th and 18th centuries, prizefighting became a major sport there – the sport being bareknuckle in character. Bill Richmond (1763 - 1829), an American-born former slave, became the first man born in America to win acclaim in England as a first-class pugilist. Tom Cribb (1781-1848), the Englishman, is considered the first to win immortality in the sport of boxing. Cribb beat Richmond in 90 minutes in 1805. Later, after winning the English championship, he twice beat Tom Molineaux (1784-1818), another American-born former slave, in what were considered Cribb's greatest performances.

As evidenced by the above, ethnic and racial considerations have long been a major theme in boxing. The first man considered a scientific fighter is described as "an English Jew" named Daniel Mendoza (1763-1836). Other fighters remained associated with their ethnic and/or national origins. The waves of immigrants that came to America from the British Isles and Europe, all coming to America competing with one another for advancement, produced not only outstanding fighters identified as "Jews," but others identified as "Italian," "German," "Scandinavian," "Polish," "American Negroes" and "Foreign-born Negroes." Of course, the only group against which there was great prejudice at times was against the Black fighters, who presently dominate the ring in all weight categories.

Amateur boxing began during the 19th century in Britain. In 1888, the Amateur Athletic Union (AAU) of the United States was founded. In 1923, the *Chicago Tribune* newspaper founded an amateur competition called the Golden Gloves. The name, Golden Gloves, was first used in New York in 1927. It has now grown into a national competition rivalling the AAU. (See Chapter 16.)

Although boxing as a sport is now worldwide, there is no accepted world-ruling body for professional boxing. Each country has its own rules, and in the U.S. each state has different rules. Most common, however, is that the bouts take place in a "ring" – which is in reality an area 14 to 20 feet square, surrounded by three strands of ropes. Professional bouts are from four to fifteen rounds in duration.

Key to this discussion is the general rule that disqualification may be made by the referee during a fight for fouls – such as hitting below the "belt," an imaginary line drawn across the body from the top of the hip bone. There are other rules for disqualification, but the above usually is recognized as the most crucial rule. Also significant for this discussion is the central aspect of technique that dictates the gloved hands must be held up in front of the body: the left hand shoulder high and extended about 12 inches. The left hand is slightly higher than the right, with the left forearm held across the chest, right fist almost touching it, and both elbows bent and resting lightly against the ribs. The right fist is held close to the chin for protection and tucked into the chest, and the shoulders are hunched. (*Encyclopedia Britannica*, 15th Edition).

Whereas the above sets forth the specifics of the formal boxing match, it is the specific symbolism and the symbolic elements in the behavior of boxing that are the major concern. Awareness at the level of the symbol and the symbolic enables us to comprehend a more significant meaning of the dynamics of the world around us.

Essentially, to the extent that the surrounding reality is not understood at the deeper levels – at the level of the symbolic – the individual and the collective remain relatively powerless. Symbols and symbolic activity impact at subconscious and unconscious levels of the brain-computer, escaping conscious level screening and control over the behavioral outflow that has been stimulated by the symbol and the symbolic. With in-depth understanding, the symbol and the symbolic can be decoded and made available for conscious use and disposal, increasing the individual's power over the self and the surrounding environment. (See Diagram I.)

Brain-Computer Level	Brain-Computer Input and Output
Conscious_____	Overt-Surface
Subconscious_____	Symbolic-Symbolic
Unconscious_____	Symbolic-Symbolic

Diagram I
Brain-Computer Level of Functioning
and Level of Input and Output
of Environmental Data

Decoding the symbols and the symbolic behaviors in boxing requires returning in time to ancient Africa, the birth place of human beings, and more specifically to the African country called Egypt – in the period antedating the invasions by the white tribes of Europe. The most important Egyptian god was Osiris, referred to as "Lord of the Perfect Black," which I interpret as a reference to his *skin color*. The symbol by which Osiris was known was the black bull called Apis. J.E. Cirlot's *Dictionary of Symbols* refers to the bull as the historic symbol of white superiority over black. However, this seems to be a conscious or unconscious attempt by Cirlot to reverse the meaning of the bull symbol since the black bull was the symbol of Osiris, a Black god. Thus, in actuality, the bull must represent the opposite: black superiority over white in the psyche of the white collective.

Moving forward in time, the sport of *bullfighting* became prominent on the continent of Europe, in Spain, shortly after the Moors (Black Africans) who had conquered Spain for seven hundred years, were finally beaten and chased back into Africa. Of course, by that time, the skin color and hair of the peoples in Spain and in southern Europe had darkened because of the dominant black genetic material which the Africans brought with them. However, the Spaniard response to being conquered by the Africans, following the military but not the genetic defeat of the latter, was to begin the obsessive symbolic ritual of *bullfighting*. A male person dressed in a "suit of lights" (which can be decoded as meaning a light- or white-skinned person), daringly prances and parades in front of a black bull (acting as though he really wants to be gored) and, finally, with the help of several others, kills the bull. The fighter (the toreador), then normally takes as souvenir the bull's ear or tail, both of which have been recognized as phallic symbols. Further, the bull is often eaten and its testicles, seen as giving power to the diner, are consumed as a delicacy.

Following the Civil War in the U.S., a country whose development was based upon the slave labor of Blacks captured from the continent of Africa, the bull-steer again takes on major significance. The victory in that war went to "the North." "The South" and the slaveholders lost the war; they also lost their Black slaves through the emancipation process. Many of the white ex-slaveholders moved westward, initially, wantonly slaughtering the massive herds of black and dark brown buffalo. The indigenous inhabitants of America, who are incorrectly referred to as Indians, called the Black soldiers, "buffalo soldiers." The source of this terminology likely stems from the similarities: the hair on the head of the buffalo is very curly, like the helix hair on the heads of the Africans (Blacks). Thus, these white cowboys and soldiers were slaughtering the symbols of Osiris, the Black god, and symbols of the Blacks.

Once the buffalo were removed from the plains, in addition to the so-called Indians who were also killed, these whites began to raise (breed) cattle (cows, ox, bull, steers). For for the most part, these cattle have been brown and black in coloration. The *superior* cattle, the angus, is mostly all black. Even more interesting is the fact that the whites who raised, bred and herded brown and black cattle, referred to themselves as "cowboys," a highly interesting word which *doubly effeminizes* these males. The word "cow," while it can be used broadly to refer to any domesticated bovine, is used most specifically to refer to the mature *female* cattle. Similarly, the word "boy" historically has been used by whites in the U.S. to refer to the Black male as a means of minimizing and degrading his masculinity. These cowboys, nonetheless, threw ropes (lassoes and lariats) around the necks of brown and black cattle (just as ropes were also placed around the necks of Black men in lynchings), and they also castrated the cattle-producing steer (as they castrated Black men who were lynched).

Cattle-raising and cattle-herding operated under the ostensible purpose of producing beef for eating. The U.S. has become one of the major beef-eating nations in the world with its favored meats being steak and hamburgers. Beef is the preferred meat of the majority of whites in the global white supremacy system and culture. Beef eaters are suppose to be or to become more powerful and more masculine.

Cattle were also put to other uses, mainly the production of leather for shoes, gloves, clothes, luggage, etc. The wearing of leather, particularly black leather, is supposed to make one appear maximally masculine and powerful. Leathers are used in the production of many articles of clothing for the military. The German military (the Nazis) in the Second World War, perhaps, exceeded all other white supremacy forces in the utilization of black leather to give the appearance of power and might.

As a result of the aforementioned facts, the black bull and its symbolic uses – clothing and food – have come to demonstrate the power that was originally seen in Osiris ("Lord of the Perfect Black"). The sport of boxing assumes the same theme of power. In this specific instance, the theme is expressed through the use of the leather gloved fists, continuing a practice begun in the days of the Roman Empire.

In current times, the fists of the boxer are covered by rounded, padded, colored leather boxing gloves. These paired gloves, poised together in front of the body at the beginning of the fight, are *symbols* of the genetic material containing skin-covered testicles – the containers of the true power of the man, the genetic essence.

The poised fists, are in direct parallel alignment with the testicles below the belt. The critical off-limits body area, which the boxer is penalized for striking, is the area of the testicles or genitals – "below the belt." Of course, this body area restriction in the boxing match is to prevent serious pain and bodily damage. However, it also is necessary to prevent the conscious association of the *symbol* with the true objects whose power is really being contested, the genetic power residing in the testicles. It is as though the "below the belt" restriction states, "the testicles have nothing whatsoever to do with this contest." In reality, however, the contest is only about the genetic power of the testicles. Some investigators also view the paired feet (often leather-covered) as symbols of the testicles that are in parallel alignment above them. This awareness contributes to a deeper understanding of the foot and the shoe fetishes seen in the global white supremacy system/culture.

Returning to the boxing arena, the symbolic contest of the genetic power of the testicles is staged in a "ring." It is referred to as a ring because it is symbolic of the female vaginal orifice. The bout also takes place on canvas, typically considered white in color.

In the recent Holmes-Cooney fight, the canvas was colored red, white and blue. This is significant because these three colors: red, white and blue are the most important symbolic colors in the white supremacy system and culture, as manifested by the colors of the flags of the majority of white nation-states. The flag on a pole symbolizes the lateral view of the phallus and the testicles, the colored cloth representing the testicles. A red, white and blue cloth symbolizes genetic material that produces white skin, through which can be seen, red arterioles and blue veins, hence the expression "bluebloods," a phrase which means that the skin is white or pale enough for the blue veins to show through. Blue veins and arterioles typically are not visible through melanin-pigmented skins. Additionally, in *Rocky*, Stallone wears red, white and blue trunks that are designed to symbolize the American flag. The trunks cover the genitals and, in this instance, genitals that produce white skin through which red arterioles and blue veins can be seen.

Finally, in regards to the boxing match, the gloved fists typically are covered with black, brown or other colored leather, as opposed to white leather. This fact reveals that, at the deep levels of the white individual and collective psyche, power is thought to be associated with color (skin color), as opposed to colorless (white) skin. In the final analysis, it does not matter which boxer (white or nonwhite) is the winner at the surface level. The color of the gloves of the winner are always non-white, and the white fighter who dons colored gloves simply identifies himself with the power and color of the bull of Osiris, which is black – not white. Thus color is always the winner at the deeper levels of the psyche – just as in reality black (skin color) is always genetically dominant to white.

Additional support for my thesis is found in an article entitled "M.D. Describes 'Fisting' as Caring Sexual Practice,"in *Psychiatric News of the American Psychiatric Association,* June 18, 1982, The article reports on the work of Thomas Lowry, M.D., Chief of the Psychiatry Department at the Kaiser Permanente Medical Center in Vallejo, California, and Gregory Williams, an occupational therapist living in San Francisco. Lowry created the term "brachioproctic eroticism" to describe the practice known as "fisting." The article states,

> 'The ultimate closeness' and 'the ecstatic and total trust' are just two of the phrases used by participants to describe their feelings during a sexual practice that, although bizarre and seemingly unlikely, is apparently engaged in by a sizeable number of persons.
>
> This practice consists of one person inserting his or her hand and forearm into the rectum of another – In the first phase of their study, Lowry and Williams distributed questionnaires at "leather" bars, homosexual conventions, specialty nightclubs, bookstores, and doctor's consulting rooms....From these data, the authors estimate that, nationwide, roughly 50,000 persons have incorporated fisting into their regular sexual repetoires. The study is reported by Lowry and Williams in the January 1981 issue of the British Journal of Sexual Medicine and was presented by Lowry at the March 1982 annual meeting of the American Association of Sex Educators, Counselors, and Therapists....The mean age of the respondents was 34.1 years, and their major occupational groups included (in descending order) professionals, businessmen, skilled laborers, and unskilled laborers. Ninety-six percent stated that they were exclusively or predominantly homosexual....

There is deep level symbolism involved in fisting, a practice that represents a form of clinical pathology of the self-concept and self-image. It is directly related to the above translation of the symbolism inherent in boxing – wherein the "fist" becomes symbolic of the testicles. Chapter 6 explains that male homosexuality is based upon the conscious and/or unconscious sense of "male-substance deficiency." This results in the highly symbolic and behavioral preoccupation with the internalization, at one or the other end of the gastrointestinal tract, of male substance in the form of semen. Lowry and Williams reveal that there is an increasing number of persons, the vast majority of whom are exclusively or predominantly homosexual, who in response to a deep sense of 'male-substance deficiency' are motivated to have the fist and forearm of another inserted into the anal end of the gastrointestinal tract.

For greater clarity, the fist and forearm in abstract form constitute a ball at the end of a road or stick. This abstract diagramatic form resembles the lateral view of the male genitalia.

The questionnaires for the data collected by Lowry and Williams were distributed in "leather" bars, along with other places frequented by homosexuals. Leather bars are settings where mostly white male homosexuals dress in black leather and/or engage in various forms of sadomasochistic sexual activity involving the use of black leather, (e.g., whips).

Having a leather whip inserted into the rectum is one form of symbolically internalizing, not only male substance but, more specifically, Black male substance (the leather being symbolic of the Black male). Being beaten by a whip, or being "dominated" by someone dressed in black leather are other symbolic forms of internalizing Black male substance through the act of submission.

The wearing of leather and the preoccupation with the use of leather objects, including boxing gloves, is the subconscious and unconscious return, through symbolism, to the white collective's perception of the dominant genetic power of the Black male. Therefore, for men who consciously and/or unconsciously sense themselves as deficient in male-substance, to act out symbolically and to don or to internalize symbols representative of the highest standard of male power – blackness – is logically correct, if not logically necessary.

18

The Cress Theory of the Holocaust (1980)

Heretofore, the destruction of the Semites of the Jewish religion and the gypsies of Europe have been presented as a confounding puzzle. Well, there *is* an answer, horrendous yes, but not at all difficult to understand; and the implications for Black people are profound.

The New York Times (June 8, 1980) in an article entitled "Brandeis to Set Up Institute on Causes of Holocaust," reported:

> Brandeis University will establish a research institute to study the cause of the Holocaust, the 15 year period in which more than 6 million Jews were killed in Europe....By autumn the 32-year-old Jewish sponsored but nonsectarian university expects to have a dozen junior and senior researchers at work planning conferences, lectures and articles on the period and the approximately 150 years of events leading up to it....."As important as they are, we no longer need any more collections of memoirs by survivors, pictures of concentration camps and research into the mechanisms of Hitler's 'final solution for the Jews,'" said Marver H. Benstein, president of the University. 'What's needed now and in the future is an attempt to account for what happened, to *explain why,* and to give some *insight into* future events if possible." (author's emphasis) Mr. Bernstein said the institute would be financed by an $800,000 grant from Dr. Laxlo Tauber, a surgeon in the Washington, D.C. area and survivor of a forced-labor camp in Hungary. It will be the only institute of its kind in this country, Mr.

Bernstein said, and the only one outside of Israel, where the Hebrew University in Jersusalem has a similar study group called, 'The Hand of God.' Unlike that research institute, which concentrates on the Holocaust years 1930-1945, the Brandeis Institute intends to look at the broader range of Western European history from about the time of Napolean's emancipation of the French Jews in the first decades of the 1800's.

'We cannot bring them back,' Dr. Tauber said of the estimated 20 million civilians, Jewish and non-Jewish, who died in Nazi labor and concentration camps, 'But I would like to see people educated to the realization that it can happen anywhere, anytime, again....'

Whereas I am not an invited scholar nor a petitioner to attend the Tauber Institute at Brandeis University, I have been a student of anti-Semitism in Europe and the destruction of the Semites of the Jewish religion since the mid-1950s. Throughout that time, I remained convinced that the treatment of the Semites of the Jewish religion in Europe and in America was intimately related to the gradual destruction of Black people as well as the millions of native peoples found in the 'Americas' by the immigrating whites from Europe – a pattern which continues to the present. Further, I was convinced that the "final solution" for the Semites in Europe was associated with the "atomic bomb solution" for the Japanese peoples in World War II, and that the anti-semitism of Europe and America was intimately related to the "apartheid" of southern Africa and to the historic pattern of treatment (mistreatment) of all of the peoples *classified* as "non-white" or "non-aryan" peoples by the peoples who classify themselves as "white" or "aryan."

One of the serious flaws in Western logic, thought and scholarship is the failure or inability to see things as a "whole." Rather, the tendency is to perceive fragmented "abstractions" that are never united as one. This pattern of thought is sharply contrasted to the Eastern mode of thinking and perception that *begins* with the perception and analysis of the whole, so as to place in accurate perspective any parts or fragments which may be isolated from the whole.

The focus on the destruction of the Semites of the Jewish religion as an abstraction outside of the context of the *totality* of the historic Western civilization and cultural imperative (the past 2,000 years, at least) explains why there has not been, to date, a comprehensive understanding of the Semitic destruction in Europe from 1933 to 1945. Indeed, the Tauber Institute at Brandeis University will not find the answers it seeks (the $800,000 grant, not withstanding) with the limited historical perspective of only 150 years of history of Semites in Europe.

Sometimes, at deep unconscious levels, people do not really wish to find answers to problems that they obsessively complain about, even when that problem has caused the death of six million people. There is the conscious awareness, perhaps, of the need to know the whole truth and to understand in depth; but below this surface, there is the more powerful need to maintain the status quo, which depth knowledge and awareness would explode in volcanic fashion. Specifically I am referring to, perhaps, an unconscious need on the part of Semites of the Jewish religion (and perhaps other Semites as well) to avoid confronting and, therefore, understanding their entire historic experience amongst the whites in Europe, in addition to their prior experience with the whites while they still resided in Africa two thousand years ago.

However, I have no such unconscious need. To the exact contrary, I perceive the existing chaos and injustice on the planet Earth to be of such horrendous magnitude that this global evil needs to be broken asunder by the surfacing of depth knowledge and insight so that the true calm of a greater justice can evolve and prevail. It is just as when a volcano spews forth the molten materials from its core, the soil upon which the ash falls becomes enriched and more fertile from that which subsequently springs forth. This essay, then, is for all Black people and for others who wish to understand the destruction of the Semites and gypsies in Europe between 1933 and 1945. It is a presentation of the critical *datum* that will totally clarify, once and for all, why there was anti-Semitism in Europe and why a "final solution" for the Semites as well as for the gypsy population in Europe was needed.

It is necessary at this point to reiterate the key issues of The Cress Theory of Color-Confrontation and Racism (White Supremacy): The white supremacy (white survival) necessity is to establish, maintain, expand and refine the power equation *white over non-white* (W/NW), white power over all peoples with an ancestral history of substantial melanin skin pigmentation that can be genetically transmitted. The white genetic phenotype can be maintained on the planet Earth only through this means (intensive "genetic-watch").

The implications of the Cress Theory are that all behavioral patterns in the global white collectivel *begin and end* with the conscious and/or unconscious consideration of white genetic survival and the corollary consideration of the global threat of white genetic annihilation by the non-white majority. Were this not the foremost consideration of the global white collective, a white population would not exist on the planet Earth; it would have succumbed to white genetic annihilation, and, therefore, never would have been an organized psychological and military defense.

So, what does all of this have to do with the mass destruction of members of the Jewish religion living in Europe and the phenomenon of anti-Semitism? First, much confusion has arisen because of the conscious and/or unconscious insistence of mixing a discussion of religion with a discussion of race, specifically as it concerns the Semitic population that practices the Judaic religion. This population migrated from Africa and has resided in Europe for the past two thousand years. The "holocaust" in Europe was the end result of the long-standing dynamic of anti-Semitism. Semite refers to a racial group. Thus, anti-Semitism was a dynamic directed specifically against a group with a distinct racial (genetic) background, which incidentally practiced a particular religion.

A *Semite* is conventionally defined as "a member of any of the people whose language is Semitic, including the Hebrews, Arabs, Assyrians, Phoenicians, Babylonians, etc." (*Webster's New World Dictionary*). The adjective *Semitic* is defined as "1. of, characteristic of, or like a Semite or the Semites 2. designating or of a major group of languages of south-western Asia and northern Africa, related to the Hamitic languages and divided into East Semitic (Akkadian), North West Semitic (Phoenician, Punic, Aramaic, Hebrew, Modern Hebrew, etc.) and South West Semitic (Arabic, Ethiopic, Amheric)." *Webster's New World Dictionary* also informs us that the prefix, "semi - "(L., akin to Gr. hemi-, Sans. sami-, AS. sam), means half, as in semidiameter.

Thus, both of the words *Semite* and *Hamite* (the later from the Greek "Hemite") could refer to peoples who were Black, but a mulatto-type mixture of Black and white and combinations thereof, hence "semi-" or "hemi-" – half Black and half white – much like the present mixed Black or colored population in the U.S., or wherever white males have sexually aggressed against African (Black) females. A fine example is the Roman (white) soldiers' sexual aggression against African women. In my decoding, the word Semite, as from the Latin prefix "semi-," means someone whose ancestry was a Black and white mixture, therefore *Black* (since Black is genetically dominant).

In *The Washington Post* (May 4, 1979), in an article entitled "Pope to View Poland's Black Madonna," Sylvana Foa reports:

.... The mysterious Black Madonna of Czestochowa is the most sacred icon in Poland. It is also one of the most haunting and beautiful works of religious art in the world. Pope John Paul II, a strong advocate of devotion to the Virgin Mary will travel to the hilltop monastery in June to show his special devotion to the strange painting depicting Christ's mother as a black woman....Art experts believe the Madonna was painted between the 6th and 8th centuries and say the style is reminiscent of early Egyptian Christians....many art historians, believe the Madonna is one of the rare black Madonnas still extant. Most of the Madonnas painted in the earliest centuries of Christiandom were black, according to historians and it wasn't until the Renaissance that it became popular to give the mother of Christ the features of a Florentine maiden ..."

223

The "features of a Florentine maiden" means the features and coloring of a white woman. Thus, religious and art history support the fact that the Semites were Black people, with the highly esteemed personage of Jesus and his mother as evidence.

In the diaspora of the Semites of the Jewish religion after the Babylonian exile 2,000 or so years ago, Semites left Africa and went to Europe. With continuing genetic admixture with the European (white) population, operating under the definition that a Jew is "anyone whose mother is a Jew," it was possible, if enough white males had sexual intercourse with a sufficient number of Semitic or colored women, for the once Black population of Semites to become progressively lighter and lighter. All offspring from these white males and Semitic women of the Jewish religion then would become Jews.

Over 2,000 years or 100 generations, the population that was once Black became significantly lightened. Just examine how relatively light in color Black peoples in the U.S. have become after only 20 generations of white male sexual aggression against African (Black) women. Just think what we could achieve in 100 generations if our goal was to become lighter and lighter with each generation, using the well-known formula: Don't marry anyone darker than yourself!

It is significant to this discussion that Karl Marx (1818-1883), another Semite of the Jewish religion, had such dark skin that his children called him "The Moor," meaning of course, "the Black." Robert Heilbroner, in his book *The Worldly Philosophers,* states, in contrasting the appearance of Marx with his co-worker Friedrich Engles, "They were very much opposites in appearance. Marx looked like a revolutionary. His children called him, 'The Moor,' for his skin was dark and his eyes deep-set and flashing."

Prior to reading Heilbroner, I always had been impressed by the great similarity in appearance of Frederick Douglas, the pre-Civil War Black orator, and Karl Marx. Frederick Douglas was the offspring of a Black woman and a sexually agressing white slave master – thus himself a Semite or mulatto.

Another Semite of the Jewish religion who was identified as "a Black" was Albert Einstein. Albert Einstein (1879-1955), the great Nobel prize physicist, as documented by Robert Clark's *Einstein: The Life and Times* was once described as "1.76 meters tall.... broad shouldered, with a slight stoop. His short skull seems remarkably broad. His complexion is swarthy...." (*Webster's New World Dictionary* defines the word "swarthy" as "having a dark skin; dusky; dark. SYN. see dusky."

The same dictionary defines dusky as, "1. somewhat dark in color; shadowy; swarthy; 2. lacking light .... dusky suggests a darkness of color or absence of light, verging on blackness. Swarthy and tawny both refer only to color, swarthy suggesting a dark brown verging on black ...." *The Encyclopedia Britannica*, described Einstein as: "...a young man, not very tall, with a wide and long face, and a great mane of crispy, frizzled and very black hair, sprinkled with gray and rising from a lofty brow. His nose is fleshy and prominent, his mouth small, his lips full, his cheeks plump ..." This was a description of Einstein in his middle thirties. Crispy and frizzled hair is one half step away from *kinky hair*. Again, we see in the person of a most prominent Semite descriptive features that are associated with the genetic stock of the African continent: swarthy skin and crispy, frizzled hair.

We now come to Sigmund Freud (1885 to 1939), a Semite of the Jewish religion, born in Austria, a physician and psychiatrist and founder of psychoanalysis. In a July 23, 1979 *Time* book review of *Freud: Biologist of the Mind* entitled "Did Freud Build His Own Legend?" Frank Sulloway revealed, "Sigmund Freud idolized Hannibal. So much that for years he was psychologically unable to enter Rome because Hannibal had never set foot in the city...." It is interesting that Sigmund Freud, a Semite of the Jewish religion, should identify himself with *Hannibal*. Hannibal was a Black man.

Encyclopedia Britannica states,

> Hannibal (b. 247 B.C., North Africa – d. 182 B.C., Libyssa, Bithynia, now Turkey), one of the great military leaders of antiquity, commanded the Carthaginian forces against Rome in the Second Punic War (218 - 201 B.C) .... After the Romans

declared war in 219 B.C., Hannibal, at the command of a force of about 40,000 and a number of elephants, crossed the Pyrenees into southern Gaul. From there he executed an incredible fear to military enterprise proceeding across the Alps into northern Italy. In 217 B.C. at the Battle of Lake Trasimene, he inflicted one of the greatest defeats suffered by Rome....

I have quoted the above sources extensively because there is a significant reason why three of the greatest Semitic thinkers of the Jewish religion have been described as *dark* in appearance or have identified *themselves,* as in the case of Freud, with Blackness. Freud even went further in his last work, *Moses and Monotheism,* written in part while fleeing from the Nazis, to describe the founder of the Jewish religion, Moses, as an Egyptian – meaning of course, a Black man. Each of these representative Semites of the Jewish religion either has identified himself or has been identified by others with Blackness, primarily because the Jews in Africa two thousand years ago were Black (African) people. That is the reason that all of the earliest paintings of the Madonna and child (Jesus and his mother) were a Black madonna and child. They were Africans.

The modern day, highly misconducted Semites of the European experience may want and may have wanted in the past to forget their Black ancestral heritage and suppress this truth, but the global white collective never has forgotten this critical fact. Always, the white collective, consciously or unconsciously, must remember this fact in relationships with "Semites" and all other peoples whose genetic history causes the whites to classify them as non-whites, if there is to be white genetic survival.

Adolph Hitler, other Germans and Europeans, all of whom are whites, were aware (consciously, subconsciously or unconsciously) of the greater origin of the "Semites" no matter how light-skinned many of them may have become after 2,000 years of miscegenation with the whites or "aryans." Hitler and his followers not only mandated the destruction of the Semites, but also the destruction of the gypsies. W*ebster's New World Dictionary* defines "gypsy" as "n. (pl. gypsies), (earlier gypscien, short for Egypcien, Egyptian: so called because thought to have come from Egypt – a member of a wandering Caucasian people with dark skin and black hair, found throughout the world..." The reader should not conclude falsely that the word "caucasian" means "white." Often, "caucasian" is used to refer to dark skin (non-white) peoples who may have straight hair. However, white means white and caucasian means caucasian.

The reason Hitler gave for making the Semites and gypsies priorities on the list of destruction was that they were classified by the whites (aryans) as "non-white" peoples, whose origin was in Africa. These non-white peoples were considered genetically inferior to the whites, but capable of causing white genetic annihilation. Therefore, it was considered essential by those who were interested in white genetic survival to destroy those in their midst whom they believed could cause white genetic annihilation. All non-white peoples can cause white genetic annihilation because of their ability to produce melanin skin pigmentation. Hitler made it absolutely clear that his objective was global white supremacy and white racial purity.

The specific fear of white genetic annihilation, while always present in the global white collective, becomes more prominent and is more frequently acted upon in times when whites have lost a war and/or when there is serious economic uncertainty. At these times the white collective feels insecure because the major props for the sense of white invincibility and for white genetic survival – their *guns* and money – seem to have failed.

Thus, after the German's loss of World War I (which was followed by political instability, high level inflation and high level unemployment), there appeared on the scene a dynamic spokesperson, articulating the need to destroy those perceived as capable of ultimate white destruction.

In the United States we are in such a period. There has been the loss of the Vietnam War (a war lost to non-white people), followed by political instability (Watergate, etc.), and there is high level inflation and unemployment. Thus, we witness increasing levels of activity of Nazis, Skinheads, the Ku Klux Klan and other spokespersons, such as Nobel prize laureate, Dr. William Shockly, articulating the need to get rid of

Black people and discussing Black genetic inferiority; some also focus in the Semites as a problem.

This behavior must not be looked upon as immoral, as though it can be challenged by moral persuasion. This logic, thought, speech, action, emotional response and perception is of *absolute logical necessity* for a people who historically have been in fear of their genetic annihilation by Black and other non-white peoples.

The term *anti-Semitism* means white supremacy (racism). A *holocaust*, the open destruction of non-white people by white people, occurs when: 1) there is a sufficient level of insecurity or anxiety in the white population relative to white genetic annihilation; 2) there is no longer a plan; or 3) it is considered too expensive to keep non-whites confined in "ghettos," "prisons," "barrios," "bantustans," "concentration camps," "on reservations" or "on welfare." Holocausts also occur when whites consider it necessary to relocate non-white peoples for labor purposes (e.g., Africans being brought to the Americas or Native Americans being moved off the land because whites want it). Presently, a holocaust is occurring in the jungles of Brazil, and the victims are the native peoples of the area, so-called Indians.

The Semites of the Jewish religion always have referred to themselves as God's chosen people. However, they have debated amongst themselves the reason they were chosen and what they were chosen to do. I have answered these questions in the following way: they were chosen to help all of the other non-white peoples of the world living under white supremacy domination to understand that no matter how much you may mix with and intermarry with people who classify themselves as white, no matter how light-skinned you may become through loss of melanin pigment, no matter how straight your hair may become, no matter how much you may shrink the size of your nose, no matter how many doctors, lawyers, judges, professors, scholars you may produce, no matter how many Einsteins, Freuds, Marxs or Rubensteins you produce, no matter how much money, diamonds and gold you may obtain, if you are classified as non-white under the conditions of white supremacy domination, when the *hammer* of white supremacy falls, you will be under that hammer.

The Semites of the Jewish religion were chosen to teach a very important moral, and that is, never disrespect or be ashamed of the *Black genetic heritage of Africa,* and speak up for, own up to, protect and defend that heritage with your very life, should conditions and events ever call upon you to do so. Be proud to be Black and be proud to be non-white. This is a profound lesson in self-respect for all of the people in the world.

19

The Neurochemical Basis for Evil
(1988)

The American philosopher William James has stated, "There is no doubt that healthy mindedness is inadequate as a philosophical doctrine, because the evil facts which it positively refuses to account for are a genuine portion of reality, and they may after all be the best key to life's significance, and possibly the only openers of our eyes to the deepest level of truth."

The Kabbalah, which literally means "tradition," is the sum of Jewish mysticism, the tradition of things divine. The Book Bahir, an 1180 A.D. document on the Kabbalah concerning Satan, states,

> It teaches that there is in God a principle that is called 'Evil', and it lies in the north of God, of it is written [Jer. I:14]: 'Out of the north the evil shall break forth upon all the inhabitants of the land,' that is to say, all evil that comes upon all the inhabitants of the land breaks forth out of the north. And what principle is this? It is the form of the hand [one of the seven holy forms which represent God as the original man], and it has many messengers, and all are named 'Evil'....And it is they that fling the world into guilt for the *tobu* is in the north, and the *tobu* means precisely the evil that confuses men until they sin, and it is the source of all man's evil impulses.

In early Egyptian (African) tradition, evil was associated with Set, the brother of Osiris ("Lord of the perfect black"). Set eventually killed his brother Osiris and dismembered his body, which his sister/wife (Isis) helped restore to life. Osiris was the great Egyptian God figure. Set is considered the white brother.

In contrast, the early Christian religion and the Bible related evil to the *fallen* angel Lucifer, a word that means light and that can be construed to mean white. However, in the Middle Ages, for some Europeans, the devil took on an appearance of a Black man with a long phallus, which has been modified as the present red colored figure with a long *tail* and a long *fork*.

In keeping with each of the above perspectives of evil, *Webster's Dictionary* defines "evil" as: "1. morally bad or wrong; wicked, depraved, 2. causing pain or trouble; harmful; injurious, 3. threatening or bringing misfortune; unlucky; disastrous; unfortunate; as an evil hour, 4. resulting from or based on conduct regarded as immoral; as an evil reputation."

The Cress Theory of Color Confrontation and Racism (White Supremacy), links whites' unjust behavior towards people of color (black, brown, red and yellow) to whites' inability to produce melanin skin pigment in the skin melanocyte. The whites' numerical minority status in the world and, ultimately, their fear of global white genetic annihilation by the genetically dominant, skin melanin producing, non-white world majority are pointed out as additional reasons for white aggression towards people of color. This thesis helps to explain the evil "kill or be killed" behaviors of the global white collective in relation to non-white people.

In 1972, I presented a paper entitled, *Melanin:_ The Neurochemical Basis for Soul*, at the annual meeting of the National Medical Association Section on Neurology and Psychiatry. I theorized that the presence of melanin in high concentrations in Blacks accounted for some of the observable differences in behavior between Black and white people (ie., religious responsiveness, rhythm, emotional responsiveness, sensitivity levels), noting the familiar saying amongst older Black people, "The blacker the berry, the sweeter the juice; if it ain't got no soul, it ain't got no use." Also, I emphasized the song by James Brown, "We Got More Soul." Further, I pointed out that the most sensitive body areas are the areas most highly pigmented.

Fifteen years ago in a paper entitled, "Blacks, Hypertension and the Active Skin Melanocyte" (*Journal of Urban Health,* 1975), I posited melanin, among other things, as a possible neurotransmitter and the skin melanocytes as the foundation of the sixth sense – the basis for knowledge of the unseen, including a deeper knowledge of "bad." I explained that if the melanocytes were sense receptors and melanin was a neuro transmitter, then the darker the skin, the higher the levels of hypertensions found. Primarily, this is true because people with darker skins are more sensitive to the energy currents around them. If those energy currents are stressful, they will be more stressed, increasing *levels* of hypertension.

In 1987, at the first Melanin Conference, I discussed The Cress Theory on the George Washington Carver Phenomenon, suggesting that the skin melanocytes of this very Black-skinned scientist (high level concentration of melanin skin pigment) enabled him to communicate with the energy frequencies emanating from plants. Thus, he was able to learn their secrets and purposes.

Since my 1972 presentation on the neurochemical basis for soul, the neurochemical basis of evil has periodically come to my mind, begging that I outline my thoughts on evil as the anti-thesis of soul. I relate soul to order, spirituality and the affirmation of life. I equate evil with chaos and destruction, especially the destruction of life. (The word *evil* when spelled backward is, *live*.) The discussion of evil takes on even more significant proportions in light of the increasing number of persons in this society who openly are proclaiming themselves to be worshippers of the Devil – Devil being the arch doer of evil – in contrast to worshipping God. Reportedly, these persons participate in the ritual murder of human beings.

The concept of evil is not at all unusual in religious and philosophical discourse. Also, evil has been a frequent subject for literary exploration. (The novel *Moby Dick* by Herman Melville is an example of the symbolic discussion of evil in classical American literature.) Evil is approached less often in the natural sciences, including modern medicine. However, psychiatry is the one branch of modern medicine that has major antecedents in both religion and philosophy and thus, the topic of evil has found discussants who consider themselves scientists and scientific.

The role of the psychiatric-physician or physician-scientist is to attempt to comprehend, bringing greater clarity and insight, the total spectrum of human behavior, which would include the special category of behavioral phenomena recognized as evil. Further, I believe that the challenge of modern psychiatry, like the challenge of modern physics, is to approach, if possible, a view of the "unified field."

Modern physics, since Albert Einstein, has sought to unite the spectrum of forces – gravity, electromagnetism, weak and strong forces – in a unified field, viewing these separate forces as outgrowths from or manifestations of a whole (a unified force field). Likewise, modern psychiatry should seek to discover if there is a united behavioral force field that can explain evil as well as other dominant behavioral phenomena.

For the ant, the greatest evil consists of killing ants. For the human being, the greatest evil consists of the obsessional degrading and killing of other human beings. All lesser evils are simply added to this (ie., destruction of other life forms, destruction of the planet and destruction that extends beyond planet Earth). With evil so defined, clearly there is an overwhelming atmosphere of evil in the world. In fact, the entire planet exists in an atmosphere of degradation and murder. To ignore this evidence of evil, this obsession with mass killing and death, is only to participate in the establishment and the maintenance of its reality – in effect, to participate in evil. On the other hand, to address this obsession with mass death and the degradation of human life in hopes of countering it is to affirm the dignity of human beings and the universe.

Ernest Becker, in his book *Escape From Evil*, had the following to say about evil: "All organisms want to perpetuate themselves, continue to experience and to live....For all organisms, then, opposing and obliterating power is evil – it threatens to stop experience." He continues, "So we see that as an organism man is fated to perpetuate himself and as a conscious organism he is fated to identify evil as the threat to that perpetuation. And what then would be the highest development and use of those [man's] talents? To contribute to the struggle against evil."

However, before there can be effective struggle against evil, the following questions must be answered: 1) What are the dynamic conditions in a society or culture that would stimulate such activity as announced as devil worship? 2) What are the dynamics in a society and culture wherein increasing numbers of Black males are being killed daily/yearly at epidemic levels? 3) What are the exact causation dynamics in a society and culture wherein the greatest percentage of its resources are used in the development and production of instruments of death and destruction? 4) What are the exact dynamic conditions in a power system or culture wherein 50 million people can be destroyed in the course of slave trade, as on the continent of Africa? 5) What are the exact dynamic conditions in a power system or culture wherein six million Semites of the Jewish religion can be destroyed deliberately or 20 million people killed in the course of a war, such as in the Soviet Union during World War II? 6) What are the dynamics in a society and culture in which hundreds of thousands, possibly millions, are doomed to die of infection with a virus that increasing numbers are concluding was deliberately man-made?

These are questions that the psychiatrist should be motivated to answer in the context of understanding the issue of evil, especially when it is recalled, as stated by Thomas Mecton in his *Raids on the Unspeakable* that,

> One of the most disturbing facts that came out in the [Adolph] Eichman trial was that a psychiatrist examined him and pronounced him *perfectly sane*. We equate sanity with a sense of justice, with humaneness, with prudence, with the capacity to love and understand other people. We rely on the sane people of the world to preserve it from barbarism, madness, destruction. And now it begins to dawn on us that it is precisely that sane ones who are the most dangerous. It is the sane one, the well adapted one, who can without qualms and without nausea aim the missiles and press the buttons that will initiate

the great festival of destruction that they, the sane ones, have prepared.

Psychiatrist M. Scott Peck, in his nationwide best selling book, *People of the Lie, The Hope for Healing Human Evil*, contends, "Science has also steered clear of the problem of evil because of the immensity of the mystery involved....we do not yet have a body of scientific knowledge of human evil deserving of being called a psychology." He also states,

> Those of us who are Caucasians seem to have fewer compunctions about killing blacks or Indians or Orientals than we do in killing our fellow white men. It is easier for a white man to lynch a 'nigger' than a 'redneck'.... The matter of the racial aspects of intraspecies killing is yet another one deserving significant scientific investigation.

He concludes, "War today is at least as much a matter of national pride as of racial pride."

Even though Peck suggests that science has steered clear of the subject of evil because of the "immense mystery involved," Herman Melville, the 19th century novelist, perhaps subconsciously, went directly to the subject of evil. He approached "evil" through the symbolism of the white whale, Moby Dick, and the crippled white ship captain who pursued him, Ahab (who is often compared to Satan). Melville uses an entire chapter of his book to discourse on "The Whiteness of the Whale." He begins,

> What the White whale was to Ahab, has been hinted; what, at times, he was to me, as yet remains unsaid. Aside from those more obvious considerations touching Moby Dick, which could not but occasionally awaken in any man's soul some alarm, there was another thought, or rather vague, nameless horror concerning him, which at times by its intensity completely overpowered all the rest; and yet so mystical and well nigh ineffable was it, that I almost despair of putting it in a comprehensible form. It was the whiteness of the whale that above all things appalled me. But how can I hope to explain

myself here; and yet, in some dim, random way, explain myself I must, else all these chapters might be naught.

Melville proceeds to detail many positive associations with whiteness: "and though this pre-eminence in it [whiteness] applies to the human race itself, giving the white man ideal mastership over every dusky tribe." He continues,

> ...yet for all these accumulated associations, with whatever is sweet, and honorable, and sublime, there yet lurks an elusive something in the innermost idea of this hue, which strikes more of panic to the soul than that redness which affrights in blood.... That ghastly whiteness it is which imparts such an abhorrent mildness even more loathsome than terrific, to the dumb gloating of their aspect. So that not the fierce-fanged tiger in his heraldic coat can so stagger courage as the white-shrouded bear or shark.

Further on, Melville contemplates,

> What is it that in the Albino man so peculiarly repels and often shocks the eye, as that sometimes he is loathed by his own kith and kin! It is that whiteness which invests him, a thing expressed by the name he bears, The Albino is as well made as other men – has no substantive deformity – and yet this mere aspect of all-pervading whiteness makes him more strangely hideous than the ugliest abortion. Why should this be so?

Again referring to whiteness, Melville writes, "...it is at once the most meaning symbol of spiritual things, nay, the very veil of the Christian's deity; and yet should be as it is, the intensifying agent in things the most appalling to mankind."

Melville's Captain Ahab sees the white whale as all evil of which he is in pursuit. In a letter to Nathaniel Hawthorne, Melville referred to *Moby Dick* as a "wicked book." My own interpretation of the symbolism in this novel, which has been regarded as the greatest of all American novels, is that the crippled white Captain Ahab represents the mutant (global) white population, afflicted with albinism (whiteness). The white whale is symbolic of racism (white supremacy), the major pursuit of the global white collective – the evil destructive goal of the global white collective. This furious, evil pursuit in *Moby Dick* ends in a disaster for all: a deadly end in which the white ship captain and all of his crew, whites and non-whites alike, are destroyed. Yet, one survived to tell the tale, foretelling the end of white supremacy as a specified power dynamic.

It is not surprising that this novel containing the symbolism of albinism and white supremacy was written prior to the great bloody conflict (The American Civil War) that had so much to do with the relationships between white (albino) and Black people. This conflict ended the power of the share holders as well as the formal enslavement of Black people by whites.

Melville's linkage of evil and dread with the condition of albinism parallels my own thesis that the absence of the neuropeptide melanin – the absence of this black pigment in the skin and other aspects of the nervous system – critically impairs the depth sensitivity of the nervous system and the ability to tune in to the total spectrum of energy frequencies in the universe. This deficiency of sensory awareness sets the stage for the absence of harmony (the chaos and destruction), which is evil. Thus, the injustice and evil of white supremacy not only has its foundation in the numerical minority status of the global white population and its genetically recessive status in terms of melanin pigment production, but the very absence of melanin in the nervous system in significant degrees (decreasing sensory input and thus sensitivity) is an additional contributing factor in the problem of white supremacist injustice. White supremacy is the greatest known evil on Earth. Likewise, racism (white supremacy) is the unified force field that encompasses all of the lesser evils we now recognize. Indeed, if the absence of melanin obstructs the nervous system's ability to tune in to the total spectrum of frequencies in the universe, rendering those lacking melanin incapable of acting in harmony with those frequencies, then it becomes incumbent upon those possessing melanin to counteract the evil.

20

Black Children and the Process of Inferiorization (June 1974)

Black people, as a collective, are becoming increasingly sophisticated. We are becoming strong enough to face many unpleasant realities and truths about ourselves and the social system and world that we live in, without denial or panic. This ability to analyze ourselves, our behavior and our reality critically is one of the signs of true mental health. Another equally important aspect of mental health is our full acceptance of the responsibility for reorganizing our own behavior in order to change things that are wrong.

Black children are our most valuable possession and our greatest potential resource. Any meaningful discussion of the survival or the future of Black people must be predicated upon Black people's plan for the maximal development of all Black children. Children are the only future of any people. If the children's lives are squandered, and if the children of a people are not fully developed at whatever cost and sacrifice, the people will have consigned themselves to certain death. They will be destroyed from without or from within – by the attack of their own children against them. And they may be destroyed by both. Black people now are being attacked in the streets (from within) by our own youths, as well as being attacked (from without) by our collective oppressor. This reality reveals the central questions of this essay, which Black people must answer: 1) Will Black children in the U.S. ever develop to their maximum genetic potential? 2) If so, who will assume ultimate responsibility for bringing about that maximal development – Black people themselves or white people? 3) If Black children are not to be maximally developed, what do Black people really think is going to happen to this large Black undeveloped mass of human beings? And, 4) Are white people in any way looking to Black people for the maximal development of white children?

In trying to understand precisely what is happening to us, let us be very clear about the following: The function of the encounter between the newborn child and the various elements of the social/environmental experience, which continues throughout the life of the individual, is to shape and mold the newborn child to fit his or her predetermined *social role*. In effect, this is achieved by the total social experience acting upon the child's genetic potential. Any established social system has assigned social roles for every child born into the system, inasmuch as children are born to parents who already are occupying "their place" in the structured social system. Social roles are related most fundamentally to how much true power one will or will not have in a given social system. True power is the key factor in the determination of "identity," which is the individual's relationship to actual power. In an oppressive social system, one's identity is either that of the oppressor or that of the oppressed.

In a social system designed to achieve white domination, the experience of that system molds white children so that they may function in the role of the oppressors, or the "functional superiors" (because that is what white supremacy is supposed to mean: that whites *will* function in a superior way as compared to non-whites). Through structured superior functioning, whites will be able to oppress others. The same social system simultaneously will mold all children classified as "non-whites" or "others" to play the role of the "functional inferiors," or the oppressed. This is why a white racist social system is completely incapable of providing total equality of opportunity to Blacks. Such a system must, for its maintenance, produce differential levels of functioning for whites and non-whites. If, for example, apparent equality is granted in the area of education, it is denied in family background. If it is given in income, it is denied in housing opportunity. If it is granted in health care services, it is denied in terms of fathers' income levels. If it is granted by law (Brown, 1954), it is denied through social practice. Et cetera.

We must stress the use of the term "functional inferiority," which is in contrast to "genetic inferiority." "Functional" is used because the genetic material of non-white children actually is not impaired, but the pre-determined and established racist social experience is designed deliberately to destroy the genetic potential for social functioning. The destruction of non-white genetic material (which is the fundamental meaning of the word "genocide" – killing genes) leads to the appearance of inferiority in the non-whites.

To describe the social process by which Black genetic potential is destroyed, thus profoundly influencing the whole life experience of every Black child, the term "inferiorization" is used. *Inferiorization* is the conscious, deliberate and systematic process utilized specifically by a racist (white supremacy) social system, as conducted through all of its major and minor institutions (including the institution of the family), to mold specific peoples within that system (namely, all peoples classified by the racist system as non-white) into "functional inferiors," in spite of their true genetic potential for functioning. Under the white supremacy system, the more melanin pigmentation present in the skin and thus the darker the individual, the greater the "inferiorization" pressure imposed by the racist system. Thus, amongst all non-white peoples, Blacks are most victimized by this process. Particularly, darker Black people receive extreme victimization – even amongst Black people themselves. This skin coloration code established by the global white collective, like other methods of Black subjugation, is essential to white genetic survival. This same code causes Black people to say "Don't marry anyone darker than yourself," preferring light-skinned persons as mates. Such socially imposed patterns of thinking yield the Black infant its first direct experience with rejection and negation by the racist social system he or she is born into; this negation will continue for the entire life span.

Simply, inferiorization means that through the structuring of thought patterns and social experiences such as poor housing, poor health care, deteriorating school systems, broken families and low income levels, a

Black or other non-white child – who could be a genius based upon genetic endowment – can be turned into a criminal who must spend his productive years locked behind the bars of a prison cell. Inferiorization deliberately turns a Black child, who could become a brilliant, universal statesman, a strong supporting father and a loving, caring protector for his wife, into a drug addict. It turns a Black female child, who could become a physician, scientist and excellent mother, into a prostitute. It turns Black parents, who could be mature, supporting, loving and kind to their offspring, into immature child-batterers and sexual abusers of their own children. It turns some Black teachers, who could love and educate Black children, into teachers who hate and cannot educate. It structures the total social experience of Black young people so that they believe it is "cool" and more important to smoke marijuana, use foul language and learn to dance than to learn to read and become expert mathematicians. It turns Black people into "clowns," rather than into true nation-builders. It shapes many Blacks, who could give maximum service to Black people, into persons whose major concern is the accumulation of money and material possessions. It makes men care more about wearing "Superfly" clothes than about learning to be excellent fathers and guides to their offspring, especially their sons. It makes Black people see themselves as sex machines rather than builders of a higher humanity.

This social process of destructive distortion is achieved through the imposition, from birth to death, of a stressful, negative and non-supportive social/environmental experience upon the people who are to be inferiorized. The negative and stressful social experience, which is structured to affect every aspect of life activity, leads to the development of a negative self-concept, a loss of self-respect and the development of self- and group-destructive behavioral patterns. Some of these negative behavioral patterns rampant among Black people today include showing off material possessions, gossiping about one-another, name-calling, cursing, squabbling, snitching and being discourteous and disrespectful to one another. When these behaviors are directed toward people who are a reflection of self (i.e., Black people towards other Black people), they indicate self-dislike and self-dissatisfaction. The high rates of Black male homicide and suicide are extreme, but all-too-common examples of this phenomenon. Black people using drugs and selling them to one another is another example of the same homicide and suicide pattern.

All of these patterns of self- and group-negating behavior, in addition to many others, become the invisible chains and shackles around the necks and ankles of the Black oppressed, holding all of us in a continuously destructive enslavement. With full justification, we can call all of these behaviors mental illness since they imply self- and group-destruction. These behaviors prevent group unity and efficient group effort. When parents, teachers and other adults practice these behaviors towards one another, they teach children how to practice them also. Black children learn that Black people do not respect each other, which also means Black people do not and should not respect themselves. The children, in turn, will teach those of following generations how to disrespect themselves and each other – thus, how to remain oppressed.

Inferiorization is essential to the process of oppression. It ensures that the oppressors need not be troubled to hold the oppressed constantly under gun and key to keep them in the oppressed state; it keeps the oppressed from effectively challenging the oppressive process and system. In this way, the oppressors mold the oppressed to share fully in the process of their own oppression. In the final analysis, the process of inferiorization is designed specifically to prevent the maximal development of the genetic potential of the non-white oppressed. Black people must learn that no system of oppression ever maximally develops those whom the system is specifically structured to dominate. Such a system only permits the oppressed to survive so that they can continue being oppressed. No system of oppression is structured consciously to destroy itself. The maximal development of all Black people would prove false the ideology of white superiority. Thus, if Black children and Black people as a whole are ever to be developed fully, Black people themselves will have to enact that development. Sufficient data and evidence are in: after 127 years of so-called emancipation, the white collective has demonstrated that it does not intend to develop Black children maximally. Still, whites are talking about Black children and Black people as being genetically inferior to themselves, and they are developing extensive social policies based solely upon such a pattern of reasoning and logic.

Instead of developing behavior patterns for further useless protest, Black people should be cultivating patterns of self-help for self-development. Since the Black family setting is the first social institution under the racist system in which the Black child begins to experience inferiorization, it is of key importance that all Black people begin to understand 1) the true function of family life, 2) how some of the most important aspects of inferiorization can occur there and 3) that the Black family is the one social institution over which we as Black people can begin to exercise some control. Control of the Black family will be evident once we gain some mastery over our individual lives. We will learn that dysfunctional behaviors can be changed through the exercise of willpower. Thus, within the family setting, Black people can begin to alter the inferiorization dynamic and create a process for the maximal development of Black children.

The functional family unit is composed of the father, mother and offspring. The ultimate role of this vital social unit is to instruct the children as to how adult males and females function, usually and harmoniously together for the maximal development of a people. Individual family units are but cellular units of a whole organism called a people or a nation. All of the units must function efficiently and effectively if the whole organism is to live a healthy existence. If a family unit cannot instruct the young in harmonious patterns of relating between adult males and females, then ultimately the people will perish because adult male and female alienation eventually leads to the end of the procreative process. Without the young, the people will have no future.

The process of instructing the young in harmonious, mutually respectful patterns of relating as well as in appropriate and constructive patterns of functioning is called *socialization* – the molding of their behavior for maximal development and functioning in a given environmental setting. The father's major task in relationship to the children is to teach adult male role-functioning through daily example, with love and kindness expressed towards the children – love and kindness being essential to efficient learning. The adult male's major responsibility is "breadwinning" and protection of the family unit and the total people. The mother's major task in relationship to the children is to teach adult female role-functioning through daily example, love and kindness. The adult female's major responsibility is child socialization and care of the home. These divisions of labor are fundamental and necessary for efficient and effective family functioning under hostile social/environmental conditions, and racism is a hostile and aggressive social environment.

Today there is much yelling and screaming about such role-functioning priorities, mostly by white women. However, we as Black people cannot allow whites to continue to set our priorities. If we ignore these necessities as Blacks, we will do so at our peril. And it serves well to remember that the intellectual performance of white children is directly proportional to the time their mothers have spent with them in socialization during the first five years of life, while white fathers play the role of primary family "breadwinners" and family and group protectors. White power has been predicated upon white male aggression and "breadwinning" activity, while white females take care of fundamental home and family-life responsibilities.

Nature has endowed men with the greater muscle mass, which makes males more efficient and effective aggressors and protectors of people, just as females are more effective and efficient at giving birth and nursing the young. In the framework of any hostile and aggressive external environment, such as oppression, the most important family unit member is the one to whom nature has given the greatest muscle mass to ward off external physical attack, should that ever be necessary. The racist social system has understood that the most potent method for oppressing and inferiorizing a people is to attack the family unit structure, thereby decreasing its ability to function as a fundamental unit for developing and socializing the young. If there is deficient socialization, the behavior of the young will be chaotic and disorganized with dependent, weak and immature personality structure. This can be accomplished best through attacking and weakening the family unit's primary support and ultimate defense – the adult male. Females can be controlled by male oppressors once the males of the oppressed group are weakened and/or destroyed. This is true no matter how many college degrees the females may have; no matter how tough, loud or coarse their language may become; no matter how "strong" they may appear. In the final analysis, females must depend on the physical strength, discipline and willpower of their men for ultimate protection. Thus, always the males represent the major potential threat and challenge to male oppressors.

The system of racism in the U.S. specifically has labeled its number one target of attack as the Black male. The Black male is not only to be intimidated and oftentimes physically destroyed, but more importantly, he must be destroyed functionally through the negation of his major breadwinning activity for the Black family. When men are not permitted to become the major breadwinners and true functional protectors for their families, a major imbalance is created between the importance of the adult Black male and adult Black female roles. Likewise, the importance of male functioning is discredited and thus subtly disrespected. As a result, chaos and disorganization befalls family-life, leaving the family as a dysfunctional "survival-unit," where mothers are forced to engage in full-time breadwinning and protector activities and are not free to perform their major tasks of child-care and socialization.

The subsequent imbalance produced between the money power and the pseudo-social (and family) power of the Black female, when compared to the Black male, eventually leads to alienation between the two of them. This alienation, followed by separation and/or divorce, causes the imbalance that leads to the now epidemic Black social-pathologic syndrome: the so-called strong Black female and weak Black male. The fundamental cause of the syndrome is the white supremacy power system. Also, this system leads to the "Black male womanizing syndrome," wherein Black males seek to compensate for a lost sense of manhood by attempting to prove they are still men via the number of women they can seduce and conquer. But this syndrome only heightens the alienation between the Black male and female, and it fails to convince the male of his manhood.

Increasingly, Black females are being left alone to rear the children. They, along with the myth of the so-called "strong Black female," are crumbling under this impossible burden. Nonetheless, the survival-units become dominated by adult female presence and all of the children are feminized, males and females alike. Even when there is no physical separation or divorce (because the racist social system never attacks the Black female with the same ferocity as it does the Black male), a relative Black male passivity is produced, leaving an overall tone of greater female power than male power amongst Black people.

This analysis should not be viewed as a condemnation of the Black male or the Black female. It is only a description of the intent of the oppressive system of racism. Most profoundly affected are Black children who grow up in this system, especially Black male children. Black male children systematically are deprived of stong male models through whom they can develop pride, useful self- and group-supporting behavioral patterns, and true respect for the Black adult male position. Large numbers of young Black male children can tell you that it is far easier and more rewarding to be a Black female than a Black male. (See Chapter 6.)

The racist social system can survive only if Black manhood is destroyed. It steadily has removed strong Black male images, such as those presented by Malcolm X and Martin Luther King, Jr. Initially, it replaced those powerful, progressive and constructive images with the powerful television and movie images of "Geraldine" and "Superfly." The racist media then followed with the message to Blacks that it is "*good times*" to see a pathetic Black adult male who never can seem to find a decent paying job and a teenage Black male son who is a clown and a criminal shoplifter who never studies, but who now has an intense interest in academic subjects. Innumerable like-examples followed. These weak Black male media images persist into the present. We return to the "pitiful times" of real life to face the fact that the average college-trained Black female has a salary scale only $300 lower than her white college-trained counterpart, whereas the Black male college graduate earns $3,000 less than the white male *high school* graduate.

All of these factors are responsible for the now epidemic proportions of Black male passivity, effeminacy, transvestism, bisexuality and homosexuality (see Chapter 6), the root cause of which is the racist system's necessity to stamp out Black manhood through distorting the dynamics of Black family life. Black people should not view these patterns of behavior as isolated criminal or immoral acts. They must be recognized as the by-product of social/political warfare against the maximal development of Black people as a whole.

Black people can begin to halt the process of Black inferiorization if the now dysfunctional female-dominated survival-units can be turned into true family units. A balance must be established between the adult male role of breadwinning and the female role of child socialization, with equal respect maintained for both roles. This cannot be accomplished by males attempting to force females to walk seven paces behind. Neither can it be achieved by males forcing females into silent submission. It can be achieved by Black males refusing to remain content with less than adequate breadwinning roles. Thus, all Black males will have to refuse being passive, dependent and female-supported to any degree. They will have to demand from the oppressor, and will to achieve, the right to be equal breadwinners with white males before white or Black females are given equal breadwinner roles with white males. There must begin a Black men's liberation movement for salary and job opportunities equal in all respects with that of white males. As a collective, Black males must realize that they have been fooled into believing that white females are their most loving allies. While white females are luring Black men into bed and to the altar, the white female collective is depriving Black men (through the white female's liberation movement) of their opportunity to function fully as breadwinners and not just as "sex-machines."

Black females must begin to struggle to achieve the opportunities enjoyed by white females – to stay home while being adequately supported by their husbands, to provide adequate socialization and needed care and attention to the children. Black females must not be fooled into believing that a women's liberation movement is their salvation. They must cease believing in the myth of the "strong Black female" who is capable of doing everything (breadwinning and socializing) all alone. Black females must understand that we always will be oppressed, as will our sons and daughters, unless Black men are liberated to defend themselves, Black females and Black children from any and all attacks and insults.

When these fundamental issues are placed in perspective, when Black men and women are struggling together for these objectives that have everything to do with the development of Black family-life, Black male children will be able to grow up respecting themselves as future men. Thus, they will recognize the purpose of disciplined study to achieve academically, and they will cease desiring to be females. Black female children will grow up respecting themselves as future women supported, protected and respected by their own men, and they will learn to respect Black men as men. Focusing on these external common objectives, Black men and women will be freed from the present destructive competition with one another and will, instead, learn to work as a team in order to compete successfully with their common oppressors for the maximal development of themselves and their children.

But, Black people must not only commit themselves to combating inferiorization through the struggle for maximal development, we must, as a part of that struggle, begin to establish standards of academic achievement and codes of behavioral conduct for Black children. These standards and codes will serve as the fundamental basis for developing Black self- and group-respect. Without true self-respect, all efforts for achievement will be in vain. In keeping with that goal, all Black children, before the age of six, should be taught the following fundamental exercises in Black self-respect by Black adult examples in the home, school, church and neighborhood:

1. Stop name-calling one another.
2. Stop cursing at one another.
3. Stop squabbling with one another.
4. Stop gossiping about one another.
5. Stop snitching on one another.

6. Stop being discourteous and disrespectful towards one another.
7. Stop robbing one another.
8. Stop stealing from one another.
9. Stop fighting one another.
10. Stop killing one another.
11. Stop using and selling drugs to one another.
12. Stop throwing trash and dirt on the streets and in places where Black people live, work and learn.

With this behavioral foundation in self-respect, Black children would be taught that academic achievement is the highest priority. Each neighborhood should give annual awards for the children in each age group, based upon public performance in reading and math achievement. This would indicate to Black children that knowledge and information are the important bases of power, along with self-respect.

Additionally, by age six, Black children must learn that Black people, as a nation, do not look highly upon young people fathering and mothering Black children before they achieve emotional maturity and are capable of completely caring for the new Black life. Making a baby should no longer remain the criteria of Black manhood or womanhood. Black manhood and womanhood should be determined solely on the basis of one's ability to be self-supporting and to function effectively under the pressures of white supremacy.

These objectives are only a beginning, but they can be achieved if every Black adult views himself/herself as one of the many parents of all Black children. These parents must assume responsibility for the maximal development of each and every Black child. That responsibility can be expressed in as simple a manner as never displaying to any Black child any form of self- or group-negating behavior. In effect, this practice will teach the child the most important lesson of all: that Black people respect themselves.

21

Racism and Black Child and Youth Inferiorization (July 1987)

As we approach the 21st century, it is essential that Black physicians – scientists, researchers, clinicians, pediatricians and child psychiatrists – understand exactly what is happening to the behavioral, emotional and physical health of Black people, specifically of Black infants, children and youth. We must know precisely where we are going and what we must do. Now, more than ever before, we need to apply a systematic understanding to our work in helping to solve the multitude of health problems (physical, emotional and behavioral) impacting Black infants, children, youth, parents and, thereby, families. By developing such a systematic approach in our perception of the seemingly myriad problems, it is possible to focus more effectively on what must be done to move towards problem solution, what must be done by ourselves as members of the healing profession, and what must be done by Black people to establish a level of health and total functioning (for the Black collective) that is second to none on this planet.

It is now 1987. It is impossible to pick up a newspaper in the United States without seeing one or more articles and references addressing the ever-worsening plight of Black people across the entire age spectrum. There are seemingly non-reducible levels of infant mortality and morbidity. There are Black infants being born with AIDS to parents who are drug-addicted and who have AIDS. There are massive numbers of Black infants being born to children (teenagers and pre-teens) who never will

251

be able to parent them effectively. The same infants and children will experience physical, social and psychological neglect. These children will experience physical and sexual abuse. They will experience being inadequately housed, clothed and fed. They will experience abandonment to welfare systems and foster homes. They subsequently will experience failure to achieve academically, and then fail to perform adequately on scholastic achievement tests. Because of their frustration from being stressed and inadequately cared for, they will fail to attend school. Eventually they will drop out of school. Many Black children and youth will become involved with drugs – either to medicate often unrecognized major depression, or to sell drugs to solve their own or their family's financial difficulties. Perhaps both. The drugs will be used to suspend briefly a grinding sense of hopelessness and doom. Then addiction sets in. Other Black children and youth will become obsessed with sexual activity to compensate for a profound sense of unmet dependency needs that immature and overwhelmed parents could not and cannot address. The outcome from this will be AIDS, other venereal diseases, male and female prostitution and another generation of teenage pregnancy and inadequate parenting. The destroyed sense of self, the negative self-image and self-concept that derive from these overwhelming and stressful circumstances lead these children and youth (who have been baby-sat by the television set), to conclude that it is acceptable to use drugs and to sell drugs to one another. And, in ever-increasing numbers, Black children and youth are concluding that it is perfectly alright to shoot and kill one another when drug deals go badly, or to kill one another for an expensive pair of shoes or sunglasses, designer sweat suits, leather gold chains or clothing. Both these activities lead to their certain incarceration.

By now, every thinking Black person is familiar with these all-too-common reports and their accompanying statistics. However, scientists and clinicians, as opposed to mere technicians, should not simply gather statistical data. The statistical data must be examined, understood and interpreted in depth, then placed in proper perspective. Such a process allows for the problems that are reflected in the statistical data to be solved and prevented from occurring in the future.

Generally, it is assumed that a society or social power system seeks to support the development of all of its infants, children and youth. This is a totally erroneous assumption in a social power system built upon racism for the purpose of white genetic survival. The assumption is erroneous even when the white supremacy system is highly refined and masked. Thus far, Black people have failed to decode fully the power system established to maintain white genetic survival. And, to the same extent that we have failed to understand white genetic survival or white supremacy, we have failed to control the symptoms that arise from this destructive power dynamic, which is positioned against the maximal development of Black genetic and constitutional potential.

In a social power system established for white genetic survival, children classified as non-white (black, brown, red and yellow) are inferiorized systematically so that they will become and remain dependent and susceptible to control throughout their lives. In the terminology of Erik H. Erikson, author of *Childhood and Society*, when the social environment supports the developing fetus, infant, child and youth into adult existence, the child's psycho-social development advances through the following eight stages: 1) basic trust, 2) autonomy, 3) initiative, 4) industry, 5) identity, 6) intimacy, 7) generativity, and finally, 8) integrity. However, each one of these eight stages has its counterpart in failure when society fails to support the child systematically. Instead, the social power system subjects the infant, child and youth to an overwhelming degree of stress. Instead of basic trust, there is mistrust; instead of autonomy, there is shame and doubt; instead of initiative, there is guilt (the sense of "I cannot" versus "I can"); instead of industry, there is inferiority (or lethargy); instead of identity, there is role confusion; instead of intimacy, there is isolation; instead of generativity, there is stagnation; instead of integrity, there is despair.

This process of failed psycho-social development, which is brought on by all levels of environmental stress that occur under white supremacy domination and impact Black people most heavily, forces massive numbers of Black infants, children and youth into the destructive chain of events that I have referred to as the process of inferiorization: mistrust, shame and doubt, guilt, inferiority, role confusion, isolation, stagnation and, finally, despair. Thus, while large numbers of white infants, children and youth receiving societal and environmental support progress through the eight stages of psycho-social development, their Black counterparts, the recipients of high level environmental stress, progress through the stages of failed psycho-social development, or inferiorization. It is within this schema that the deteriorating picture of Black life (from infancy to adult age) must be understood. This is not the accidental development of an underclass. This is planned inferiorization for the purpose of white genetic survival. Most important, clinicians caring for Black infants, children, youth and their families must understand that this destructive dynamic is historically and solidly situated, and it is on-going.

However, it is not possible to comprehend the process of inferiorization of Black youth and the seriously compromised functioning of the Black adult without a specific understanding of racism as the struggle for genetic survival on the part of the genetically recessive global white minority population that currently controls power in the world. Because few Blacks or other non-whites understand racism at this level, they fail to understand white supremacy as actual systematic warfare being conducted by people who classify themselves as "white," against people whom whites classify as "non-whites."

Few Blacks or other non-white people are aware that white people are conducting major discussions on the white birthrate. Few Blacks or other non-white people are aware that white scholars and experts are discussing the projection that by the year 2073, whites will represent fewer than 3% of the people on the planet. Few Blacks or other non-white people are aware that white experts are projecting that within six to nine generations, non-white people will represent the majority of people in U.S. Few Blacks or other non-white people are aware that these white experts are concluding that they will be left in a state of peril if these facts are ignored.

The war for white genetic survival is conducted simultaneously on nine battle fronts: economics, education, entertainment, labor, law, politics, religion, sex and (military) war. The war is conducted through all forms of behavior. In addition, within each of these areas of activity there have evolved myriad institutions, all of which further the goal of white supremacy.

Because Blacks and other non-white people have failed to understand racism as white genetic survival, they erroneously have believed that they could be integrated into the white supremacy system and that they could depend upon whites to maximally develop Black infants, children and youth in the same manner that white people promote the maximal development of white infants, children and youth. Blacks and other non-whites have failed to understand that if white people were to do this, it would mean active white participation in white genocide. Black people must master this perception of racism (local and global) as a war for white genetic survival, a system into which non-white people never can be integrated.

Under the stress of white supremacy, numerous offspring prevent the possibility of adequately meeting the needs of each individual child, as each child crowds out the opportunity for emotional nurture of the others. This crowding prevents high level psycho-social development from taking place. This promotion and insurance of failed psycho-social development is the process of inferiorization, which in turn promotes and ensures local and global white genetic survival.

What then is to be done? What short- and long-range strategies and tactics do Blacks need to employ in order to neutralize the ongoing white supremacy thrust for white genetic survival, which is achieved through Black infant, child and youth inferiorization? As an initial response to this important question, all Black people must abandon the illusion of integration and face the difficult reality that most Black people prefer to ignore: you do not win a chess game if you have no knowledge of the exact objective and rules of the game. It is imperative that all Black people understand they are not in a benign environment of benevolence and support, and that the surrounding highly structured environment is deadly; a very specific warfare is being waged against Blacks and other people classified as non-white in this social system. Further, all must understand that the specific war is racism for the purpose of white genetic survival – by any and all necessary means, inclusive of chemical and biological warfare. (Chemical warfare is designer drugs, such as crack and PCP. Biological warfare entails the production of cultural and ethnic organisms in viruses such as AIDS.)

Additionally, Black people must recognize the following points:

1) The war of white genetic survival achieves a major effect through inferiorization or failed psycho-social development, creating dependency, negative self-image, negative self-concept and vulnerability.

2) The war of white genetic survival attacks the functioning of Blacks in general, but most specifically attacks the Black male, as it is the Black male who most specifically threatens white genetic survival at a level the Black female is unable to approach.

3) Blacks must learn to counter the thrust of white supremacy and Black inferiorization effectively.

4) Blacks must discuss openly those means by which Black male infants, children and youth can be supported and developed maximally in order to counter the attack of white supremacy on Black male development and functioning.

5) Black male infants, children and youth need their fathers constantly present to support the behavior and identity of Black male children. And, because of the historic removal of Black fathers from homes, classes are needed to promote high-level functioning of Black males in their roles as fathers.

6) The white supremacy attack upon the Black male causes a collapse of Black family life and a distortion in the role of the Black female. This, in turn, causes a distortion and collapse of the support system for Black infants, children and youth, thereby beginning the process of inferiorization.

7) Blacks must think about and openly discuss, not how to beg white people to stop racism (because white people will have to continue their efforts for white genetic survival), but instead, how Black people can organize their own behavior on an ongoing basis, specifically to neutralize white supremacy and its impact on the development of Black offspring.

8) It is futile to beg white people to give grants and funds to foster the maximal development of Black people. To do so is to ask white people to commit white genocide.

9) Blacks must be able to discuss openly the logical necessity for Black inferiorization in whites' struggle for white genetic survival.

10) The singing of "We Shall Overcome" will not combat white supremacy or Black inferiorization any more than singing any song will help to solve a problem in medicine or physics.

11) Immature and overwhelmed fathers and mothers cannot promote psycho-social development and counter Black inferiorization in the next generation.

12) Single female teenagers cannot promote psycho-social development in male or female offspring. And, most certainly, they cannot develop male offspring. They only can prepare these male offspring to spend their lives in penal institutions, while preparing their own daughters to become teenage mothers.

13) No Black female should become a mother before 30 years of age. No Black male should become a father before 35 years of age. Each Black family should have no more than two children, no closer together than three years apart. And, both Black males and females should, at a minimum, complete high school and become fully self-sufficient before marriage and parenthood. These structures are specifically for the pur-

pose of countering the thrust of Black inferiorization and failed psycho-social development, under the conditions of white supremacy.

14) Maximal development of the collective Black genetic and constitutional potential will take place by the efforts of Black people alone – through their knowledge, understanding and behavior.

It is my hope that eventually every Black person in the healing profession will master an understanding of the etiologic chain that leads to Black inferiorization. Furthermore, it clearly would be to the benefit of Black people if Black professionals, in their efforts of healing, pass on this knowledge to their Black patients – enabling the patients to neutralize the impact of white supremacy on their lives and achieve a development of their Black genetic and constitutional potential, second to none.

22

Black Child-Parents:
The New Factor in Black Genocide

The levels of collective self-consciousness and self-respect that a people carry can be determined accurately by the standard of care and development it demands for *all* of its young – the future of the people. It is virtually impossible, in the final quarter of the 20th century, for 99.9% of Black teenage male and female persons to raise children who will be emotionally strong, stable and capable of functioning effectively under the *stress* of a racist society. The very dynamic that produces the pathological situation wherein children attempt to have and rear children is designed to ensure Black functional inferiority. Yet, 25% of all Black children born today in the U.S. are born to Black teenagers. This means that, at the very least, 25% of all Black children will suffer in terms of their development and will be impaired in their potential to function effectively under the stress of racism. I refer to the failure to ensure the maximal development of the genetic potential of all Black children, as well as the ultimate waste of this genetic potential, as *Black genocide.*

During the American slave era, Black teenage females were forced to breed baby after baby and were prevented from actively caring for the development of these slave babies. There was no concern for these human beings reaching maximal levels of their genetic potential. This lack of concern for the development of these young human beings was enforced by racist slavemasters and slavemistresses. Today, just as in the slave society, Black teenage girls are caught up in a similar destructive dynamic: producing human beings who subsequently are subjected to low-level development and treated in inhuman ways.

The more complex a social system becomes, the higher the level of emotional maturity and formal education needed to negotiate that system successfully. Often, the ultimate level of functioning reached by children is correlated with the level of emotional maturity achieved by the parent(s) prior to the birth of the child. In brief, emotionally immature and poorly educated parents raise children who are more likely to fail than children of emotionally mature and well-educated parents. Although income is an important factor, it is a less important factor than emotional maturity in successfully rearing a child – particularly a non-white child living under the conditions of white supremacy.

The following comments have been made to me by Black teenagers who either already have become parents or are contemplating becoming parents:

1) "Dr. Welsing, I'm sixteen, I know I'm grown."

2) "Dr. Welsing, I'm gonna have my baby. Nobody's gonna take my baby from me. I'm not going to let those doctors kill my baby. I'm not gonna have no abortion."

3) "Dr. Welsing, all of my friends have babies; I want something of my own too. I'm not going to have an abortion. I'm going to love *my* baby."

4) "Dr. Welsing, my baby's gonna love me. I want somebody to love me. My mother and father don't love me. Nobody loves me. My parents act like teenagers, they don't know what they are doing."

5) "Dr. Welsing, I know I can take care of a baby!"

6) "No, Dr. Welsing, my boyfriend doesn't have any job, but he's gonna take care of me and my baby. He says he can. He's 17. He's gonna get us an apartment. No, we didn't finish school; we don't go to school anymore. I mean we go, but we don't go to no classes."

7) "Dr. Welsing, if I had it to do over again, I wouldn't have no baby when I'm young. I just didn't know no better."

8) "Dr. Welsing, my boyfriend, he's gone. I thought he wanted the baby too."

9) "Dr. Welsing, I'm19 . My boyfriend, he's 19. He gets mad at my baby – it's *our* baby – when he cries. He hit the baby one time. Sometimes I feel like hitting the baby, too."

10) "Dr. Welsing, I just didn't know how to be no father. I never had my own father at home."

11) "Dr. Welsing, my girlfriend can take care of that baby by herself with the welfare."

12) "Dr. Welsing, my mother had me when she was fifteen. I don't see why she's telling me I don't want my baby. I don't see why I can't do what she did."

All of the above statements have been made by teenage *children*. These are not unusual statements. Teachers, social workers, doctors and counselors working with young people have heard similar comments as they talk to Black teenagers in the U.S., where the incidence of Black children parenting children has reached epidemic proportions.

Elaborate programs are being established to counsel teenage parents (especially teenage mothers); special education and prenatal, obstetric and gynecological programs are being established to assist the child-mothers; classes on nutrition are being organized; courses on sex, anatomy and physiology are given. And, while all this is happening, no one is raising the most critical question: "Can Black *children* (teenagers) be *effective* mothers and fathers to persons who must function in a highly complex, technological society that is extremely racist and oppressive to Black and other non-white peoples?" Another critical question that has not been answered is: "Why are so many teenage children engaging in this high degree of sexual activity and producing children for whom they are unable to provide sufficient care?" Is there an underlying social dynamic that is forcing on children this pattern of destructive behavior that borders on homicide – most certainly, emotional and psychological homicide? If so, what is it? What are the implications for future generations if this pattern of behavior continues? Are we prepared to reap the whirlwind?

In my clinical view, having functioned as a psychiatrist for adults and children for the past decade, I have found that there is an absolute difference between simply having a child (being able to give birth as a female and being able to initiate the reproductive process as a male) and possessing the developed concrete ability to socialize a new human being for high-level functioning in a complex social system. Based upon my experience in the private practice of adult and child psychiatry, as a psychiatrist in public mental health centers and as a psychiatric consultant in the system of welfare services to families and children in a large metropolitan area, I believe it is impossible in the late 20th century for a Black teenager to be an adequate parent (*mother* or *father*). Further, if Black people are ever to evolutionize their situation from oppression to justice and liberation, they will have to shift their present patterns of behavior radically such that marriage will not be considered before the age of 30. In keeping with this approach, *childbearing* should not be considered before the age of 32 to 35. This will provide both parents sufficient opportunity to maximize levels of emotional maturity and to work to overcome deficits experienced in emotional development during their own early years.

There is an African proverb that states, "The hand that rocks the cradle rules the nation." I will paraphrase it: "The level of *emotional maturity* in the hand that rocks the cradle determines the fate of the nation." A people on their sojourn through time (history) are somewhat like a ship on the ocean. If many people aboard the ship have extensive knowledge of the sea and navigation, that ship will have an excellent chance of reaching the desired destination. On the other hand, when the people aboard a ship lack knowledge of the sea and navigation, more than likely the ship – should the sea become at all rough – will flounder into destruction.

Black people in the U.S. are in a parallel condition. The critical decisions that Black people make now about Black children becoming the parents of other Black children will determine whether the ship reaches its destination intact or flounders off course and sinks, bringing almost certain death to all. If present conditions persist, history will record that Black people living in the U.S. failed to survive the 20th century A.D. This failure will occur, not simply because they were a captured and oppressed people, but because they permitted themselves to become a blind people without any social vision or understanding. History may record that Black elders, fathers and mothers had no vision, and therefore the Black children became stupid, thinking that they could nurture something as precious as the life of a new human being. As a result of all this, Black people perished.

In the Old Testament of the Bible, the prophet Isaiah says, "Where there is no vision, the people will perish." *Vision* means the ability to understand the present in its totality and to organize one's behavior in the present to meet successfully the challenge of circumstance, present and future. A people that does not understand, and thus fails to teach each generation that potential mothers and fathers *must be able* to carry out certain *basic* functions (going far beyond mere material provisions) in relationships with their children is a people without vision. A people amongst whom just anyone produces a child, at anytime, without any serious thought or consideration, without any group recognized standard for parenthood, is a people on the brink of disaster. Black people in the U.S. are at such a crisis point.

Many Black people's understanding of the roles of mother and father is limited to the view of mothers as females who simply give birth to children and fathers as males who simply impregnate women. The act of creating new life is taken so lightly that school children sing and joke about it, being provided such songs by their elders. Record companies make millions of dollars playing cheap songs about what fun it is to bring a child into the world, when this should be the most highly respected exchange between a man and a woman.

Yet, for us as a people, the definition of a parent is becoming limited to a person who has participated in producing an offspring, even though many of these persons are unprepared to participate fully in the development of those offspring. In effect, no real progress has been made from the time when *we* formally were considered as *breeders* of human beings who were viewed as having no true human worth, merely things to be used and misused. Thus a Black mother can be a 10-, 12- or 16-year-old female. A Black father can then be a 13-, 14- or 15-year-old male.

The following statistics are reflective of the extent to which these limited definitions are operative amongst large numbers of Blacks. Teenage mothers account for about half of the out-of-wedlock children born to both Blacks and whites in 1976. Approximately 25% of all Black children are being born to teenage mothers. Virtually all unwed teenage mothers (93%) keep their babies. Twenty-five percent of teenage mothers get pregnant again within a year after their first baby and 15% within the second year. This tendency of repetition condemns many girls to a life of poverty, poor education and welfare. In all too many cases, teenage mothers do not finish high school, and they find it more difficult to get jobs. Their children also are condemned to lives of poverty and stress.

Teenage motherhood presents many serious complications. Large numbers of these teenage mothers are poor and ignorant of medical needs. They do not receive adequate prenatal medical care or nutrition. Those girls in their early teens who become mothers are not physically fully developed and, therefore, they are less able to bear the physical strains of having a baby. According to recent figures from the Department of Health, Education and Welfare, teenage mothers have higher death rates, more anemia, more toxemia, more hemorrhage and lower-weight babies than women in their twenties. Also, the babies of teenage mothers are more likely to be born with birth defects than those of women in their twenties. The above statistics must be viewed in the context of what is happening to Black children irrespective of the age of their mothers. For example, more than half of the Black children born in the U.S. during 1976 were born to unmarried women, according to a new report by the National Center for Health Statistics. Just 13 years ago, 26% of all Black children were born to unmarried women. Today, 40% of all Black children live in families headed by women, compared to about 12% for white children. Six years ago, the figure for Blacks was 30%. Female-headed households now have become the new poverty group in the U.S. Almost 33% of all Black children now receive benefits from Aid to Families with Dependent Children.

Another indicator of the magnitude of the problem facing Black people is reflected in the facts that follow. The District of Columbia has a higher percentage of Black citizens than any other major political unit in America today. It has a Black mayor and a city council that is predominantly Black. It has the highest percentage of educated Black people of any city in the world; it has a university that is referred to by some as "the capstone of Black education," and it has the *major* Black medical center and Black college of medicine in the world; it has all of the highest level elected Black officials in all of the U.S. working every day. Yet, this same city has the highest rate of infant mortality of any state in the country. Even the state of Mississippi has a lower rate of infant mortality. Further, there is a wide disparity in Washington, D.C. between Black and white infant mortality: 27.7 Black babies die for every 1,000 born, while there are only 7.5 white infant deaths per 1,000 births. This high number of infant deaths is not caused by teenage pregnancies alone. However, they do contribute.

The point of this discussion about teenage parenthood is not to imply that teenage people engaging in sexual activity are dirty or immoral or that sex is dirty or immoral. This discussion is concerned with questioning whether Black children are capable of fully understanding and carrying forth effective parenthood. Particularly, are Black children prepared to function *together as mothers and fathers* under the conditions of racism, which is exceedingly complex and creates high-level stress for non-white people?

Greater insight into this question is provided by the following conclusions: 1) Examining numerous case histories of current Black teenage parents, I have noted one major common denominator – a great percentage of the *mothers* of the current teenage mothers were themselves teenagers when their *first* children were born, just as their own mothers were teenagers when they were born. In other words, the prior generations consisted of child-parents. Many believe that parenthood, when it occurs in childhood, causes the child-mother to achieve emotional maturity rapidly. 2) In actuality, the child-mother's emotional development *stops* progressing when she becomes responsible for another life. It may not resume until the child-mother is relieved of *all responsibility* for parenting and can continue her own maturation with the guidance and support of *mature* adults outside of the family circle. If this burden is not removed, there even may be emotional regression due to the overwhelming sense of frustration brought on by the responsibility and stress for which the child-parent is unprepared. The child-parent may begin to act more immature than she did prior to the delivery. Any level of responsibility towards the newborn then becomes too great for the child-parent to handle. Some child-parents show a very short period of seeming responsibility towards the newborn child, only to collapse after 6 to 12 months of "imposed" responsibility. Many of these child-mothers begin to develop resentment, anger and hatred towards their children. The children are aware of these negative feelings, although they are unable to articulate their experiences of emotional rejection and deprivation.

The impact of this rejection and deprivation soon is displayed in the children's disturbed behavioral patterns, particularly in the school setting, where attention and behavioral controls are required. Eating problems, extreme temper tantrums, stubbornness, excessive activity and excessive crying may manifest before these children reach the age of school attendance. This vicious cycle begins when the mothers, due to their own lack of emotional maturity, fail to meet the dependency and emotional demands of their newborn children. In 10 to 14 years, the new emotionally starved children begin to act out sexually, attempting to have these long-standing dependency needs met via sexual intercourse. If it is a female child, very shortly thereafter she becomes pregnant. She blindly believes she needs and wants a baby to satisfy her needs. As a result, another generation of emotional starvation is set in motion. Another generation is prevented from achieving emotional growth and maturity. Often, the emotionally starved male child turns to drugs, frequently heroin. The penis in the vagina for the female *child* and the heroin needle in the vein of the male *child* are both symbolic substitutes for the desired breast or bottle in the mouth that failed to take place sufficiently in early infancy and childhood. When these methods fail, often the young person turns to alcohol. Sometimes alcohol is used from the beginning. All of these symbolic substitutes for the mother's care are destructive.

Beyond these activities, the child who eventually is abandoned by the child-mother becomes convinced that he/she is worthless and not worthy of deep "mother-love." The child concludes that something must have been wrong with him/her from birth for the mother to have abandoned him/her. Either the mother released the baby to the care of relatives, the welfare agency, the adoption agency or foster parents. The child is not able to understand that the mother was too emotionally immature to become a parent. The child only recognizes that 1) he/she was given away by the mother, 2) the mother could not provide him/her adequate care or 3) the mother physically abused him/her (or allowed a boyfriend to do so). The child summarizes it all as "I must not be worth anything." All the substitute care in the world by grandparents and others does not remove this wound and deep-seated doubt about the self that remains with the child for the length of his/her life, producing a severe distrust of and alienation from others. This is one of the major reasons that many persons enter psychotherapy as adults, primarily with symptoms of depression. Children must enter psychotherapy because of the same problem, but the depression is masked by disturbed patterns of behavior.

The emotional and psychological underdevelopment of an entire people can become chronic and permanent once this dynamic effects a sufficient percentage of the population. As I have previously stated, 25% of Black children being born in the U.S. are a part of this cycle of emotional underdevelopment – the basis for functional inferiority. Blacks would be horrified if anyone suggested the outright slaughtering of 25% of Black children. Again, Blacks scream genocide when outspoken white supremacists suggest sterilization of 25% or more of the Black population. Yet, the aforementioned pattern of child-parenting, presently widespread in the Black population, achieves exactly the same results. The only difference is that with Black child-parents, the Black child's death is more painful and drawn out – a living death. It is a living death in this highly complex society to be left unable to sit still in school and achieve academically because of incorrect socialization. It is a living death for a child to be shifted repeatedly from one foster home to another. It is a living death for a child to walk the streets addicted to drugs or alcohol. It is a living death to be a school drop-out. It is a living death to walk the streets as a prostitute. It is a living death to sneak around the street as a thief. It is a living death to suffer the depression of unemployment because you are uneducated and unskilled. It is a living death for a child to be attacked by teachers and others for being "bad," meaning his/her behavior is unsocialized. It is a living death for a child to be confined to a psychiatric hospital. It is a living death to spend a lifetime locked up behind the bars of a juvenile detention center or a prison cell. Depression that results from not having had sufficient, patient and confident mothering is also a living death. Many of these syndromes of living death lead to forms of actual death such as suicide, drug overdose and homicide. More often than not, these deaths are the direct result of children parenting children.

All of the above are related directly and indirectly to the dynamic of white supremacy, which necessitates Black functional inferiority. However, many of the above patterns of living death can be controlled, countered and combated effectively only if the Black community – the entire Black collective – is *determined* to re-program its individual and collective knowledge, understanding and behavior toward the *total elimination* of Black child-parents. This re-thinking will increase the educational and emotional maturity levels of *all* Black parents maximally, first by elevating the acceptable (meaning, acceptable to Black people) chronological age of Black parents for first births. In this way, Black people consciously can start to neutralize the emotional and psychological basis of Black functional inferiority that can begin as early emotional deprivation based on parental emotional immaturity. By solving the emotional and psychological basis of Black functional inferiority, we will be placing ourselves in the best possible position to solve the *socio-political* basis of Black functional inferiority – racism. By first consciously controlling the emotional and psychological basis of functional inferiority, Blacks can begin to consciously and scientifically control and determine the future of the Black collective.

All age groups in the Black population *must* understand that the most critical factor in the development of a child is the level of emotional maturity achieved by the parents *prior* to the year of birth of the *first* child. This level of emotional maturity is proven by the parents' mastery over the external conditions of racism, as expressed through patterns of behavior that are self- and group-supporting in all areas of people activity.

The levels of emotional maturity of the mother and father, coupled with their levels of functional respect for and cooperation with each other, provides the foundation upon which emotional and psychological development occurs in the child. The level of emotional maturity in the mother determines the degree of *sustained* patience with which she can relate to the infant. The level of emotional maturity achieved by the father prior to the birth of the child determines the level of emotional support he is able to give the mother so that in the first several years of life she can give high-level emotional support and attention to the child. This support will allow the mother to meet the child's dependency demands completely. Also, it is important that the father is capable of exercising patience with the child and capable of meeting the child's dependency demands.

For example, oftentimes a person 14 to 18 years of age has achieved only three or *fewer* years of emotional maturity, particularly in the Black population where there have been many child-parents in previous generations and where many single mothers must leave young children in poor care in order to go to work. In the event that the mother is emotionally immature, she will be incapable of meeting the dependency demands of the child. Similarly, if the father is emotionally immature, he will experience the child's dependency demands as an irritation and will find himself competing with the infant child for the mother/wife's attention. These two immature parents often place inordinate demands upon one another, as each is looking (unconsciously) to the other to be the idealized mother that he/she never had. These demands cannot be met, and thus these two child-persons end up with extreme frustrations and irritation towards one another. Not only were they unable to provide emotional support for one another at mature levels, but they were unable to provide a basis for the emotional and psychological growth of the new generation.

If the parents lack the emotional maturity needed to meet the dependency demands of the newborn child throughout its early years of development, when the child becomes of sufficient age to move outside of the home, he/she will search the environment for a sense of closeness and human warmth in an attempt to make up for the areas in which the parents failed or were lacking. Soon, similarly emotionally deprived male and female children will find one another. Having long ago discovered their genitals, they will begin to seek physical closeness with one another. They will do this through sex, not for the purpose of creating and caring for new human life, but because it seems to them that they have found the means for satisfying their long-standing hunger for emotional warmth, security and the desire to be close to another human being. Mother could not give this sense of prolonged closeness – either because she was too immature and impatient or too busy working. Father could not give this sense of closeness because he was too emotionally immature, impatient, tired or overwhelmed. And grandmother, also, became too tired and overwhelmed. So, unconsciously the children seek to gratify this need for warmth through sexual contact with one another. But this does not work because they are emotionally starved children who lack the emotional development, stability and maturity to remain stable, emotionally supporting partners for one another. Often the resulting pattern is that the teenage male leaves the teenage female in search of another playmate. The girl has a baby, believing that the baby will be something of her own to hold on to, to be close to. Or, she believes that the baby will make the teenage male stay – or return. When the baby fails to provide the child-mother with a sense of belonging (because babies cannot give; they can only demand) and fails to make the child-father stay or return, the unconscious search for dependency-need-gratification and human closeness begins all over again. The result is another pregnancy. The cycle continues.

These children who have become parent-children are in search of mature, patient and quiet maternal and paternal love, warmth and instruction that they have not had from adults. Much of the difficulty adults have in relating to these young persons comes from the anger they have developed towards a whole society and world of disappointing adults who failed to provide them with what they needed as dependent children. A child's need for emotional sustenance from mature adults cannot be satisfied with material purchases and provisions. It must be given directly to the child through mature and patient support and understanding. It must be given to the child consistently over a sufficiently extended period of time, such that the child gradually weans himself or herself from the need for high-level support and need-gratification.

The ability of parents to provide high-level emotional support for a child cannot be obtained from anyone's crash course designed to prepare the already pregnant teenage mother and father for their new responsibility. These highly complex tasks cannot be prepared for by course work or book-reading alone. These tasks must be learned through the child's own developmental experience over a period of years. It is a sham to allow these teenagers to believe that they can somehow learn to be long-term, effective parents when they are only emotionally immature children. Teenage children who become parents know absolutely nothing about meeting the emotional and developmental needs of a child. They are looking to have their own needs gratified, needs that never were gratified fully when they were infants and small children.

It is imperative that all Black persons in leadership positions fully understand the emotional and psychological basis for sustained achievement in individuals. Early dependency-need-gratification during the first six years of life is the essential foundation upon which all other stages of emotional and psychological development (such as self-confidence, initiative, sustained school achievement, sustained work achievement and self- and family-support) are built.

All of the well-intentioned demands for *excellence* in school achievement and performance will be for naught if this critical factor of early dependency-need-gratification is ignored in early infancy and childhood. A child whose dependency needs have not been gratified is a child who will be unable to learn, even if a school breakfast has been provided on a plastic plate. The large percentages of Black children who attend public schools in urban centers, unprepared to sit quietly and allow the teacher to begin academic instruction, are in many instances the offspring of persons who were teenage children when they attempted to begin parenting. No teacher, no matter how highly motivated, can meet the unmet dependency demands of a classroom one quarter full of children who have been parented by children. Yet, these dependency demands *must* be met if the children are to pay full attention and learn.

Further, it is the exceptional child-parent who can help a child with his/her homework patiently or encourage that child to be patient while he/she learns to read, write or do mathematics. And, it is the rare child-parent who is able to sacrifice personal desires in order to attend PTA meetings so that teachers and parents can work together in helping children to learn. The immature child-parents will find it far easier to get lost in the fantasies of television, drugs, alcohol or in the rhythmic beat of rock and roll music – the "rock" music being used, I am certain, in the attempt to make up for the mother's failure to hold, cuddle and rock the child in infancy and childhood. Child-parents, in general, are concerned with the normal interest of most *children* – simply *fun* and *games* and *parties*. Also, child-parents who have their own unmet dependency needs, often will find themselves too preoccupied with having these needs met through constant sexual activity. They are then useless for meeting the continuing needs of young children.

Blacks, as a people, must understand that Black child-parenting under the stress of racism is *group-destructive behavior*, and as such it cannot be condoned by the people; it must be controlled. Only older Black persons can parent and instruct Black children toward *success* under the stress of racism. In others words, correct behavior for Black people attempting to end their oppression under racism is to prevent, by all possible means, children from giving birth to, or parenting, children.

When the Black collective begins to understand that *power* is directly related *not to money* but to correct behavior pattern organization, behavior discipline and behavior control on the part of the individual and the collective, the Black collective will be well on its way towards a new level of political understanding (power) and maturity. These attempts to evolve correct patterns of behavior under the specific circumstance of racism become the tactics and strategies in all areas of life activity to achieve the ultimate goal of liberation and justice.

It is incumbent upon every Black person to begin to see the long- and short-range implications of all patterns of behavior in which Black individuals and the collective engage. This recognition is necessary in order to evaluate accurately whether the given pattern of conduct aids or detracts from the goal of Black liberation. If the behavior detracts from the long-range objective, it must be eliminated. If the behavior enhances the achievement of the ultimate goal, it must be reinforced among the people by their own individual willpower.

The Black collective must find ways to surround all Black children and young people with sufficient emotional support, warmth, encouragement and constructive activity. When this is done, they will not have to abuse the act of self-reproduction, and they will mature to the point that they eventually will be able to dignify the birth of every Black child and lead those children toward full development. If Black people wait for grant funds to become available for this to be achieved, all will be lost.

We should take it upon ourselves to establish a five-year plan for the total elimination of Black child-parenting, so that by the year 1984 there will be no Black child-parents in the U.S. Simultaneously, we should take it upon ourselves as a collective to decrease Black infant mortality and Black maternal illness and death drastically. We cannot say that we respect ourselves until such fundamental objectives have been achieved, as they constitute the basis for developing a future for the collective. We cannot state that we have reached maturity as a people until we are ready, willing and able to take 100% internal responsibility for achieving our articulated goal of libertaion and justice. We cannot teach the children a level of maturity and responsibility that we, as older persons, have failed to achieve.

23

The Crisis in Black Male/Black Female Relationships: Is it a False Problem? (July 1985)

Disenchantment with the institution of marriage. Disharmony. Disrespect. Separation. Divorce. Single female-headed households the norm. The absence of male models for developing Black male children and youth. Epidemic levels of teenage pregnancy. Thousands of children abandoned to foster care and adoption. Black male bisexuality and homosexuality. Black female bisexuality and homosexuality. Increasing numbers of Black females with more education and income than their Black male counterparts. Hardly any Black persons knowing five happy Black couples.

Given these dynamics as ever-present realities in the Black community, it would seem that there is a crisis of immense and serious proportions in the Black male/Black female relationship in the final decades of the 20th century. This crisis has far-reaching ramifications that touch every aspect Black life, extending into facets of the larger social order. During the past decade, this apparent problem has been seminared, dialogued, discussed, debated, probed and shouted about from every conceivable angle. Innumerable remedies have been proposed. No matter from what angle this issue is approached, the problems don't disappear. Instead, they seem to multiply, and the alienation between the Black male and the Black female just increases. If Black male/Black female alienation is not resolved, is there hope for a meaningful future for the Black race?

Case in point: Already some Blacks are discussing "the relationship between the Black male and the white female" or "the Black female and the white male." These discussions indicate that alienation has grown to the point of Black racial suicide.

In the title of this chapter, I ask if this dilemma between the Black male and the Black female is a "false" problem. Are we, perhaps, focusing on the wrong issues in the attempt to end Black male/Black female alienation? A "false" problem is one that, on the surface, appears to be valid, but upon closer scrutiny is only a symptom of the true problem. In the present discussion, this means that the discord between Black males and Black females and the failure to establish long-lasting harmonious relationships are caused by another problem. When the underlying dynamic is exposed, analyzed and understood, it is possible to remedy the symptom (false problem). Only then can short-term and long-term tactics be developed. When the underlying cause is discovered, addressed and neutralized, the false problem begins to wither away. If we are successful in finding the true cause of the alienation and neutralizing that cause, then Black male/Black female alienation will yield to true harmony.

The largest unified movement presently occurring amongst Black people is the demonstrations against "apartheid" in South Africa. Although many people use the word "apartheid" only in reference to South Africa, the fundamental meaning of apartheid is white supremacy – white rule and domination over Blacks and other non-whites. This very same dynamic (with its many variations depending upon the particular geographic location) – in its more highly refined forms – exists worldwide, wherever and whenever whites have come into contact with peoples who possess the genetic potential to produce melanin in their skin. Amongst many other horrible things, the system of white minority rule in South Africa "legally" enforces prolonged separation of the Black male and the Black female, causing fragmentation of Black family life. Similarly, under the American slavery system (a phase in the establishment of the white supremacy dynamic), Black males and Black females were forbidden by law to marry and stabilize their relationships.

To further prevent their unity, often Black males and females who became intimate were sent to different plantations by their slaveholders.

Besides the example of South Africa, the surface appearance of white rule, during the past 125 years, has been altered. However, the fundamental dynamic of white supremacy has remained untouched. Tragically, too few people wish to come to terms with an in-depth analysis of the global behavioral phenomenon of white supremacy, although the vast majority of the world's people (non-white) are victimized by it in all areas of their life activity: economics, education, entertainment, labor, law, politics*, religion, sex and war.

Failure to analyze the white supremacy dynamic deeply is a tragedy because this dynamic is the fundamental cause of the failed relationships between Black males and Black females. It prevented marriages of Black males and Black females during American slavery, and it currently separates the Black male and the Black female for 11 months out of each year in South Africa. This same white supremacy dynamic has kept Nelson and Winnie Mandela apart for over 20 years.

Because whites fear white genetic annihilation, and because only males can initiate sexual intercourse forcefully, during slavery Black males were oppressed more harshly than Black females. This pattern of greater pressure on the non-white male is historic and continues. This explains why Black males are victimized harshly by police brutality and arrest and also illuminates why they are victimized most harshly by the educational system. Because of their extreme victimization in these two areas, Black males have the highest levels of unemployment and under-employment, the highest rates of prison incarceration, the highest incidence of school failure and school drop-out rates, the highest incidence of alcoholism, the highest rates of drug use and addiction, the highest homicide rates, the most rapidly increasing suicide rate and the shortest

---

*Here the word "politics" includes all people relationships. Black male/female relationships are included under this heading as well as under the heading of sex. Other aspects of these relationships fall under any of the other headings.

life span. Also, the Black male most often finds himself outside of the Black family structure in the epidemic condition of homelessness.

This excessive and disproportionate pressure on the Black male by the global white supremacy system produces a grave imbalance between the Black male and the Black female, even though both are victimized by white supremacy. This imbalance has produced what some incorrectly call "the Black matriarchy." However, this is not Black matriarchy, but white genetic survival necessity and its fear of the potential for genetic annihilation that the Black male represents.

This conscious and unconscious struggle for white genetic survival by the global white collective necessitates certain basic and specific relationship patterns between whites and Black males and whites and Black females in all areas of life activity. An appropriate analogy is found in the game of chess. The white king, the companion white queen and all of the other white pieces on the chess board must move in certain specific patterns against the black king, the black queen and all of the other black pieces if the white king is to checkmate the black king. That is, of course, the main objective of the game of chess. And in the game of chess, white always makes the opening (aggressive) move.

The black king and the black queen must move in tactical and strategic harmony with one another if they are to counter the white assault successfully and defend their side of the chess board effectively. This harmony is particularly crucial if they are to checkmate the white king!

If someone with *no in-depth knowledge* about the game of chess sits down at the chess board to play the black side of the board while an expert in the game of chess sits down on the white side of the board, the player on the black side of the board surely will lose the game. He or she will be checkmated *repeatedly*. The player on the black side simply does not understand the game.

If, however, that same person, who repeatedly has lost all previous games, takes it upon himself/herself to sit down and master the game of chess (and then to master playing on the black side of the board), through continuous hard work and study, he/she will have an excellent chance of being victorious. With consistent and continuous study, he/she can become an expert, establishing a pattern of continuous wins and successes.

It is much easier for white supremacy to control female-headed households, wherein Black females must confront a white male-dominated power system alone. Further, these female-headed survival units eventually produce more passive and effeminized male offspring or male offspring with dysfunctional behavioral patterns, who, in many cases, eventually will be incarcerated as anti-socials, continuing the necessary Black male/Black female separation.

Stabilized union between the Black male and the Black female means the eventual end to white supremacy. When the Black male and the Black female simply define their joint struggle in terms of achieving education, housing, jobs and money, rather than as specifically countering the global and local dynamic for white genetic survival (white supremacy), we are attempting to function with the wrong game manual and with all of the wrong rules. While we have remained confused, the global and local white collectives consciously and/or unconsciously have mastered white genetic survival strategies – in all areas of life activity. Thus, we as Blacks are being "checkmated" continuously by the local and global white collectives. We are the victims of white supremacy who spend most of our time squabbling, struggling and fighting with one another. Thus, matters go from bad to worse, especially in such critical areas as the Black male/Black female relationship, the very foundation of the Black nation.

Until now, we have attempted to function as united Black males and Black females with no knowledge of exactly how the white supremacy dynamic *must* drive the Black male and the Black female apart. Therefore, we have failed in the past and we continue to fail in this relationship. If we understood white supremacy, the number one priority for *each* Black male and Black female would *not* be to reach out for one another with designs of dependency, love, lust or marriage. Instead, we would seek to master specific patterns of perception, logic, thought, speech, action and emotional response that would counter the white supremacy dynamic scientifically. We would codify such behaviors and practice them day and night. We would become single-minded in our activity, knowing that unless global and local white supremacy is attacked continuously and effectively, the Black male/Black female relationship has no chance of surviving.

Black males and Black females would be in a continuous exchange of information, knowledge and understanding (like true team members) about how to counter white supremacy more effectively. This quality of exchange could take place as much as we exchange phone numbers, jokes, dance steps, trivia and (in all too many instances) drugs. There would be much less time to look into each others eyes and become bored, and then start quarreling and fighting. Instead, both persons would be looking outward, beyond themselves, to counter local and global white supremacy, which is the real problem annihilating the Black collective.

Actually, people grow closer together as long as they remain focused outwardly in the same direction. By maintaining a like-minded focus, Nelson and Winnie Mandela of South Africa have evolved possibly the strongest marriage known to Black people worldwide. They deserve recognition as the model for the Black male/Black female relationship. They are looking outward, beyond themselves, to fight white supremacy. By specifically fighting white supremacy, they prevent that force of injustice from driving them apart.

When both the Black male and the Black female take up the struggle for justice against white supremacy, they are endowed with the strongest possible insurance that they will remain united. They are united in a common effort against injustice, and simultaneously they express the strongest possible statement about respect and love for themselves as individuals. In doing this, the Black male and Black female are declaring that they have conferred upon themselves the highest possible value, which is essential if there is to be self- and group-defense.

The new answer to the Black male/Black female relationship dilemma is for the Black male and the Black female to make serious, conscious struggle against white supremacy their number one priority. Fortunately, Neely Fuller has written a textbook for victims of white supremacy (*The United Independent Compensatory Code/System Concept*) that details specific behaviors that the Black male and female must adopt in order to combat effectively the force that is driving them apart. Fuller suggests that the most critical question is how Black males and Black females spread their time (energy), how they use each of the 24 hours in the day. He recommends: 1) constructive conversation, 2) constructive work, 3) sufficient eating and sleeping, and 4) sexual intercourse no more than twice a week. These suggestions deserve our full consideration. If energy use was limited to just these activities by each Black male and Black female, certainly we would become more responsible towards ourselves as individuals, which would translate into more responsible interaction with one another. It is critical that we realize our present patterns of behavior permit white supremacy to exist. Directed radical change in Black behavior, as suggested above, will alter permanently the face of white supremacy, its victimization of the Black male and the Black female and the destruction of the Black male/Black female relationship.

24

Black Women Moving Towards the 21st Century
(May 1975)

Today, the world is going through a period of great turmoil and change. Individually, we are aware of this turmoil because social and environmental chaos brings an attendant increase in the stress we feel in our daily lives as women workers in all capacities: wives, mothers and individual members of a total collective that for 400 years has been oppressed. Yes, this is a difficult period for all of us "hue-man" beings, and it would not be an exaggeration to say that we are in a time not only of turmoil, but of *crisis*.

During periods of crisis and stress, the easiest thing to do as an expression of our pain, despair and hopelessness is to moan, groan, cry or attempt to escape through alcohol, other drugs, fantasy, laughter or just fun and games. However, another possible behavioral response, which channels the body energy upward and onward as opposed to downward, is the use of the crisis as a stimulus for analysis, challenge, responsibility, growth and great creativity.

The word *crisis* evolves from the Greek word, "krisis," which means *decision*. A period of crisis is a time for decision: an unstable or crucial time or state of affairs when the decisions that are made and acted upon become all-important for determining future events. Both men and women throughout the world have key roles to play in the resolution of this crisis, but my singular emphasis here is on the role of Black women.

Before specifically defining our present period of crisis and our response to it, we must contemplate our *identity*, the self-image that we carry in our brain-computers. For all that we can imagine doing and all that we *will* do or *fail* to do is a result of that picture of "self," derived from our total experiences from birth onward. That picture becomes the basis for all our behavioral patterns. Unfortunately, a major part of these self- and group-images for all too many of us Blacks consists of a brief and inaccurate history. Accordingly, this history began 400 years ago when we were brought to North America in the holds of slave ships by the "very advanced" Europeans (whites); it continues with the "advancement" that we have made since our emancipation in 1863 in becoming full-fledged "Americans"; and, finally, this history insists that many of us now are just like the whites. There is a proverb that states, "The tree grows strong and tall *only* to the extent that its roots are deep and firmly planted in the soil." If Black people are at all disappointed in our present level of achievement, it may be because our roots are not planted deeply enough in the past – resting upon such a shallow, inadequate and faulty data input of only 400 years of history.

The facts of our true identity are that we, as Black people, are persons whose dominant genetic and historic roots extend to Africa, "the land of the Blacks." Men and women of science today, with few exceptions, are satisfied that Africa was the birth place of humankind and that for many *hundreds of centuries thereafter* Africans, meaning Black people, were in the forefront of *all* human progress. As John Henrik Clarke states, "It can be said with a strong degree of certainty that Africa has had three Golden Ages. The *first two* reached their climax and were in decline before *Europe* as a functioning entity in human society was born."

Factually speaking, this means that Black women and Black men are the parents of the entire family of people – black, brown, red, yellow and white varieties. Black people can and have produced all of the colors of mankind, including white. White skin is simply the product of a recessive genetic mutation to skin albinism. Whites cannot be the parents of humankind because whites can only produce white. But Blacks can produce a range of colors from as black as the proverbial ace of spades, to as white as the proverbial driven snow. Not only are Blacks the genetic parents of all people in the world today, but Blacks produced the first scientists, architects, musicians, mathematicians, astronomers, astrologers, philosophers, statesman, priests, prophets and generals. Indeed, Africa produced some of the first fighting women generals.

I am reminded of some ancient and important wisdom of Africa, as seen in the following two proverbs: 1) "When you educate women, you educate a nation," and 2) "The hand that rocks the cradle rules the nation and its destiny." With this wisdom of our Black ancestors in mind, let us examine the current world crisis and the role of Black women in its resolution. What is the nature of this crisis?

Critical in the history of white supremacy was the decision not to control Black and other women of color, but to control the men of color. Men are the initiaters of the act of reproduction. Ultimately, women are dependent upon their men for protection because of the greater physical strength of men compared to women. If one simply controls the men of a people, the women are controlled also. Thus, the white collective went about the business of systematically developing a plan and power mechanism worldwide to bring all of the world's men of color under their ultimate control. Once this was established, the men of color were informed overtly as well as subtly that if they ever should seek to alter the power relationship of *white* over *non-white*, they would have to fight and many would die. Thousands upon thousands of Black men in the U.S. were lynched and castrated to drive home the message that white men intended to control the "balls" in this world, both on and off of the court!

White males understood that they needed white women as well as Black women to help them achieve and maintain this power relationship. White women always have known what they stood to gain – their own survival as whites. Black women have been confused and less clear in fully understanding how they have been led to cooperate in this deadly power game of white supremacy. Further, Black women do not understand fully that they have nothing to gain and everything to lose if this deadly game continues.

The first lessons to Black women were harsh and cruel ones of sexual assault and abuse, taking their children away and forcing them to watch their men being lynched and castrated. But then these harsh lessons were followed by milder treatment of Black women as compared to Black men. Black women were given extra food, money, clothing and other gifts for their special personal favors to the masters. They were rewarded for correctly teaching their children to conform to the masters' wishes, as well as for telling their men to calm down and be patient so that they too could be rewarded. Perhaps we (Black women) really became seduced by the illusion of power, being so close to white males.

We have told ourselves that these behaviors were survival tactics and the only way that we could have "come this far." But as our survival increasingly is becoming threatened, we are forced to wonder if we have been mistaken in our analysis and our strategy. But, again, there is something to be learned from our African past. And we must never forget that those who do not learn from "history," "their-whole story," are bound to repeat it.

The specific *story* to which I refer is that of the African (Black) queen, Cleopatra. Born in 69 B.C., Cleopatra came to the throne that she shared with her brother, Ptolemy XIII, when she was 13 years old. Egypt was then a Roman protectorate. It was beset with internal strife and intrigue. Cleopatra aligned herself with the Roman general, Julius Caesar, whom she *thought* would reinforce her power and help her people. She saw her political and sexual relationship with Caesar as a maneuver to save Egypt from the worst aspects of Roman domination. This maneuver failed in spite of her second Roman lover Mark Anthony, who came after Caesar's death. Her suicide is a profound statement about the series of decisions that she made. Egypt fell and became a Roman colony. And all of the harsher aspects of Roman rule, which Cleopatra had sought to prevent, settled over Egypt and the Middle East.

There were other Black queens in Africa who fought the white invaders to their death; they did not submit or cooperate with their oppressors. Instead, they moved to resist and destroy that oppressive process. They urged their men to do likewise, thus leaving their marks as heroines and warriors for their people who died in honor. These Black women have not been known simply as "beautiful" queens who committed suicide in their own disgrace.

This brings us to the pertinent question: Should we continue our alliance with the present "Romans," or having learned from the past, should we choose an alternate course? In the context of all that we may want to call progress and material prosperity, we must face the reality that today, Black men die younger than white men, white women and Black women. Black men are the most frequent victims of homicide and they are being killed by one another in increasing numbers. The suicide rate for young Black men is the only Black suicide rate greater than the rates of whites. Black women and Black children are the most frequent victims of rape and other physical assault and violence. Black infant mortality remains two to three times the figure for whites. Black women are more often left alone to care for their children than any other female group in the country. Nearly one-third of our so-called "Black family units," which I refer to as "survival-units," are single-parent families. In the Washington, D.C. metropolitan area, there are over 60,000 Black male children growing up in homes without fathers or other surrogate father figures. We continue to have the highest rates of separation and divorce and, thus, family dissolution. We continue to have some of the highest rates of teenage parenthood, and thus, immature and inadequate parenting of the next generation. We continue to have high levels of juvenile delinquency, gang wars and drug addiction. Young Black people continue to leave school in record numbers prior to high school graduation. There is a virtual epidemic of low reading and math scores amongst our young people, and as a result, these youngsters are leaving school with totally inadequate preparation for this highly technological, computerized and industrialized social system.

Black people are in a very serious economic depression, while whites are still at the stage of recession. Blacks remain the last hired and first fired, in spite of the supposed achievements of "affirmative action." The relative levels of Black unemployment and white unemployment have not changed since 1945. The housing situation for urban Blacks is not improving. Black men continue to be sent to prison in record numbers, out of proportion to our population percentage. Black men presently constitute 90% of the state prison population. And we now witness the nationwide return of the death penalty.

What must we as Black women do? It is my conviction that the African proverb "The hand that rocks the cradle rules the nation and its destiny" is true. Black women are the mothers and, thus, the first teachers of Black females and Black males alike. With increased consciousness of their importance as the *first teachers*, Black women can determine whether future generations of Black children will be warriors or if we will continue to be slaves living in a highly refined state of psychological oppression, which is no less a death than direct physical destruction. Black women as mothers and teachers can teach the first powerful lessons in pride and respect for cultural, historical and genetic Blackness, while steadfastly refusing to impart any part of the white oppressors' lesson in Black self-hate that we learn as children: "If you're Black, stay back; if you're brown, stick around; if you're yellow, you're mellow; and if you're white, you are all right." Black mothers must cease making their first concern whether or not their babies will have light skin and straight hair.

The newborn infant can tell from the mother's first touch whether she is pleased or disappointed with its color, appearance and gender. Certainly later the child can tell the mother's respect for Blackness by the comments she makes about who is a pretty girl, who is a handsome boy and who has the proverbial "good" and "bad" hair. All of these lessons that we have been taught by our white oppressors to teach our young we must refuse to teach ever again!

But Black women as mothers and first teachers can take their consciousness to an even higher level. They can give the first lesson in what constitutes Black manhood. They can teach all of their sons that they are not their "babies" or their substitute lovers. Black women can be the first to inform their sons, with loving kindness, that they did not bring them into the world to be oppressed. Rather, they brought them into the world to be free men, warriors who have to war to be free, and to die if they so happen to die in the fight for their right to be full men under the stars.

Black women must cease saying to child psychiatrists, "I'll never tell my 'baby' anything like that!"

Black women can teach their sons and their daughters that the definition of a Black man is not simply someone who can buy things (a nice home, a car, a yacht and clothes), but rather someone who will respect, support, protect and defend himself, his woman and his children. And finally, Black men are those who will do whatever is necessary to ensure their families' respect, support, protection and defense.

Black women as mothers and teachers consciously can teach their daughters that Black women, as the mothers of all mankind, are the alpha and the omega of women on this planet. They were here in the beginning, and if humankind remains, they will be present in the end. Black mothers can teach their daughters that they should never seek to look like or be like anything other than themselves. They can set the standards of what women will be like on this planet. For this is their responsibility, coming from the tradition of the first mothers and queens. Black women can teach their daughters that respect is not *given* to women by men, but that Black women carry in themselves the highest possible level of self-respect that commands respect from men and women of all races. Black women can teach their daughters how they possibly assist in the destruction of Black men and Black people by allowing Black men to hide out in the vagina. To allow this hiding out (attempts to climb in the womb to be babies or fetuses again) when they know the men should turn and face their oppressors, is an extreme level of self-destruction.

Likewise, Black women can teach their daughters never to refer to Black men as "baby" and never to allow Black men to refer to them, when adult women, as "mamma." Thus, they systematically can refuse to reinforce the image the white man wants reinforced: an adult Black male baby and thus the proverbial "mother-fucker." It is clear that a "baby" will never track down "The Man." Finally, Black women can teach their daughters that they can change the tide of Black destiny by only giving their most intimate pleasures to the providers who also prove themselves as warriors against all enemies of the Black collective.

These lessons will not be practiced until we Black women reach a new level of respect for ourselves. We must struggle as individuals to build this essential new Black self-respect through the following exercises: 1) We must stop gossiping about one another; 2) we must stop name-calling one another; 3) we must stop squabbling with one another; 4) we must stop competing and comparing ourselves with one another; 5) we must stop making babies of our sons and lovers and then calling them incompetent behind their backs; 6) and instead of looking into the mirror each morning asking, "Mirror, mirror on the wall, am I the fairest one of all?," we should begin to ask, "Mirror, mirror on the wall, am I fooling my Black self at all?"

We do not have many choices remaining. The time is short and the crisis situation, though not of our own making, is upon us. Will we continue to be the "Cooperating Cleopatras" or will we be the fighting, struggling warrior-queens? Racism, now as in Cleopatra's time, is war against Black people, against the Black family, against Black men, against Black women and against Black children, throughout the world. There is no war in history that has gone away with a wish or a prayer. Wars must be fought with the willpower, knowledge, courage and determination of people.

There is not a Black problem that I mentioned in this book which is not related to the reality of white domination of Black people. We are not "Americans," just as the Jews were not considered "Germans." In code language, both "German" and "American" mean white! We, as Blacks, are the victims of the Americans, like the Jews were the victims of the Germans. We are the victims of those who classify themselves as white. The Jews gave their response to their white oppressors. What will be our response as Black women? How will we decide to influence the course of Black destiny as we rapidly approach the 21st century? Mothers of mankind, the decision is ours.

25

The White Supremacy System, the White Supremacy Mind-Set and the AIDS Holocaust (1988)

Medicine, if it means anything at all, means to ascertain the fundamental (rock bottom) causation of disease. Ultimately, the fundamental cause of a given disease determines what must be done about it. Otherwise, one is treating various symptoms of a disease. Sometimes a disease may be a symptom of something else. AIDS (Acquired Immune Deficiency Syndrome) is recognized as a disease, but AIDS also may be a *symptom* of yet another disease, which must be determined.

In relationship to the present epidemic/pandemic caused by the AIDS virus, four questions must be raised and answered, if at all possible: 1) *Could* a government, a specific power entity, cause such a phenomenon as the present AIDS epidemic/pandemic, in which 75 million plus deaths have been projected? 2) *Would* any government cause such a phenomenon, and why? 3) Are there any precedents of a government causing such massive levels of deaths? 4) If indeed there is a precedent, what are the parallels between that precedent and the present AIDS phenomenon?

Raul Hilberg's *The Destruction of the European Jews* provides insight into both the Jewish holocaust and the AIDS epidemic/pandemic:

> As time passes on, the destruction of the European Jews will recede into the background. Its most immediate consequences are almost over, and whatever developments may henceforth be traced to the castrophe will be consequences of consequences, more and more

remote. Already the Nazi outburst has become historical. But this is a strange page in history. Few events of modern times were so filled with unpredicted action and unsuspected death. A primordial impulse had suddenly surfaced among the Western nations; it had been unfettered through their machines. From this moment, fundamental assumptions about our civilization have no longer stood unchallenged, for while the occurrence is past, the phenomenon remains.

Before the emergence of the twentieth century and its technology, a destructive mind could not play in fantasy with the thoughts that the Nazi were able to translate into action. The administrator of earlier centuries did not have the tools. He did not possess the network of communications; he did not dispose over rapid small arms fire and quick working poison gases. The bureaucrat of tomorrow would not have these problems; already, he is better equipped than the German Nazis were. Killing is not as difficult as it used to be. The modern administrative apparatus has facilities for rapid, concerted movements and for efficient massive killings. These devices not only trap a larger number of victims; they also require a greater degree of specialization, and with that division of labour the moral burden too is fragmented among the participants. The perpetrators can now kill his victims without touching them, without hearing them, without seeing them. He may feel sure of his success and safe from its repercussions. This ever growing capacity for destruction cannot be arrested anywhere.

...we saw how the Nazis had built upon the experiences of the past. Now there are means which will allow still others to seize upon the Nazis' experience, so that it in turn may yet become a precedent for the future.

...in the words of President Truman, 'Hitler's persecution of the Jews did much to awaken Americans to the dangerous extremes to which prejudice can be carried if allowed to control government actions.' With uncommon perception, the President saw that the retention in mid-twentieth century of discriminatory barriers signified the maintenance of a springboard, and the preservation of a target, for destruction.

The New York Times editorial reviewing *And the Band Played On*, by Randy Shilts, states:

And the Band Played On applies withering hindsight to society's shortcomings, almost none to its successes. It (the book) overlooks the scientific feat of identifying the AIDS virus and developing an antibody test, achieved in record time. It gives no credit to the equally striking social achievements. Most Americans have so far refused to panic in the face of a terrifying disease, or to oppress *the barely tolerated minorities that are its focus.*" (Emphasis mine.)

In another article, *The New York Times* reported:

Geneva, November 14 (Reuters) – The World Health Organization has raised it estimates of AIDS cases throughout the world by 50 percent and says finding a vaccine may take longer than experts thought.

...Halfdan Mahler, the organization's director general, painted a bleak picture at the start of the conference on acquired immune deficiency syndrome, which destroys the body's ability to fend off disease and is always fatal.

'My scientific sources tell me that a vaccine may be even further away than we thought a year ago, and development of therapeutic agents has been frustratingly slow,' he said.

Mr. Mahler said, 'Available evidence indicates that the virus is continuing to spread and the number of AIDS cases climbs steadily.'

The health agency estimates that 5 to 10 million people in the world are carriers of the human immuno-deficiency virus, which caused AIDS, but have not as yet developed the disease.

"If you do not understand White Supremacy (Racism) – what it is, and how it works – everything else that you think you understand, will only confuse you."
— Neely Fuller, Jr.
The United Compensatory Code/System/Concept

In the size of the lie there is always contained a certain factor of credibility, since the great masses of people – will more easily fall victim to a great lie than to a small one, since they themselves...lie sometimes in little things...Thus such an untruth will not at all enter

their heads...therefore, just for this reason, some part of the most
impudent lie will remain and stick.
— Robert G.L. Waite
The Psychopathic God: Adolf Hitler

"What's past is prologue."
– William Shakespeare

George Santayana, the American philosopher, has left to posterity the
challenge, "Those who do not know history and do not learn from history,
will repeat it."

From the aforementioned information, I conclude the following:

If you attempt to understand biological and chemical warfare without
understanding white supremacy, you will only be confused.

If you attempt to understand the killing of gypsies in Germany, under
the leadership of Adolph Hitler, without understanding white supremacy,
you will only be confused.

If you attempt to understand the killing of homosexuals in Germany,
under the leadership of Adolph Hitler, without understanding white
supremacy, you will only be confused.

If you attempt to understand the holocaust of Semites of the Jewish
religion in Europe from 1933 to 1945, wherein 6,000,000 Semites were
slaughtered under conditions of mass deceit with the awareness of other
Western (white) powers, without understanding white supremacy
(racism/anti-Semitism), you will only be bewildered and totally confused.

Anyone who has not mastered an understanding of Germany under the
Adolph Hitler's leadership and the holocaust of Semites, cannot possibly
understand the AIDS holocaust of 1980 to 1991, wherein 50,000,000 to
75,000,000 deaths of Black people on the continent of Africa and else-
where have been planned and projected.

If you attempt to understand the AIDS holocaust, without understanding white supremacy, you will only be confused; and you may be
dead.

The word *holocaust* is defined in this paper as "the massive, planned
slaughtering (by whatever necessary means), under conditions of major

deception, of people classified as non-white, conducted by people who classify themselves as white, for the specific purpose of depopulation of non-white people, under the specific conditions of white supremacy domination."

All information, events and data that are not placed in proper context or do not establish precise relationships are only nonsense. Nonsense, because it deceives and causes confusion, can be used for deadly purposes. Much of the discussion heretofore about AIDS and much of the information that has appeared in the electronic and print media about AIDS are experienced as largely nonsensical to increasing numbers of people, especially Black people, including those in the U.S., which thus far has the largest number of documented cases of AIDS, but also in Africa, which has the largest number of projected deaths.

Most disturbing and most nonsensical is the obsessive insistence, on the part of people who classify themselves as white, that Black people in Africa caused the spread of the AIDS virus throughout the world from their contact with the African Green Monkey (the Vervet Monkey).

My effort, therefore, is to place the discussion of AIDS in what I consider to be its only proper and logical context. I am attempting to neutralize much of the nonsense that has developed worldwide concerning this topic in the past five or so years. AIDS is a deadly disease, which after its sudden appearance has already killed thousands of people. The projection is that it will kill many, many thousands more, indeed many millions. I hope thtat by cutting through the nonsense surrounding the discussion of AIDS and taking a more logical approach to the epidemic (and now pandemic) disease, many lives throughout the world will be saved.

From 1933 to 1945, Germany – a leading country in Western civilization under the leadership of Adolph Hitler – with the assistance of politicians, doctors, lawyers, professors, judges, scientists and the general population, conducted open warfare against and planned the extermination of Semites of the Jewish religion who were citizens of Germany and other countries of German-occupied Europe.

As persons who were referred to in Germany and throughout Europe as Semites, the Jews were not considered to be white people or aryans. As Semites they were considered to have their genetic roots amongst Africans – Black people on the continent of Africa.

Indeed, the word *Semite* is derived from the Latin prefix "semi," which means half. Semites were the products of the genetic mixture produced when white Greek and Roman soldiers invaded Africa and raped African women, who of course were Black. Semite means the same as mulatto. Thus they were considered to be half Black and half white, or colored people. Thus, a yellow colored star was placed on their outer clothing by the German government in the Hitler era.

The terms *anti-Semite* and *anti-Semitism* most fundamentally refer to a destructive ideological, psychological and behavioral state of "anti-color" waged by people who classify themselves as white against those who are classified as non-white, even when those non-whites have lost much of their skin coloration in some instances.

Semites who left Africa and eventually attempted to settle in Europe, miscegenated further with white-skinned people on the continent of Europe and continued to lose much of their melanin skin-pigmentation.

However, because of the dominant character of the African (Black) genotype, including hair texture and type and facial features, there continued to exist evidence of African genetic heritage. Because of the dominance of African or Black genetic heritage, genetically recessive white-skinned people of Europe continued to fear the possibility of white genetic annihilation caused by the Semites. Thus, there was a 2,000 year history of white hostility towards Semites, or coloreds, of the Jewish religion on the continent of Europe, in spite of short periods in which the hostility of whites towards the Semites was less intense.

Following Germany's loss of World War I and the major decline of the German economy, which caused a sense of extreme and profound dislocation and vulnerability amongst the German people, latent hostility began to escalate towards the Semites. Again, these people were long recognized as being able to cause white genetic annihilation because they carried the dominant Black genetic material from Africa, although it had been much diluted over a 2,000 year period.

It should be noted that the most fundamental of all vulnerabilities is white genetic vulnerability or the fear of white annihilation.

Hostility against the Semites intensified even though the Semites sought to identify with and be accepted as white people. They wanted to be Germans or other Europeans, but they were told they were Semites, even if one their parents was white or even if they were married to whites (aryans).

Hostility also was directed against gypsies who were also darker-skinned people and whose very name means "out of Egypt." In addition, hostility was directed against homosexuals because, in the logic of Adolph Hitler and other white supremacists, homosexuals represented weakness on the part of the white (aryan) male, who already was feeling vulnerable.

Adolph Hitler, who came to power in Germany in 1933, became the most forceful articulator of that most fundamental of all fears of the global and local white collective – the fear of white genetic annihilation caused by people classified as non-white.

Indeed, it can be said that Adolph Hitler was the highest crystalization of the white supremacy mind-set based upon the fear of white genetic annihilation and its companion thought, white genetic survival by any necessary and conceivable means.

Hitler, because he tapped into the deepest fear, was able to have the support and sympathy of masses of other people who, like himself, classified themselves as white – then and now. They understood Hitler's call, at conscious as well as deep subconscious levels, for white genetic survival. This is the perceived threat that the Semites of the Jewish religion residing in Europe represented to Germans and other Europeans (whites).

Hitler and his followers referred to the Semites as *tiermensch* (German, for "subhuman"). Amongst many other horrendous accusations, Hitler accused them of carrying and causing disease. Indeed, he referred to the Semites as being "viruses."

From the book *The Psychopathic God: Adolph Hitler* by Robert G.L. Waite, I quote:

> Toward the end of February 1942, just after the Wannsee Conference which organized the 'final solution' to the jewish problem, Hitler listed himself among the great benefactors of mankind who had isolated dangerous disease germs: 'The discovery of the Jewish virus is one of the greatest revolutions that has ever taken place. The fight we are carrying on is of the same nature as that waged by Pasture and Koch during the last century. How many diseases have their origin in the Jewish virus! We shall retain our health when we eliminate the Jew.'

Hitler further accused the government that preceded his own, the Weimer Republic, of "surrendering the German nation to 'syphilization' by Jews and Negroes."

And thus, in Hitler's pattern of perception and logic (the white supremacy mind-set), he planned for the extermination of the Semites as the "final solution" to the problem of white genetic survival, by getting rid of the source of white genetic annihilation.

Through a monstrous pattern of lying and deceit, promoting the "Big Lie" through a very sophisticated government propaganda apparatus, it was propagated that the Semites were the source of all of the problems that threatened the German and European peoples.

Thus, mass level destruction was planned against the Semites. This process was participated in by all levels of the German and European societies. Adolph Hitler's leadership of Germany from 1933 to 1945 in the war against the Semites has become the standard for the ultimate conduct of governmental and state white supremacy.

In 1932, the year before Adolph Hitler came to power in Germany, in Tuskegee, Alabama, U.S.A., another destruction was being conducted against people who were classified as non-white by people who classified themselves as white doctors, scientists and government officials. This planned destruction was the Tuskegee Syphilis Study.

From 1932 to 1972, a total of 40 years, United States Public Health, Macon County Health Department, Tuskegee Institute, Veterans Hospital in Tuskegee and private physicians in and around Macon County deliberately planned to withhold treatment from more than 400 Black men who were suffering from syphilis. It was *verbalized* that the program would be a means for getting rid of the Black people in the U.S. (This destructive deception recently ended, under pressure, in the year 1972.)

Very shortly thereafter, the disease which we now refer to as AIDS began to surface in the U.S. The populations focused upon as being infected with the AIDS virus were first the white male homosexuals and subsequently Black and Hispanic people. More specifically, the projected source of the virus was/is said to be African people who had been bitten by the African Green Monkey or the Vervet Monkey.

In 1969, a book entitled *A Survey of Chemical and Biological Warfare*, by John Cookson and Judith Nottingham, was published by the Monthly Review Press. The book is described on its cover as follows: "Derived from a three year study conducted by a British biochemist and geneticist and a British political scientist, the text affords a comprehensive review of materials used, and policies adopted by authorities in the U.S., Canada, Great Britain and West Germany." It also states that it "...provides one of the most comprehensive views on the subject of chemical and biological warfare written for the layman. The authors, who are well qualified, produced a vast amount of documentation of the use and research on these types of weapons." On p. 322 at the bottom of the page, the authors state,

> The question of whether new diseases could be used is of considerable interest. Vervet monkey disease (African Green Monkey Disease) may well be an example of a whole new class of disease-causing organisms. Handling of blood and tissue without precaution causes infection. It is unaffected by any antibiotic substance so far tried and is unrelated to any other organism. It causes fatality in some cases and can be venereally transmitted in man. In the words of Dr. C.E. Gordon Smith, 'It has possible potential as an infectious disease of man. It presumably is also of BW (biological warfare) interest. New diseases are continually appearing (chikungunya and o'nyong-nyong fever for example). In addition to these there are the possibilities of virus and bacteria being genetically manipulated to produce 'new' organism.

On p. 110 in the same book (bottom of page), they state,

Just recently a great deal of useful work has been done on the Vervet Monkey Disease (African Green Monkey Disease) which caused seven deaths in Germany. Reports of progress were: 'sent to 40 laboratories all over the world; 9 of these have been supplied with infective material and/or antisera [vaccine]: 4 in the USA and one each in Germany, Panama, South Africa, Uganda and the USSR. A non-infective complement fixing antigen has been prepared to the WHO (World Health organization) reference laboratories.'

–Hansard, May 1968

In another book, *A Higher Form of Killing (The Secret Story of Chemical and Biological Warfare)* by Robert Harris and Jeremy Paxman, published by Hill and Wang (1982), on p. 219, the authors state:

The claims continued. In January 1978, a correspondent with Reuters news agency reported from NATO headquarters that 'scientific experts' had informed him that the Russians were developing 'three horrific new diseases for warfare...Lassa Fever, which according to the sources, kills 35 out of every 100 people it strikes, Ebola fever, which kills 70 out of every 100, and the deadly Marburg fever (Green Monkey Disease).

Over and over again the name "African Green Monkey" shows up. This is not a "monkey" biting Africans and causing disease, but a weapon of biological warfare developed in laboratories by people who classify themselves as white. This charge, however, is denied, and blame is projected on to African (Black) people.

Adolph Hitler propagated his "Big Lie" against the Semites of the Jewish religion, which became his pretext for the planned slaughter of 11 million. He actually succeeded in killing six million, all in the name of white supremacy (racism/anti-Semitism) for the express purpose of white genetic survival.

In the late 1980s, there has been grave concern throughout the world that the white birthrate is declining as the birthrates of all non-white people continue to increase. It is at this time that we witness the sudden appearance of AIDS, primarily effecting Black people in Africa and Haiti.

As truth always surfaces, in time we will know the full details of the massive deception of the AIDS holocaust, when the current "Big Lie" is unveiled.

Recommended reading

Cookson, John and Nottingham, Judith. *A Survey of Chemical Biological Warfare*. New York: Monthly Review Press, 1969.

Jones, James H. *Bad Blood: The Tuskegee Syphilis Experiment*. New York: The Free Press, 1982.

Lifton, Robert Jay. *The Nazi Doctors – Medical Killing & the Psychology of Genocide*. New York: Basic Books, 1986.

ALSO AVAILABLE FROM THIRD WORLD PRESS

Nonfiction

*The Destruction Of Black
Civilization: Great Issues
Of A Race From 4500 B.C.
To 2000 A.D.*
by Dr. Chancellor Williams
paper $16.95
cloth $29.95

*The Cultural Unity Of
Black Africa*
by Cheikh Anta Diop $14.95

Home Is A Dirty Street
by Useni Eugene Perkins $9.95

*Black Men: Obsolete, Single,
Dangerous?*
by Haki R. Madhubuti
paper $14.95
cloth $29.95

*From Plan To Planet
Life Studies: The Need
For Afrikan Minds And
Institutions*
by Haki R. Madhubuti $7.95

Enemies: The Clash Of Races
by Haki R. Madhubuti $12.95

*Kwanzaa: A Progressive And
Uplifting African-American
Holiday*
by Institute of Positive Education
Intro. by Haki R. Madhubuti $2.50

*Harvesting New Generations:
The Positive Development Of
Black Youth*
by Useni Eugene Perkins $12.95

*Confusion By Any Other Name: Essays
Exploring the Negative Impact of The
Blackman's Guide to Understanding
the Blackwoman*
Ed. Haki R. Madhubuti $3.95

*Explosion Of Chicago
Black Street Gangs*
by Useni Eugene Perkins $6.95

*The Psychopathic Racial
Personality And Other Essays*
by Dr. Bobby E. Wright $5.95

*Black Women, Feminism And Black
Liberation: Which Way?*
by Vivian V. Gordon $5.95

Black Rituals
by Sterling Plumpp $8.95

*The Redemption Of Africa
And Black Religion*
by St. Clair Drake $6.95

How I Wrote Jubilee
by Margaret Walker $1.50

Fiction

*Mostly Womenfolk And A Man
Or Two: A Collection*
by Mignon Holland Anderson $5.95

The Brass Bed and Other Stories
Pearl Cleage $8.00

Poetry and Drama

To Disembark
by Gwendolyn Brooks $6.95

Earthquakes and Sunrise Missions
By Haki R. Madhubuti $8.95

I've Been A Woman
by Sonia Sanchez $7.95

My One Good Nerve
by Ruby Dee $8.95

Geechies
by Gregory Millard $5.95

Earthquakes And Sunrise Missions
by Haki R. Madhubuti $8.95

Killing Memory: Seeking Ancestors
(Lotus Press)
by Haki R. Madhubuti $8.00

Say That ⁻iver Turns:
The Impu   Gwendolyn Brooks
(Anthology⌐
Ed.by Haki R. Madhubuti $8.95

Octavia And Other Poems
by Naomi Long Madgett $8.00

A Move Further South
by Ruth Garnett $7.95

Manish
by Alfred Woods $8.00

New Plays for the Black Theatre
(Anthology)
edited by Woodie King, Jr. $14.95

So Far, So Good
Gil Scott-Heron $8.00

Wings Will Not Be Broken
Darryl Holmes $8.00

Children's Books

The Afrocentric Self Discovery and Inventory Workbook
By Useni Perkins $5.95

The Day They Stole
The Letter J
by Jabari Mahiri $3.95

The Tiger Who Wore
White Gloves
by Gwendolyn Brooks $6.95

A Sound Investment
by Sonia Sanchez $2.95

I Look At Me
by Mari Evans $2.50

The Story of Kwanzaa
by Safisha Madhubuti $5.95

Black Books Bulletin
A limited number of back issues
of this unique journal are available
at $3.00 each:

Vol. 1, Fall '71   Interview with
                    Hoyt W. Fuller

Vol. 1, No. 3   Interview with
                    Lerone Bennett, Jr.

Vol. 5, No. 3   Science & Struggle

Vol. 5, No. 4   Blacks & Jews

Vol. 7, No. 3   The South

Order from Third World Press, 7524 S. Cottage Grove Ave *Chicago, IL 60619. Shipping: Add $2.50 for first book and .2⌐ for each additional book. Mastercard/Visa orders may b⌐ placed by calling 1(312) 651-0700.*